A Yankee Jeffersonian

A Yankee Jeffersonian

Selections from the Diary and Letters of

WILLIAM LEE of Massachusetts

Written from 1796 to 1840

Edited by MARY LEE MANN

THE BELKNAP PRESS of
HARVARD UNIVERSITY PRESS
Cambridge, Massachusetts 1958

Library of Congress Catalog Card Number 58-12970

Printed in the United States of America

This book is dedicated to the memory of
William Lee's granddaughter,
my dearly loved mother, Mary Elizabeth Lee Mann,
who treasured this diary and the family letters
for many years.

Foreword

It is seldom that the student of history encounters such a delightful find as this. Of course many adjectives could be applied to the record which William Lee so diligently made, in diaries and letters, from the period of Washington's second administration through the second term of Andrew Jackson in the White House. It is entertaining, it is instructive, it is illuminating; but the word delightful best sums up its fresh and beguiling quality. A document of this kind should combine historical values with a strong flavor of personal feeling, and is all the better if it expresses certain eccentricities and dogmatisms. This book does not have the weight of the diaries of Gouverneur Morris or the rich anecdotal flow and insight into character of Mrs. Smith's *First Forty Years of Washington Society;* but it deserves to be placed on the same shelf with those two immortal works, and adds something to their picture of America in its republican infancy, and of Europe in the Napoleonic era.

William Lee was well qualified to play the part of historical observer, and circumstances befriended him. This clearheaded Yankee, educated at Phillips Academy, never impressed everybody as brilliant; but he was shrewd, sensible, perceptive, and without being cynical was always realistic. Among our many political and literary diarists it is refreshing to find a businessman, a keen New Englander frankly intent on making a fortune — at one point he assures Mrs. Lee that it will yet be hers — who after seeing that a consulship in France can be combined with a commission merchant's calling, realizes that he ought to make some record of the remarkable events and scenes under his eyes. The early pages of this book, with their account of many matters that would interest a businessman more than a diplomat or writer, recall Arthur Young. They have the practical quality of his travels in France. Lee was fortunate in sojourning in Bordeaux when shipping and commerce presented painful issues between the American and French governments; he was still more fortunate in gaining the entree to Napoleon's court in Paris. He knew intimately Monroe and Talleyrand, Joel Barlow and Jefferson. He brought his European experience back to provincial America, and lived in the Washington of Monroe and John Quincy Adams with his memories of Paris as the capital of the Empire.

The personality of the diarist is also in many ways fascinating. He was a staunch republican, who at Versailles thought primarily of the injustices of the old regime; the peasantry had paid for all the luxuries of those robbers called nobles. He was a puritan, shocked by the indecent dress of the actresses at the Comédie Française. But like John Quincy Adams, with whom he shared a memorable day, he rapidly became a man of the world, a cosmopolite, whose tastes steadily broadened and who before long could qualify as a connoisseur in various fields. As a Francophile, in spite of himself he rebelled a little against Anglo-Saxon manners and aims. Throughout life he was something of an idealist, and his scheme in his middle years for establishing a factory in Washington to employ Swiss refugees appealed to the idealistic strain in Jefferson. Always he was a man of character, with firmly held convictions as to good conduct public and private, and with a ready detestation of the cruelties, squalors, and vices of which he saw so much on the European continent. His humor appears in his depiction of his Scots fellow traveler in France, and his compassion in many a passage. Altogether, he was and is a man worth knowing.

Readers will be grateful to Miss Mary Lee Mann for rescuing this remarkable document from the total obscurity in which it has long lain, and to Harvard University Press for presenting it in so attractive a form. The editing, in completeness, taste, and scholarly exactness, is worthy of a text which will be read with pleasure, and treasured as a scholarly source of unusual value.

Columbia University   Allan Nevins
September 1958

Preface

Entrepreneur, public servant, and lifelong democrat, William Lee of Massachusetts lived through the colorful and crucial years from 1772 to 1840 that saw the beginning and early growth of the American republic. Although Lee was not himself a chief character in American history, he gives us through his diary and letters a candid and telling glimpse of the struggles by which the hard-won independence of the young republic was assured. His activities as commercial agent of the United States at Bordeaux spanned the administrations of Jefferson and Madison, and his career as auditor of the Treasury in Washington brought him into close association with two other presidents — Monroe and Adams. His own record reveals him as a man of character and charm, an upright citizen and an able public servant.

On another, more private, level, William Lee's diary and letters give an intimate picture of a devoted American husband and father in the early nineteenth century: deeply attached to the wife who followed him to foreign shores, eager to form his daughters in the graces and accomplishments of proper young ladies, full of ambitious projects that might better his position.

The diary and letters passed from William Lee to his elder son, William Barlow Lee, who in turn handed them on to his son, Dr. William Lee of Washington, D.C. With a lively appreciation of the career and the writings of his ancestors, Dr. Lee preserved the letters in two large bound volumes; and it was these, together with the diary and another volume prepared by Dr. Lee's nephew, Charles Addison Mann, Jr., that I inherited from my mother — Dr. Lee's sister, Mrs. Mary Elizabeth Lee Mann. The three volumes of Lee's letters, as well as a number of unbound letters, a memorandum book running from 1794 to

1816, and the two small notebooks that comprise his diary have all been presented to the Library of Congress. Another small group of letters was given earlier to the Columbia University Libraries, in whose Special Collections they may be found.

Other letters from Lee are contained among the papers of Thomas Jefferson, James Madison, and James Monroe, and in other collections of papers covering the active period of his life. Quantities of his letters appear in the records of the Department of State for Bordeaux, in the National Archives; a number of others are filed at the Archives Étrangères in Paris. In addition to his letters and personal records, Lee wrote a great many articles for the *National Intelligencer* of Washington, D.C. The Rare Books Room at the Library of Congress houses two of his other works — a small pamphlet called *The Hog,* describing for Lee's son the many uses of that animal, and a short treatise on the War of 1812, *Les États-Unis et L'Angleterre.*

In compiling and editing this collection, I found that a manageable and readable volume required the omission of entire letters that were needlessly repetitious and of parts of others that were too detailed or that were simply statistical. In the text that follows, Lee's spelling of proper names, his punctuation, and his capitalization have been regularized in most cases, but his original syntax has been preserved throughout.

My thanks are due to Dr. St. George L. Sioussat, formerly Chief of the Manuscripts Division, Library of Congress, for his sustained interest in the compilation of these papers and for his invaluable advice. I am also deeply grateful for the kind assistance of Professor Allan Nevins of Columbia University, for his practical suggestions on method, for his repeated encouragement of my efforts to make the diary and letters available to scholars and to the public, and for his graciousness in writing the foreword.

Deciphering William Lee's handwriting — a difficult task at times — was aided by the valuable suggestions of Dr. Elizabeth G. McPherson and Dr. C. Percy Powell of the Manuscripts Division, Library of Congress, both of whom showed keen interest in my undertaking. To Dr. Julian P. Boyd, of Princeton

University, editor of *The Papers of Thomas Jefferson*, I am indebted for a list of Jefferson-Lee letters to be found outside the Library of Congress. Dr. Carl L. Lokke, Archivist in Charge, Foreign Affairs Branch, General Records Division, National Archives, kindly made available to me the material in this section, and gave his help in various important ways. Mr. Roland Baughman, Head of the Special Collections of the Libraries of Columbia University, has generously given permission to publish a letter in his care written to William Lee by Captain (later Admiral) Charles Baudin.

In my research for the explanatory notes I was helped immeasurably by the cooperation and advice of all members of the Library of Congress staff with whom I came in contact. My thanks go in particular to Mrs. Ann D. Brown, Stewart Dickson, and Beverly H. Brown of the Thomas Jefferson Room; and to Mrs. Marion J. Hughes and Mrs. Alice D. Guyer of the Genealogical Room. My work was further facilitated by the many courtesies extended by Colonel Willard Webb, Chief of the Stack and Reader Division.

The Redwood Library of Newport, Rhode Island, has also furnished me with many volumes which have served as sources for much of the information to be found in the explanatory notes.

I should also like to thank Professor Richard B. Morris of Columbia University for directing upon this volume his broad historical scholarship and for making useful suggestions as the project was nearing its end.

Mary Lee Mann

Jamestown, Rhode Island
March 14, 1958.

CONTENTS

ILLUSTRATIONS

The first of these two pages of the diary of William Lee contains the concluding part of an entry dated March 5th, continuing with one dated March 6, 1796. Lee's phonetic spelling of places is worth noting; for example, Suresnes is spelled " Souren." The second page, dated March 18th, contains an account of a visit to a library, " lately called the King's." This account has been omitted from the text because there is a description of this same library, now called the " National Library," in Lee's letter to his daughter Susan, December 17, 1809.

The exequatur was the official recognition given to William Lee in September 1801 by the government of France. The signatures of Napoleon Bonaparte, Talleyrand, and Maret, duc de Bassano, are noteworthy.

The small crayon portrait of William Lee was executed in Paris in the year 1812 by John Vanderlyn (1775–1852), well-known American artist of that period. It shows Lee in his consular dress, said to have been one of his own design. In one of his letters to his daughter Susan (page 148), Lee noted Napoleon's favorable comment concerning his attire. The portrait is signed by Vanderlyn, and on the back William Lee has written " To the best of mothers, best of friends, and best of wives."

SUSAN PALFREY LEE. *Original miniature owned by Cassandra Lee Arnold Keer (Mrs. Alexander W. Keer), great-great-granddaughter of William Lee.* 123

Susan Palfrey Lee was the daughter of Colonel William Palfrey and Susan Cazneau, his wife. Mrs. Lee was thus of French Huguenot origin through her mother. Painted on ivory, the miniature of Mrs. Lee in the dress of the Empire, probably done while she was in Paris in the winter of 1806–1807, was signed "Dagoty." This was undoubtedly Pierre Edouard Dagoty, a French miniature painter born in 1776. The painting is very probably the one described by William Lee in his letter of August 27, 1824 (see page 220), as an object of close attention by Baron de Maltitz because of its resemblance to Lee's daughter Mary, the Baron's future wife.

"ONE HOUR TOO LATE." *Original letter in the Special Collections of the Library of Columbia University.* 154

The note containing this phrase (see page 158) was written by William Lee on the outside of a letter dated July 16, 1815, which he received from Captain Charles Baudin (1784–1854). Captain Baudin was in direct charge of the attempt to save Bonaparte from the English by taking him to America on the *Bayadère*, a well-armed sloop of war which was at the mouth of the Gironde. William Lee and Count Clausel, two of the other plotters, were undoubtedly as much chagrined as Baudin was to hear that their plan was not to come to fruition because Napoleon had decided to give himself up to the English. This he did on July 15th, as reported by Baudin. Napoleon had supreme confidence that he would be liberally treated by the British nation.

Count Clausel was pursued and condemned to death, and had to escape to America, where he remained until 1825. Baudin was for a time engaged in commercial business at Le Havre, but he returned to the Navy, reaching the rank of admiral. The role of Captain Baudin in this plot is described by Thiers in his *Histoire du Consulat,* XX, 339, 545, 551.

LETTER TO HIS SON. *Original letter in the Lee-Palfrey Collection at the Library of Congress.* 155

In this letter to his elder son, William Barlow Lee, dated February 16, 1816, William Lee shows great interest in the boy's education and general welfare. Young William, then eleven years old, had been sent to Mr. Croix's boarding school at Sainte-Foy-La-Grande in the Department of the Gironde. This place was the seat of a Protestant Consistory, and the school was probably a Protestant one. How long before 1816 young William had attended the school at Sainte-Foy is not known; the last reference to schools in Lee's letters was to one in Paris in 1812. Not long after this letter, in June 1816, the Lee family left France. We know, however, from another letter not included in this book that William Lee sent the saddle to his son.

MARY ELIZABETH LEE, BARONESS DE MALTITZ. *Litho-graph owned by the editor.* 218

The lithograph shows the Baroness as a young married woman and was probably produced in Germany between 1827 and 1836 while her husband, Baron de Maltitz, was attached to the Russian legation in Berlin. "Maria Elisabeth, Baronin von Maltitz," appears at the bottom of the picture. There are no records that tell about an original picture from which the plate may possibly have been made, but on the left-hand side, near the large puffed sleeve, appears the name "L. Sebbers" as the artist who painted the portrait. This was undoubtedly Julius Ludwig Sebbers, who was born in Brunswick in 1804 and died at Berlin in 1837. He worked with porcelains at Munich and Brunswick, but he spent his last years in Berlin, where he did some portraits and lithographs. The lithograph, printed by Lemercier of Paris, whose name is at the right, is one of several copies still in existence.

SUSAN'S MINIATURE OF MARIETTE. *Miniature owned by the editor.* 219

Susan Palfrey Lee, elder daughter of William, was considered an artist of considerable skill. An example of her work is the miniature on ivory of the Lee's French maid, Mariette. Although in its present appearance the miniature shows little color, it was perhaps originally more highly colored. The delicate flesh tint still holds its quality, but the background, once dark blue, has become intensified with age and appears almost black. By using a magnifying glass on the dark background at the left, the signature "Susan Lee" may be discerned. The features, turban, and ruff show that Mariette was indeed a French woman.

A Yankee Jeffersonian

I

YOUNG ENTREPRENEUR AND TRAVELER

1796–1798

The first entry in William Lee's Diary, January 1, 1796, marks his departure from the United States for commercial business in France. Information on Lee's life to this point is scattered and scant, but from the book by Lee's grandson entitled *John Leigh of Agawam (Ipswich) Massachusetts, 1634–1671* we learn some interesting facts about Lee's paternal ancestors. The John Leigh (or Lee) of the title, great-great-grandfather of William, was an independent and free-thinking Englishman, the tradition about whose character and emigration to the American colonies is described in this same book:

John Lee was of an ancient and honorable family of the city of London, and lived with his parents, being well instructed in the principles of the Christian religion . . . [he] was a very comely person, and every way handsome, and gracefully beautiful, and has so good learning . . . Our John had an elder sister . . . [who] was afraid John would get himself into trouble with the rabble . . . against the king. [John was therefore persuaded] to emigrate to Boston, in New England, . . . [for there] he could worship God in public without being complained of and free from Popery and all mobs. . . .

In 1634, according to the records of the Colony, John Lee was fined for " speaking repchfully of the Gov'r."

John Lee's son, Joseph Lee, and his grandson, Henry Lee, were both born at Ipswich. But Henry's fourteenth child, the first William Lee (father of the William Lee of this book), spent much of his life in Canada. " When a young man [he] was employed in connection with the movements of British troops against Canada in the old French wars of 1754 to 1763, in the construction and management of the batteaux used on the lakes and rivers . . . and in consequence of his satisfactory conduct was placed in the dock yards at Halifax, Nova Scotia, as foreman of the carpenters of the Royal Navy Yard. In 1814 he was pensioned and retired. . . ."

In 1770 this William Lee had married Mary Cobb, daughter of James and Hannah (Rich) Cobb of Truro, Cape Cod, Massachusetts. Their son, the William of this volume, was born in Halifax on December 31, 1772. At some point — the date can only be surmised — young William detached himself from the milieu of British loyalists and became a full-fledged American citizen, the more vehement as if to disprove the contention, " once an Englishman always an Englishman." With the aid of his first cousin, the Reverend James Freeman of Boston, William was sent to Phillips Academy in Andover, Massachusetts. In 1790, at the age of eighteen, he established himself as a commission merchant in Boston, " being connected with Messrs. Lyman and Williams." William Lee was married by this same Reverend James Freeman on June 26, 1794, to Susan Palfrey, daughter of Colonel William Palfrey, who had been aide-de-camp to General Washington and paymaster general of the Continental Army; en route to France to serve as consul general in 1780, Colonel Palfrey was lost at sea. William and Susan Lee's first child, Susan Palfrey Lee, was born in Boston the April following their marriage, in 1795.

The beginning of 1796 found William Lee embarking for Bordeaux on mercantile business, leaving his wife and small daughter in Boston. He spent two years in France, England, and Holland visiting, observing, and transacting business. These activities, however, were complicated by the ambiguous relations between the United States and Europe. Relationships with France were particularly uneasy. Despite the Franco-American alliance so important in the winning of the War of Independence, and despite the good offices of Benjamin Franklin and Thomas Jefferson as ministers to France, the friendship between the two nations gradually deteriorated. The course of the French Revolution, the renewed outbreak of old strifes between England and France, and the young American republic's desire to stay out of European conflicts — all these weakened the alliance. For some years before 1796 French privateers had been attacking American ships, and by November 15, 1796 — Lee had been there a year — France broke off diplomatic relations with the United States.

Despite the stormy political climate, Lee made several important associations with distinguished Americans which proved helpful to him during the rest of his career. With Mr. and Mrs. Joel Barlow, Lee began a lifelong friendship that led eventually to Lee's entrée to the court of Napoleon. Another renowned compatriot, James Monroe, who was American minister to France from 1794 to 1796, wrote to James Madison that Lee " was much my friend in Paris."

The material that follows is made up of Lee's diary, the texts of its two original ledger volumes combined for the sake of continuity. The first volume begins with Lee's departure from New England and ends with the entry of October 14, 1796, describing a visit with Mr. Daniel Parker to the environs of Paris. Presumably Lee remained in Paris until he set out for Holland on January 3, 1797. With the entry of that date the second volume commences. This part of the diary primarily recounts Lee's observations of the Dutch people and their customs. Particularly interesting to students of American history is his description of an all-day excursion to Broek made in the company of John Quincy Adams, John Marshall, and some others. On this trip (also noted in the Adams *Memoirs*) began a friendship between Lee and Adams which was to last until both were old men in New England. A letter from Lee to Talleyrand in November 1797 indicates that Lee was in Paris at that time. But after June 22, 1797, there are no diary entries until March 18, 1798, when Lee left Paris for the United States.

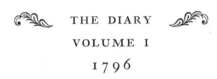

THE DIARY

VOLUME I

1796

Friday, January 1. At eleven o'clock this morning I embarked on board the ship *Mary*, Benj. Homans, Master, bound for Bordeaux, the wind being WNW and a fine breeze. At sunset we were up with Cape Cod, from which the Captain takes his departure.

May I never forget my present feelings! How painful is the reflection that every hour, nay every moment, drives me farther from happiness, the society of my affectionate wife and little one and all I hold dear! O God! Thou dispenser of every good and perfect gift, grant I beseech Thee success to all my lawful undertakings, that I may be able to return to my family and enjoy the sweets of domestic happiness.

Sunday, January 17. We are now but a few leagues to the westward of the Azores. So far we have had a remarkable rough passage; continual squalls from WNW to N for six days past with hail and sleet. For the most part we have been laying to. I have been very dull. The thoughts of home rush upon me, displaying all the sweets which the society of my dear amiable wife is capable of bestowing.

Sunday, January 24th. This week past has been very boisterous. The wind has been from W to N and at times very heavy, accompanied with hail and sleet. Homans says he never experienced more disagreeable weather in all his passages. Indeed we have not had a pleasant day since we left Boston. Two or three seas have come on board, but have done no damage except washing away the whole of the quarter boards, deranging the things on deck, and throwing the boats to leeward.

The sailors, poor fellows, have not had much comfort. Their beds and all their clothes have been wet for this fortnight past. I am much depressed and a little frightened. I now think that nothing would tempt me to cross the ocean again in the winter months. Many vessels must suffer in this rough weather. The tackle of our own is in a very bad state. The ropes look white and are very much chafed.

The little anxiety I have felt this voyage will I hope have a good effect should Providence permit me to finish it fortunately. To be again blessed with a fireside of my own, with my dear family around me, would be unsupportable happiness.

Wednesday, January 27th. This morning looks pleasant; there being a small breeze and a middling sea. On Monday last at two o'clock, the sea increasing and the wind rising with great violence from WSW, we were obliged to heave to. At five o'clock in the afternoon, we were alarmed in the cabin by the boatswain's bellowing out that the last sea which struck the ship had carried away the bowsprit, and opened the decks forward, so that the water came in ten hogsheads at a time. The Captain and all of us run on deck, where we found the people had collected aft. Homans and his mate went forward and soon returned, having found the sea had done little or no injury; the foot of the bowsprit having only just started with the violence of the shock, which pressed the okum out of the seams. The sea at this time run amazingly high, and it lightened very sharp.

The sailors are much alarmed. None of them are good seamen, an unfortunate thing for us; for had we have had a good crew, the Captain is of opinion that we would have made our passage in fifteen or eighteen days. Not one of the men can steer the ship when it blows hard. The great demand for American seamen, with the high wages given, has induced many to take to this element for a livelihood that would do better to plough the earth than the seas. Masters of vessels ought to be more careful in procuring men. They now take anything that looks like a sailor, and many suffer for it.

The wind continued with great violence all Monday night and yesterday until this morning, when it abated. And how happy do I feel with the change! How manifest has been the providence of God toward us! Those beautiful lines of the poet have often occurred to me:

> He
> Tho' chang'd thro' all, is yet in all the same,
> Great in the earth as in the aetherial frame,
> Warms in the sun, refreshes in the breeze,
> Glows in the stars, and blossoms in the trees;
> Lives thro' all life, extends thro' all extent,
> Spreads undivided, operates unspent;
> To Him no first, no low, no great, no small.
> He fills, He bounds, connects, and equals all! [1]

What trifles will at times affect us! Last night I dreamed that I met Mr. Freeman, who informed me that little Susan was thrown out of a chair and killed. It grieved me very much and I woke in tears, but could not banish the vision from my thoughts. But what are dreams? Nonsense.

Thursday, January 28th. The wind was moderate the whole of yesterday, and continued so until about six o'clock of this evening, when it began to increase with sharp lightning and heavy thunder. The horizon looks very black and dreadful. One of the men was so benumbed with the lightning, as he was taking out the pump spears [pump-rods], that it was full an hour before he could use his right arm.

Saturday, January 30th. The wind continued blowing excessive hard all Thursday night. Yesterday morning it lulled for a few hours, which gave us some hopes of a change of weather; but at twelve o'clock we were again forced to heave to. We indeed experience very serious gales! At sundown the wind increased with great violence and blowed harder than I ever heard it either at sea or on shore. At twelve o'clock in the night, we shipped a sea which again threw the boats to leeward, but the reef-tree saved them. It even drew the large iron bolts out of the deck, to which the camboose [caboose] was secured, washing it to leeward and destroying the camboose house, binnacles, water jars, at the same time washing a man overboard, who luckily recovered by a rope, though not without being much hurt by the rubbish which went overboard with him. His legs are considerably bruised, his face cut, and his eye dangerously wounded. This gale blew without cessation the whole night, but abated this morning. We are in a bad condition. The ship looks like a wreck. The Captain is now employed in dressing the wounded man; the mate and people are repairing the damages we have sustained, putting the decks in order and bending a cable. Two good days would probably put us in port.

Sunday, February 7. The weather has been more moderate for eight days past. The squalls have not been so heavy. The wind has varied from SW to NW, accompanied with rain only. We have been laying to [a] great part of the time, Capt. Homans fearing to run until he could procure a good observation, which he did on Friday last; and at four o'clock in the afternoon the water appeared to be colored. The mate sounded and found we had eighty-five fathoms.

Tuesday, February 9th. At three o'clock in the afternoon we made the land and the Cordouan Tower or lighthouse at the entrance of the river Garonne. Not having sufficient time before dark to run in, the Capt. hauls off until morning.

Wednesday Feb. 10th. At eight o'clock in the morning the Capt. made sail, the weather looking very unfavorable. He crowded canvas, determined to push for the port, fearing a lee shore, should it come on to blow hard, and well knowing the incapability of the ship to beat off in her present condition, with sails worn out, rigging chafed, and sailors disabled. The lighthouse, when we made sail, was between three and four leagues distant.

At eleven o'clock the ship struck on a reef of sand, called the *Olive Bank*, below the entrance of Passe de Graves and NNE from the lighthouse three miles. Here we lay for half an hour, the sea breaking round us. One or two very large ones threw the ship over the bank, when she floated. Her rudder by this time was gone, and a number of pieces of her bottom seen on the water. There was also six feet of water in the hold. The reef to windward breaking the force of the sea, preserved us, and while the ship was drifting in shore, we collected a few things and threw the boats overboard. Four men took to the yawl, and the rest of us, thirteen in number, to the long boat, having full two miles to row in a rough sea. We had also a shoal place to go over. We here escaped miraculously from several very heavy seas, which the boats, being light, rose to. The yawl went on shore, high and dry. The long boat, being larger and having thirteen persons on board with the luggage, struck the sand some hundred yards from the shore, when we all jumped out and held on the gunnel, until the surf threw us up on the beach, where thirty of the inhabitants were collected armed with pitch forks, spades, &c. When they found we were Americans, they appeared friendly.

After collecting our things, and leaving the mate and people to watch the motions of the ship, and guard what was saved, the Captain, Mr. Savage and Mr. Peters, two passengers, with myself proceed[ed] for Soulac, a village three miles off. One of the principal men conducted us to his house and made us a good fire by which we changed our clothes. We had a very fatiguing jaunt from the water side to the village over sand hills much worse than those of Cape Cod.

In the evening some of the sailors came to the house to inform us that shortly after we left the ship, the seas threw her down on her beam ends, carried away the main and mizzen masts, and

7

opened the decks so that the cargo (part of it) was floating on shore, which the inhabitants, being four or five hundred in numbers, were stealing as fast as it landed. So soon as the tide made, the sea increased, breaking at times over the mast head, the reef to windward affording no shelter.

Thus ends a voyage: a very disagreeable one. Capt. Homans is the greatest sufferer. I am very sorry for him. He is really a very deserving man; a man of good sense and information, and well acquainted with his business. Had he not have been a good seaman, we should never have made the land. He has treated me with a good deal of politeness and attention.

Thursday, February 11. I had a good night's rest. After breakfasting on bread and wine, the common fare here, I went to the wreck,² and a most sorrowful sight it was. The ship had beat into a thousand pieces. The remains lay high up on the sand so that I walked around them. The conduct of the inhabitants is a disgrace to human nature. There were at least four hundred men, women, and children employed in carrying away the goods. The beef they put into sacks. After taking the heads out of the casks, they took away as many as eighty firkins of butter, an hundred boxes of candles, and destroyed full three hundred barrels [of] oil, thinking the barrels contained provisions. They also cut up the cables, rigging, and sails, and robbed the sailors' chest which floated on shore. Our being present had no effect. We thought it as much as our lives were worth to oppose them.

These people plundered at least 3000 pounds worth of property before we found a means to put a stop to it. I imagine from their dexterity that they are accustomed to this business. Many of them had instruments with which they easily drew the bolts from out of the planks of the ship. Numbers of them were mounted on stilts three foot from the ground, which enabled them to wade into the water and to go to and return from their huts with great dispatch, traveling as fast as the common trot of a horse. I never saw a more miserable set of beings to appearance, and from their conduct I judge they are as destitute of principle as clothing. As for humanity they are total strangers

8

to it. My entrance into France is not a pleasing one, nor have I received a favorable impression of the people.

I felt very melancholy at sight of the wreck. How very fortunate we were to get on shore! Had we have remained on board one hour longer, or run on shore in the night, or lost our boats, as we came near to twice, we must certainly have perished. How grateful ought we to be to our Heavenly Father for having spared our lives! It was what I little expected when the ship struck. And O my S[usan]! In all my distress I thought of you, thought of your situation, and of what you would suffer when you heard of my misfortune. But by the goodness of God I have been preserved. I hope to make you happy, dear, deserving girl.

At noon I returned from the wreck to the house of M. Drouinand, leaving the Captain and crew endeavoring to save all they could. After dining on bread and wine, I took young Peters, a lad of fifteen years of age, and set off for Verdon to take passage for Bordeaux. Soulac is a village of some extent. The houses are miserable, built of stone one story high, roof with tile, and no floors. There are also a number of huts. They, the inhabitants, are extremely poor. The soil is wet and low. They are preserved from the sea by sand hills, some of which are very high; the whole about three miles in extent. There are no grapes here about. They have a number of sheep and cattle. They also raise considerable grain.

Friday, February 12. We arrived at this place, Verdon, at about four o'clock in the afternoon of yesterday, when we found we could have a passage in a boat that was to have sailed this morning; but the wind prevented.

Verdon is a small village of perhaps seventy houses. It is about a league from Soulac on the banks of the river Garonne. Here is a small garrison, consisting of one hundred men. These are the first French soldiers I have ever seen. I do not wonder at their numerous victories, if the whole French army is composed of such fine men. There is a small fortification here of ten forty-eight pounders and a howitzer. A custom house is also established

9

here, and there is a frigate stationed opposite the village to protect the trade. All the vessels coming in take their pilots from this place.

At the mouth of this river is built on a body of rocks, four and a half miles from either shore, a lighthouse called the Cordouan Tower, said to be one of the finest in the world, composed of stone, and of an astonishing height, so as to be discovered from sea long before you can see the land. There are also a number of beacons to direct the pilots, the channels being very crooked, of which there are five. Some of them a man must have a thorough knowledge of before he can enter. These channels are called *passes*. It was at the beginning of the southermost that our vessel struck.

At the house where we lodged last night, the old man and woman appeared very kind, and abused their neighbors very much for their vile conduct. After we had been in bed about an hour, a young man entered, whom we supposed to be the son. He said he had just come from the wreck, and his ass was well loaded with butter and cordage; and was going to tell what he had done and how much he had stolen, when the old woman told him to stop for that there were two of the unfortunate persons in bed in the room and that one of them understood French. By this I found (together with the two soldiers who brought my trunk from Soulac asking Mr. Peters if I had any gold about me, and the landlord of the inn, where we got supper last evening, saying the wreck was so far off that he could not bring what he wanted) that we were among a set of villains, and really began to feel uneasy, for I had considerable gold with me.

We took our breakfast and dinner at the inn: one of the most dirty ones and full of the most ill-looking devils I ever saw. They charged us for our poor fare, three meals, more than would have boarded us a week in Boston. After dinner the boatswain and five seamen came from the wreck, and at four o'clock, the wind veering fair and the tide making, we all sailed for Bordeaux. We had a fair wind and passed about fifty vessels that were proceeding up the river. In three hours we landed at Pauillac, ten leagues from Verdon and half way to Bordeaux.

Saturday, February 13th. I had an excellent night's rest and partook of a good breakfast: the first coffee, sugar, butter and cream I have seen in France. The people eat, drink, and sleep on their wine. It serves them with bread for breakfast, dinner, and supper.

This is quite a large commodious tavern. The town, I am told, consists of about two hundred houses. They are built of stone, roofed with tile and floored with large stones and brick. The street on the edge of the river is very handsome, the houses being four stories and well ornamented. There are at least fifty vessels before the town waiting for the tide. Most of the crews are on shore in the taverns and grog shops, which are numerous; it being the half-way place, where vessels are obliged to anchor; for it takes in general two tides to get up the river.

At one o'clock we sailed for Bordeaux. It rained so hard that I had but a poor view of this delightful river. I saw a number of handsome houses beautifully situated and which must be enchanting in summer.

We passed the ancient city of Blaye. . . . All the large ships stop here in going up the river to take out their guns. Some miles above Blaye, a sudden squall came on with such fury that it whirled the sand off of the bank, to which we were near, full fifty foot into the air. We were very lucky in getting our sails down before it reached us. Two boats above us in the river were upset and some men were drowned. At seven o'clock we landed at Bordeaux.

Sunday February 14th. I lodged at Mr. Peters', one of the first merchants here. In the morning, when taking a walk, it appeared very singular to me that every kind of business should be going on. I cannot think it right to consider all days alike. There ought to be some distinction. There can no good arise from this subversion of all order. Mr. Peters invited me to go to the theatre. I made some objection, but quieted my conscience with the old saying: "When you are among the heathen, do as the heathen do." I did not tarry long, for I really felt disagreeably, and thought I had better be at my lodgings. The house is very handsome and was well filled.

Monday, February 15th. I have engaged lodgings at the Hotel Tremelle,[3] an elegant house that belonged to a marquis of that name, who was guillotined, as many others were, for no other reason than that he was a man of property. Opposite my chambers is a famous fortification, called the Trumpet Castle,[4] built in Louis XIV['s] time by the celebrated engineer Vauban. It is an immense structure of hewn stone. The walls are thirty foot high. It is said that, when the accounts were shown to Louis, he asked if it was built of gold. This fort is situated on the banks of the river, where it is not more than half a mile broad, and in the center of the street running along the water side.

Tuesday, February 16th. Last evening I went to the theatre. The house was crowded. There were a vast number of women of the loose sort. I am told no others frequent this place. It is a sink of debauchery. You pay but fourpence sterling for the best seat in the house. The lowness of the price permits all classes. There is no distinction of persons. You must sit down with a smutty rascal, who stinks of garlic enough to knock a horse down, and who, if you do not look sharp, will pick your pockets. I begin to dislike this liberty and equality. I think myself superior to a bawd or a pickpocket.

This theatre was finished about fifteen years since, and cost 500,000 pounds sterling. It is a superb building. The theatre part holds three thousand persons, but there are a number of other apartments. To describe it I am not capable. The uniformity, harmony, beauty, and elegance of it struck me so forcibly that I shall ever remember it.

Wednesday, February 17th. I went with my friend John Gray [5] to see the remains of an amphitheatre built by the Roman Emperor Gallienus, who flourished about [250] years after Christ. Great part of the walls of this astonishing building (as it must have been when entire) are standing. Four of the arches are whole and of great height. What surprised me most was to see the stones of which these walls are built so decayed, and the large brick, which is lodged between the stones for ornament, remain firm and hard as flint. These brick must be of a very superior part to what is now made.

Thursday, February 18th. Last evening I went to the Comedy and heard the famous Madame Sereuser,[6] who is said to have the finest voice and is called the best singer in France. The scenery was good, particularly one where a number of angels came down in a cloud and took up M[adame] S. The dress of the actresses I do not like. Their arms are generally uncovered and one of their breasts. There were a number of elegant dancers, but their figures disgusted me. The petticoats of these dancers were of muslin, their chemise of the same, the bottom of which was bound with lace and, though longer than the petticoat, did not come much below the knees. A silk net covered part of their arms, their breasts, and the lower part of their bodies, of a flesh color, so that at a distance I thought they were half naked; for this cobweb covering was drawn over them so tight that you could discover every muscle. They performed admirably, and displayed their hips at every move. Such indecent representations can never lead the mind to virtue. All the exhibitions I have been at appeared to me to be calculated only to inspire libidinous thoughts.

Friday, February 19th. I walked round to see the city, and was shown a large cathedral [7] that was erected by Edward, the Black Prince. It is truly Gothic. The niches, which are very numerous, are crowded with images. Some of these statues are much injured, particularly those that bore crowns or mitres. This church has two steeples. The whole makes a very rude, confused appearance. There are a number of little shops now opened in this once holy place. Near this church stands a monument, for what purpose raised I could not learn. This is also going to ruin. It is built in the same form as the cathedral. There are a number of antiquities here which I think would please the literary and curious.

Bordeaux is situated on the river Garonne (which takes its rise in the Pyrenees mountains). There is a communication between this river and the Mediterranean by means of a canal,[8] the work of Louis XIV, and is about sixty miles from the sea. The navigation up the river is difficult; but the ships, when at Bordeaux, have a fine harbor and deep water. Vessels of seven and eight hundred tons lay within twenty yards of the chatroons [9] or water streets. The modern part of this city is very handsome. The houses are built of white stone four stories high and well ornamented. It lies along the river in form of a semicircle. The street along the side of the river is very beautiful.

I admire the construction of these houses. On the lower floor are the stores; above this is the counting house, and the other three stories are the apartments for the merchant's family. All of these houses have balconies annexed to them, from which you have a fine prospect of the shipping and boats, which are numerous, and the high land on the opposite side of the river (southerly), which is well cultivated and adorned with handsome country seats.

For the interior part of the city I cannot say much. The houses are some of them very high, to which they have no yards. This renders the streets extremely dirty, which are also very narrow and wretchedly paved. Bordeaux is said to have contained, in the year 1790, 100,000 inhabitants, but, by what I can learn, there are not at present arising from a destructive war more than eighty and certainly not more than ninety thousand. It has always been considered one of the richest cities in France. It is at present a place of great trade, though not to be compared to what it was formerly. Should France regain her colonies, from which this place derived almost all its riches, it will no doubt preserve its preeminence. The country around Bordeaux is noted for the superiority of its wines. They have delicious fruits and manufacture excellent brandy.

Saturday, February 20th. I went into the public walks. These must be handsome in summer. At present the trees are bare. There are some fine ornaments about the walks, but most of them have been destroyed as they appertained to royalty. I also examined two frigates that are building. They appear to be fine ships, and I think the French are justly entitled to the character they have obtained of constructing the strongest, handsomest, and fastest sailing ships in Europe. I am told that a few months ago the English took to pieces a French ship for the model.

Sunday, February 21st. The weather for a few days past has been very pleasant, and much like the beginning of May about Boston. I observe that all classes of citizens think more of Sunday than of *Decade*,[10] and not much of either. The public walks have been full of people the whole day until the theatre opened, when they all flocked to it. I have seen more women to-day than I ever saw before in the same time. Most of them appeared very handsome and were well dressed, and walked very well.

Last evening I was at a ball given by Mr. Theo. Peters. The supper was truly elegant. The whole entertainment cost five hundred *louis d'or*. The ladies appeared to great advantage, and I thought some of them were beautiful. They were dressed with exquisite taste and displayed their forms, which were in general good, in the most favorable manner. Gambling was here carried to a great height. Several persons lost so much as one hundred *louis d'or*, and one man in particular won five hundred.

Monday, February 22nd. Walked out to see more of this truly handsome city. . . . The stone of which they build in this city is procured from a mountain a few leagues below on the north side [of] the river. It is quite soft, porous and white, and when exposed to the air hardens. I was surprised to see so many holes in this mountain, and was told that when they dug out the stone they had another object in view: that of making cells to dwell in. I saw at least one thousand of these caves that were inhabited by the poor people.

Tuesday, February 23rd. Rode out with Madame Peters to her country seat. The day very fine, the country not remarkably beautiful. Mrs. P. is not a handsome woman, but an amiable one, blest with a fine family of children, whom she delights to make happy. She is the only domestic character I have met with in France. He [Mr. Peters] is a very extraordinary character. Six years ago he was obliged to leave Holland, his native country, on account of his political principles. He fled to Bordeaux, where he remained for two years a clerk, and frequently has been under the necessity of going without a dinner for the want of money to purchase it. He has by his industry acquired a fortune and is said to be worth 200,000 sterling. I have seen twelve hundred beggars at his door receiving *assignats*.[11] It is a custom with him to distribute more or less every day.

At one o'clock a number of gentlemen came out with young Peters to dine. Among them was a General Hutor, a young man of five or six and twenty, a very well-dressed, pleasing officer. After dinner we visited the seat of a Jew. Human invention cannot surpass this place in beauty. The walks, images, statues, ponds of fish, grottos, fountains, with a hermitage and temple of reason seem to surpass all imagination. Nor is the furniture of the house less superb than the gardens. All seem to be the work of the most florid fancy. At dusk we returned, passing a wood. One of the Frenchmen in company told us he once hid himself in it for ten days, having killed a man in a duel, and then went into the particulars with all the *sang-froid* imaginable. I went to the theatre this evening with Gen'l Hutor, and was introduced to a seat with the municipality.

Wednesday, February 24th. All day preparing for my journey to Paris. Wrote my affectionate wife a long letter.

Thursday, February 25th. Passed the river Garonne at the upper part of the chatroons at two o'clock for Paris with the courier. I see I shall not be pleased with the French mode of traveling. The carriage is very clumsy, horses very bad, and roads execrable.

March 1st. Arrived last night at twelve o'clock in this great city, Paris, having been four days and a half on the road, riding day and night: a journey of four hundred English miles through the most delightful country in the world. For the first hundred miles the weather was pleasant and the men and women were out cultivating the fields. The middle and latter part of the journey I suffered a good deal with the cold, being confined in a little box, in which the courier and myself could just squeeze, and where I could not find room to stretch my legs. In this place I also slept, and whenever I got out of the carriage, I could hardly walk. My knees, feet, and hands were much swelled, and my teeth so sore with the cold that I found it difficult to bite a piece of bread.

The weather was so very pleasant at Bordeaux that I did not prepare for nor expect a change. The inconvenience was not so great as I expected to feel from this jaunt, and I attribute my not taking a violent cold to the jolting. The roads might be easily made very good, and I imagine in peaceable times there are none better; but they have now something else to attend to. A person would never suppose from the appearance of the people that they were visited by any calamity. They are in general very cheerful and wear the picture of health. I saw none of those meager devils that some English authors mention, nor none that resembled the pot-gutted, bloated Americans and Englishmen that I have met. They are far from being in a starving condition. I found wine, bread, beans, and poultry in abundance.

From the great impositions I found I was likely to meet with, I judged it most prudent to agree to pay the courier three *louis d'or* for my sustenance and for the postilions. This, with ten more I gave him for my seat, brought me to Paris. The French have a vile trick of imposing on strangers. They are in general very dirty. Horses, cows, oxen, jackasses, sheep, poultry, men, women, and children all live under one roof. In general you pass through the stable to get into the house.

We passed through innumerable villages, the streets of which were very nasty and narrow, the houses built in general with stone, having no floors. Some of them were of mud with thatched roofs. . . . I stopped at the following towns: Angoulême, situated on a high hill in the department of Charente, at the foot of which runs the river Charente. The river gives birth to numerous manufactories, particularly the paper. They have wood in abundance. This is what the country I traveled through to this place appears to be destitute of. The roads on entering the city are lined with trees. The poplars attracted my notice, they being very large and in great numbers. Every little village I have seen in France has a mall. I saw a fowl at Angoulême, which weighed without the feathers eight pounds. They sew up their pullets and, by stopping evacuation, they fatten in a few days and grow to a large size. The capons too, which you meet with at every inn, are of a fine flavor.

On the 28th [February], we came to the town of Poitiers in the department of Vienne. This place is situated on a hill at the foot of which runs the river Clain. The gardens and trees beautiful; churches large and Gothic. There are two very handsome guard houses at the entrance of the town. Some of the streets very narrow, and infested with beggars. This class of people are pretty numerous throughout France. I was told that there was a number of antiquities here, particularly an amphitheatre. This place contains 15,000 souls.

The next place of note which we arrived at was Tours, in the department of Indre-et-Loire, on the river Loire, and without exception the most delightful place I ever beheld. The great street, leading to the bridge, is better than half a mile long and lined with houses four and five stories high, built of white stone and beautifully decorated. The bridge, which is thrown over the Loire, runs in a line with this street and is said to be the handsomest in Europe. Three of the arches have been carried away with the ice and I counted twelve remaining ones. This bridge must be at least, when finished, eleven hundred feet long. This place is famous for its silk manufactories and red wines. Its population is said to be 25,000. The delightful groves and walks, ponds and rivulets, round this place must make it an enchanting summer residence. . . .

We rode from Tours along the river Loire upon a causeway thirty foot high, edged with hewn stone and about sixty feet wide. Whether this ridge was natural or artificial I could not learn: perhaps both. We passed a vast number of flat-bottom boats; some of them large enough to carry one hundred tons. We posted along the river until we arrived at Orléans. This is quite a large, ancient, opulent city on the river Loire in the department of Loiret. It is said to contain upwards of 40,000 inhabitants.

Here the famous Maid of Orleans lived. There are a number of handsome churches, particularly one in the Gothic style. There are also many antiquities. The streets are spacious. Their commerce is very considerable, and consists of wine, brandy, corn and sugar: this last article is brought raw from Nantes and Rochelle; 100,000 hundredweights of loaf sugar is sent from this place in the course of a year. Sheep skins are also dressed here in great quantities, and they also manufacture great numbers of hose of all kinds. The environs of this place are beautiful, and the bridge leading to it justly admired.

Here we leave this beautiful river, having rode along its banks for twenty-five French leagues, and cross a country where not an inch of ground is to be seen uncultivated, until we arrive at Paris. I lament very much my not being able to tarry longer on this road. My finances would not allow my traveling agreeable to my wishes. When I got out of the carriage in Paris, I was conducted to the municipality, who examined my passport and permitted me to seek lodgings.

After hunting some time, I found a dirty chamber in the Hotel d'Angleterre. Here I lodged two nights and took my meals with my friend J. Putnam.[12] The master of the house had the impudence to charge me six crowns for sleeping two nights in his house. He took three. I find I shall pay dear for being an American. A stranger is well known in Paris. If he goes into a shop to buy anything, he is sure to be asked triple the price they would charge a citizen for the same article, and they are so polite, agreeable, and affable, that a person acquainted only with the rough-hewn, honest, natural, American manners cannot escape from their impositions.

March 5th. I have at length found good lodgings at the house of Madame St. Hilaire.[13] I have for inmates: Mr. S. Broom, Senr. of New Haven, Connecticut, a very worthy good man; and Mrs. Barlow, a very amiable woman, wife of Mr. J[oel] Barlow, now negotiating our treaty with Algiers; Mr. Tupper and wife of Boston; Dr. Brockenbrough of Virginia; Mr. Gelston of New York; and Monsieur Garilhe, member of the Assembly of Five Hundred. Their society is very agreeable.[14]

I find a vast number of Americans in Paris: among them from Boston are: Mr. R. Codman; S. Williams; J. Higginson; J. Waldo; [15] J. Putnam.

The snow has fallen two foot, and the weather is as cold as we commonly have it in Boston in midwinter.

March 6th. Dined with the American minister, Mr. Monroe,[16] and on the 9th with Fulwar Skipwith,[17] American consul, at his house at Suresnes, a place about five miles from Paris. Agoing to it I passed a bridge called Neuilly, the most beautiful one I have yet seen. It is perfectly level; of white stone, and seems to be as light as a swan on the water. . . .

March 18th. Having no business to do, I have employed myself in reading, writing my friends, and running about the city. . . . I went to the gallery of paintings in a building which joins the Louvre to the Tuileries. The collection is one of the best, if not the very best, in the world. There is here two hundred and fifty feet of the room hung with the battles of Alexander by Le brun; [18] but as I have been but once to this place, and shall probably find myself there often, I will not mention the particular pieces until I am better acquainted with them.

March 19th. Went to the Grand Opera, and saw the representation of Telemachus in the island of Calypso; [19] the dancing beautiful at times. There were fifty nymphs on the stage dressed in a modest manner adorned with flowers. The part of Telemachus was performed by the celebrated Vestris,[20] the best dancer in the world. He is a very stout muscular man. He performs with surprising agility. I have seen him spring fifteen feet, fall upon one leg, spin round upon his heel with great rapidity, and rest in the graceful attitude of a flying Mercury. His feats are really astonishing. I am told that he was offered 2000 sterling a year to perform in London. In this piece the best singers in France performed: Mons. Lays.[21] His voice is very melodious and powerful, and his manner natural.

This is called the handsomest house in Paris, much of the form of the Boston theatre, but not so elegant. It holds five thousand persons and has three rows of boxes. The stage is very large, and the scenery the best in Europe, and managed with great expertness. The scenes rise from under the stage, slide in sideways, and fall from aloft. There are seventeen theatres in this city open every night in the week and generally crowded. The poor put their children to bed, and go to the play from a principle of economy, as they can go for the sixteenth part of a dollar: much cheaper than wood and candles for an evening.

I have not seen a drunken person in Paris, and I have heard Americans that have resided here two years make the same remark. Nor have I seen a quarrel in the streets; and the city is as quiet by eleven o'clock at night as the town of Boston, and more so. This appears very singular to me, especially as there is at present 50,000 troops in and about the city under arms.

March 20th. I took breakfast this morning with citizen l'Hauteval,[22] after which Williams and myself walked round the city. This is both Décadi and Sunday; the streets full of people. We went into a large Gothic church, and [I] was surprised to find them performing Mass. This is the first religious ceremony I have seen since I have been in this country, and I was pleased to find that there are yet in France some persons left who wish to preserve a system of faith and worship. The Roman Catholic religion is better than none, and the observation of Bacon that the errors of superstition are not more dangerous than those of free thinking is very just.[23]

We walked round about the city and came to the Place de [la] Grève,[24] where the guillotine stood. The lamp iron, on which so many men swung did not escape my notice. From there we went to Jardin des Plantes. They are but just beginning to decorate this place, and the museum was not open. I saw here two camels, two white bears, and several monkeys of singular species.

In the evening I went to the Italian and Vaudeville Theatres. The former is quite a handsome house. There are four tiers of boxes in form nearly of an oval. These boxes are decorated with wreaths of flowers, gilt. The stage is rather small and the scenery very good though not equal to that of the Grand Opera. They were performing *Romeo and Juliet*.[25] This piece is an opera with something of Shakespeare's plot, and appears quite ridiculous to one who has ever seen it in English. This house contains three thousand persons. Vaudeville is a very indifferent house. I am informed that from three to eleven hundred persons are employed in each of the theatres in Paris, and that the Grand Opera, where there are eleven hundred performers, costs the nation every night upwards of 3000 crowns.

March 26th. I went last evening to the Theatre of the Republic, formerly Théâtre Variétés. This is by far the handsomest house in Paris, and when the preference is given to the Grand Opera, it must be on account of its scenery, and being the most fashionable resort.

Paris was said to contain 800,000 souls some time past. When bread was scarce, the convention decreed that a certain quantity should daily be distributed to the poor. This drew vast numbers from the country, and I am informed that there are at present in this city 950,000 inhabitants. It is called six leagues in circumference, contains between 35,000 and 40,000 houses and five thousand streets. Most of the houses are five stories; many six, and some seven stories. The streets are narrow and very dirty. There are four handsome squares and many superb houses; but these a person cannot see unless you enter the courts; the stables in general being in front, through which you enter by an arch into fine yards. Almost every genteel house has something of a garden to it. I admire the style of building. They finish inside with plaster of Paris, having very little wood, except the doors and some floors. The stairs are generally stone with iron balustrades ingeniously wrought. The rooms are very high: from fifteen to thirty feet, and extravagantly finished. I have seen the squares called Place Royale, Place Vendôme, Place des Victoires and Place de la Révolution.[26] This last was the fatal scene of the execution of Louis XVI and his Queen.

The palace called the Tuileries is a magnificent building. . . . From this palace the French monarch [Louis XVI], when pressed by the mob, 10th August 1792, went to the National Assembly, from thence to a prison, and from thence to the Place [de la] Révolution, and from thence most Frenchmen think to Heaven; for all the worthy men yet love his amiable character; though they think he was no statesman and that it was necessary he should suffer.

The gardens of this palace are handsome. In the center are three basins. Round the center one are some handsome marble statues of admirable workmanship. At the bottom of the garden is a thick grove of trees which shade you from the sun. I am informed that in this place all kinds of debauchery was formerly carried on, but it is not so now. You are not permitted to enter this garden after dark. From this grove you cross Place de la Révolution, which leads you into the Elysian fields [Champs Élysées]. There are very extensive walks and groves much resorted to. From this enchanting place you may drop into the Boulevards, now the most fashionable walk, and [one which] reaches nearly all round the city. The road or street has a double row of trees on both sides, always crowded with company and the center with carriages.

March 28th. Went to see Notre Dame. The ornaments of this celebrated church are destroyed and taken away. Nothing remains but the bare Gothic walls. I mounted the tower. From this height I had a view of the churches of: St. Sulpice, St. Eustache, St. Gervais, St. Étienne du Mont, old Ste. Geneviève,[27] St. Séverin, St. Roch, and Val-de-Grâce. All these churches, and some of them are very handsome, are entirely stripped. The bells are run into cannon; the decorations are taken down and deposited in the National Museum, but not without being greatly injured: particularly the marble statues. . . .

From Notre Dame I went to the manufactory called the Gobelins or tapestry. I am not capable of describing their manner of working. They copy the pieces of the best painters with so much accuracy that you cannot tell the difference. The threads are placed perpendicular and horizontal; the bobbins hang and lay on the wrong side on which they work. This manufactory was established by Louis XIV, and can only be supported by a court. It takes one man from four to six years to finish a piece three yards square. The threads are woolen. . . .

I begin to think the people of Paris are not so honest as they are said to be. A thief, a few days past, was carried before a justice for stealing something out of a house. The justice remarked that he had had two hundred and eight persons before him that day for the like offense; and that in one section.

I have been at the Grand Opera, and have seen the celebrated pieces of Panurge and Psyché.[28] The music of the former is enchanting, but you are often disturbed by some impudent coxcomb, humming in your ear. If I had understood French enough, I should certainly have said to one of those puppies, as Dr. Moore[29] once did, " I am sorry, Sir, that that woman's execrable singing prevents my enjoying your agreeable voice."

Went into the Luxembourg gardens. Here is destruction indeed! Some of the handsomest trees in the world are cut down. Near a whole grove is destroyed. The palace they are now repairing. What use they can make of this house and all the other palaces of the King and nobility I cannot think. They are now inhabited by the military, and by officers of the government. The more I see of Paris, the more I am convinced that it has run its most flourishing, though perhaps not its most happy days. Nothing but Royalty and a court can support a place like this, situated so far from navigation, and with so trifling a communication with the sea.

Should republicanism thrive in this country, men of letters and merchants will be the most respectable class of citizens. There will be no such characters as noblemen. Men of letters, despising property, can never add to the gaiety of the city; and riches, being the merchant's moving principle, he will remove to the sea coast where he will find it more convenient to acquire them. Government will retire to some other place to avoid being routed by the mob, and Paris will dwindle to almost nothing. The present government is as despotic as that of Algiers. It is supported by the sword entirely. They have fifty thousand troops now under arms in the city. They have endeavored to destroy the clubs but find it impossible. I am informed that there are yet many in this city who talk hourly for a dictator, and only wait a favorable opportunity to declare their sentiments.

March 30th. Went to see the ruins of the Bastille. Saw nothing but rubbish with the statue of liberty in the center; but even this was a gratification. Passed the gates of St. Martin and St. Denis. The last is worth seeing, and is seventy-two feet high. These gates were built to perpetuate the victories of Louis XIV, and are adorned with sculpture representing his battles. I have seen the wall that surrounds this city, and always till now thought it was erected for the defense of the place, but find it was built to prevent smuggling; for formerly every sort of merchandise paid a heavy duty on entering the gates: between 25 and 30 per cent. In 1791 the duty was taken off,[30] and the gates taken down.

   This is *Décadi*, and the troops of each section being ordered out, rendered it quite a gay day. The Spanish ambassador, who arrived in the city a few days past, was this day presented to the nation. The Frenchmen are not pleased with his extravagant equipage. The member of the Council of Five Hundred, who lives in the house with me, said if he was King of Spain he should feel mortified. He thought his sending a minister here was as much as saying, "I thank you for killing my cousin."

March 31st. Went with Williams to the Council of Five Hundred, where we obtained admittance by giving the doorkeeper a few hundred livres. This convention is called a moderate one. "Moderate" is the term given to the present members of government. If this term be just in comparison to the ruling in Robespierre's time, they must have been terrorists indeed, for a more turbulent assembly than the present one I never saw. A member will mount the [rostrum] to speak. If a word is found amiss, the whole assembly cry out, "Down! Enough! Silence!" The man will sometimes insist in speaking, saying he has a right to speak, and it is their duty to hear. Then they will bawl out, "No man has a right to tire the patience of his audience, nor will we hear with patience nonsense." The president rings his bell for order. All won't do, and the speaker is obliged to return to his seat, sometimes in the greatest rage imaginable. Scarce a day passes without three or four such scenes. There is neither decency nor deliberation in their debates, and their language resembles flashes of lightning from a troubled sky.

There are here some of the most ill-looking dogs I ever saw: men with short hair, beards that a razor has not touched for some weeks, clothes ragged and dirty, and shirt collars open. Others are *petit-maîtres* [coxcombs], and some few are decent looking men. Among the last I was surprised to find Tallien.[31] He is a tall man of a middling good form, and rather a handsome face; upon the whole an engaging person. His wife, formerly his mistress, is the handsomest woman in France, and of fine abilities. She has humanized this man and totally changed his principles; so that he is now one of the most moderate men in the Assembly, and says very little. He is by no means a popular character. He voted for the death of the King, denounced Robespierre, and was concerned in some of the principal scenes of blood, which, to look at him, you would not think him capable of. I judge him to be about thirty-two years of age. There are several black members.

April 1st. Went to the theatre in rue Feydeau, formerly Théâtre de Monsieur. This house has been shut for some time past by the Directoire, because it is frequented by the aristocrats, and opened this evening. This is the best company of comedians in France. The applause they met with on their appearance on the stage exceeded anything of the kind I ever heard. This company was once before imprisoned by Robespierre, and were also applauded in like manner when restored to the boards. Parties run high, and the conversation to-day is revolution and counter revolution.

May 24th. Went to Versailles in company with S. Bouin and J. Bussey,[32] and after viewing the beauties of this place, returned

to Paris by the way of St. Cloud. Versailles was built by
Louis XIV. It has a low situation. The palace is not so elegant
without as within. I went through a number of very large rooms
richly gilt and finished with marble. The paintings are by the
first masters, and merit great attention. Many of the apartments
are stripped of their decorations; but there are sufficient left to
show the extravagance of the court, and the folly of mankind.
I do not believe the world can produce such magnificence. The
gold work, marble pillars, colonnades, statues, water works, &c.
surpass all imagination, and would make even a man accustomed
to a luxurious style of life sigh at the depravity of human nature,
and weep for the misery millions of his fellow creatures must
endure to support the vices of a set of robbers, generally called
nobles. To set down those things which made the most impression upon me would be needless. It is sufficient to remember that
I have been at Versailles. . . .

Friday, June 3. Left Paris at three o'clock in the afternoon for
Cognac. Enchanted with the country. Nothing remarkable on
the road. My carriage broke down at Tours, Poitiers, and Jarnac.

Tuesday, June 7th. Arrived at Jarnac. Passed some of the finest
views between this place and Angoulême I ever saw: a country
so well cultivated that not a spot of barren ground to be seen for
ten leagues. Found good quarters at Jarnac at the house of an
agreeable man, Mr. J. J. Delemarin, Junior, who speaks excellent
English. Jarnac is a small place containing about two thousand
per[sons], situated on the river Charente.

Thursday, June 9th. Set out for Cognac with Mr. Delemarin,
and arrived in the evening. This is two leagues from Jarnac. Saw
the château Francis I was born in. Cognac is a very old town,
walled round; contains about three thousand inhabitants. It is
much celebrated for its excellent brandies, the best of which is
made for about four leagues round Cognac, and from 30 to
40,000 pipes [large casks of two-hogshead capacity] are yearly
exported. This article is distilled by the peasants from white
wine. Almost every family has a distill. A cask of white wine is

worth about four crowns. Six hogsheads of twenty-seven velts [33] each will make one hogshead of brandy of twenty-seven velts of four degrees or 10 per cent below what is called *London proof*. A hogshead of brandy is made in twelve hours.

Slept at Cognac at Mr. Angier's. There are four or five rich merchants here. They all speak good English. Charente washes by the town, and is very convenient for transportation. Fine society here.

Friday, June 10th. Left Cognac for Charente. Dined at Saintes, and passed on through an arch on the bridge said to be a triumphal one erected by J. Caesar. Arrived at Charente in the evening. This is a small place, cont[aining] about fifteen hundred inha[bitants]. The river here is thirty feet deep at high water and fifteen at low water. Ships lay here and load. The roads are bad from this to Cognac. Saintes is something of a town; contains about twelve thousand inha[bitants]. The peasants in this country, men and women, are very ugly and dirty.

Sunday, June 12. Went to Rochefort and obtained admittance into the dock yard, where they are building one three decker and several second rates. There are four or six dry docks here, and the yard appears to be well stocked with materials. Saw the galley slaves or convicts, about four hundred in number, chained two and two: miserable looking wretches indeed! They are kept close at work. Those that have a trade are permitted to work at it. There are two priests among them. Rochefort contains about sixteen thousand inhabitants. The houses are not so high as in the other cities I have seen. The streets are broader, but very dirty. The hospital is a fine building. Mass quite thronged.

Monday, June 13th. Leave Charente for Cognac. Meet on the road a wedding procession. It is the custom among the peasants of this country, immediately after the marriage ceremony is performed, to parade about accompanied by their friends. The pair, attended by the bride maid &c., go hand in hand. Their companions are dressed with different colored ribbons and flowers. Their music consists of a violin and a shrill screech at

the discharge of a musket which the master of ceremonies car-
ries. I was much diverted with the appearance of the band and
the silly, ridiculous figure the pair set. When we passed in the
carriage, they fired off the gun, and squalled out. We returned
the salute with a pistol and, *Vive the Republic!*

Tuesday morning arrived at Jarnac and *Wednesday afternoon*
leave it to finish my business at Cognac and Charente. *Thursday*
arrived at Charente, finish with the ship *Lyon* and return to
Jarnac. . . .

Tuesday, June 21st. Left Jarnac at five o'clock in the morning
for Paris. Nothing particular on the road except being drove
three or four posts by drunken postilions, it being haying time
and plenty of brandy circulating. The hail fell last Sunday at
Sorigny as large as eggs, and destroyed from three to four hundred acres of wheat. Sleep at Orléans three hours on Wednesday
night, fearing robbers that are at present cruising on this road.
Arrive at Paris at four o'clock in the afternoon of Thursday,
having rode three hundred and seventy-two miles in sixty hours.

Thursday, June 27th. Leave Paris in co[mpany] with Mr.
Champlain for Havre. The appearance of this country very different from that towards Bordeaux. The views are not so extensive; the houses more in the American style, and not so crowded
together in the villages; the roads through which are broader,
not always paved, and cleaner. The peasants are a handsomer
race of beings than those of the south, though their dress is as
singular, particularly the cap worn by the women. The under
part of this ornament resembles the cap worn by the savages in
North America, or like the fool's cap. They are generally decorated with tinsel, and from the peak hangs flappets of gauze or
muslin. These caps are very high, and the female looks longer
from the bottom of the waist to the tip of [the] cap than from
the waist to the feet.

Arrive at Rouen at dusk, about seventy miles from Paris, the
capital of Normandy. The situation of this city is low but beautiful and romantic, encompassed by high and lofty mountains.

The river Seine flows through meadows that present agreeable and picturesque scenes. Vessels of two hundred tons can come up to this place. Over the river is a bridge of boats of five hundred feet in length. This rises and falls with the tide. Although paved, it opens to large vessels, being so contrived that one part of it rolls over the other. It is constructed on fifteen or twenty boats, and may be taken to pieces in a short time, as it often is when the ice is about coming down the river. The quay is a good one and large vessels may tie to it and load.

Rouen is a rich city, and contains from 60 to 70,000 inha[bitants]. The houses are crowded together and streets narrow. They build considerably here with timber. In this place the great Joan of Arc was burned for a witch. I should like to spend a few days in this city, as it abounds in curiosities, and has so many beautiful views.

Pass from Rouen on to Havre in the night, and arrive at eight o'clock in the morning of Friday. In twenty-four hours from Paris about one hundred and fifty miles. At Havre we are detained from embarking for Guernsey by an embargo which continues until Saturday. Havre is a dirty hole, the houses badly built and squeezed together. It is said to contain fifty or sixty thousand inhabitants, but I should never imagine it held half the number from its appearance. It is situated on low ground upon the [right or north] side of the river Seine. Ships cannot approach it but at high water. There are two basins dug out for the convenience of vessels. The water is confined in by gates. These basins will hold five hundred to eight hundred ships. The piers which extend into the sea are well built, and must have cost great labor and expense. The road where vessels lay before the town is not sheltered and a very dangerous one in any wind.

From the hill on the back of Havre you have a fine, extensive view of the sea, river and country. There are two light-houses . . . [which] are thought to be good ones. Upon the whole the situation of Havre in respect to inland commerce overbalances the disadvantages it labors under in respect to navigation. These evils will some day or another be in a great measure lessened by the cutting of channels and basins, and I think this place will be one of the great commercial cities of France.

I leave it with Capt. Champlain on the *first of July* for Guernsey in the sloop *Aurora*. Wind ahead, but proved more favorable in the night, so that on the morning of the second, we entered the Race [34] very imprudently with a foul wind. The third night the wind blew fresh, and the Capt. thought best to get out of the strait. . . . The tides drove us up so far that to our great surprise we had got among the rocks on the end of Alderney. Orders were given immediately to wear ship.[35] The noise on deck roused me up, when I never was more frightened in my life. The tide, which is here very rapid, whirled round the rocks with a tremendous noise. The sea was rough and it was so dark that you could not discern the head of the vessel. We had the luck to wear ship, when we threw the lead and found five fathoms of water. How we got clear of them I cannot think. It is a great wonder we were not all lost.

On the *fifth July* we got into Guernsey at dusk. Guernsey is a pretty little island. The soil is good: better than the climate, which, though a healthful, is not a pleasant one: subject to rains and continual fresh gales, with cold mornings and evenings. It produces good grass of a short kind and corn; [36] though some of the latter not sufficient for consumption, one third being imported from England. Cider is made in considerable quantities, and they have much small fruit. The Chile strawberry is well worth notice from its size. I measured the largest to be found in a plate of this fruit, and it was five and three quarters inches in circumference. . . . The town of St. Peter's [St. Peter Port], the capital, has in it about eight thousand souls; is situated on the east side of the island. The streets are narrow and dirty; the houses built of stone, brick, and wood. This island has been annexed to the crown of England since the battle of Hastings, and is still subject to the ancient laws of Normandy, and is understood to be within the County of Southampton.

Guernsey is . . . defended by ledges of rocks. . . . Of art, there are four castles and one handsome fort on a hill to the [south] of the town. Cornet Castle is opposite the town and affords protection for the shipping in the road. The port is formed by stone piers thrown up in a very rude manner, about thirty foot high. The vessels enter at high water (the tide flowing from sixteen to twenty feet) and are left dry. This port will contain about one hundred sail of merchantmen. All French produce is introduced into England through this island. Upon a moderate computation, there is now more than a pipe of spirits to every mouth in the island. The inhabitants of St. Peter's follow the smuggling business very briskly. They employ a number of luggars [luggers] in this trade. The brandy they take is run off into small kegs of about five gallons each and the tobacco leaves &c. put up into small bales so as to be handled easily.

The language of the islanders is broken French and English. The butter here is of a very extraordinary good quality; and they abound in fish, particularly the conger eel, some of which I have seen as large as my thigh and long in proportion. The inhabitants are divided into several classes, and all the parade of family &c., which you find in England, is also discoverable here. They however enjoy a great share of liberty. They pay few or no taxes, and do just as they please.

Sunday July 31st. The sloop *Apollo* calls for me, and about four o'clock in the afternoon I embark for Southampton, where we arrive about noon next day, having a good passage, and passing the shipping off of Portsmouth Spithead &c., which afforded an agreeable sight, there being many first rates [37] and others in the road; more than I ever saw at one time before.

In the evening of August 1st take post chaise and go on for London, and arrive in the morning of the 2nd at about eleven o'clock. Run about this mart of the world for only two days, and met with many old friends. After finishing my business, I leave it on Thursday [the] 4th at nine o'clock in the evening for Southampton, with as much confusion in my head as in the streets of the city. I passed Hounslow Heath [38] at midnight without any molestation, though I did not feel so easy as when traveling in France: a country with which [this], or what I have passed over from Southampton to London, will bear no comparison.

Monday, August 9th. We have been detained at Southampton this three days past for want of passports from the Duke of Portland or some other fellow in power. To-day we were determined to wait no longer, and went on board our vessel to go down the river, but the custom house officers would not permit the Captain to get under way. We therefore left the vessel, and ordered her down the river to lay at Portsmouth for us. Forbes, Champlain and myself took post chaise, and in two and a half hours from the time we got into the carriage at Southampton we were on board the sloop off of Gosport, having rode twenty-four miles, and sailed about seventeen. The road from Southampton to Gosport is pleasing, but barren when compared to the fertile fields of France.

August 10th. At noon arrived at Dieppe. We made the harbor in the morning early; but the tide would not permit us to enter for some hours after. Landed here, and was directed under guard to the municipality, who examined our passports and permitted us to go on to Paris.

Dieppe is larger than Havre; at least contains more houses, and much handsomer ones, all going to ruin. It contains about eighteen thousand inhabitants, most of them miserably poor. Their chief employment formerly was fishing, which has now failed in a degree. They have no commerce and barely subsist.

August 11th. Leave this wretched place in the afternoon; ride all night; sup at Rouen toward morning, and pursue my journey along the fertile banks of the Seine through Vernon, Bonnières and St. Germain to Paris. This road equals, if not exceeds, that along the Loire and river Charente. There cannot be any country superior.

October 14th. Leave Paris in company with Parker, Codman, Tudor, and Cutting [39] to spend a few days at the former's place at Dreux, about fifty miles from Paris, on the road to Brest, and certainly thus far a delightful one. Visit while here a château, formerly belonging to Madame Pompadour, now *soumissionné* [tendered for a contract] by Mr. P[arker]. Also go to Anet [40] and view the botanic park, gardens, waters &c. of the late duc de Penthièvre: a charming place, the house very ancient and highly finished with gold painting &c. Ride through the forest of Dreux, in the center of which is a hunting lodge of an octagon form; each side having a window which looks through an avenue, say each seventeen miles, through the wood. After spending several days here very agreeably, returned to the city.

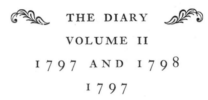

THE DIARY

VOLUME II

1797 AND 1798

1797

January 3rd. Depart from Paris for London. At noon stop at Chantilly, and view the famous hunting seat of the Prince of Condé. This place, like all the other seats of the nobility of this country, is crumbling into dust. The park here is very extensive and afforded the finest game of any place in Europe. The ancient castle is situated in the middle of an artificial basin of water, over which is thrown a bridge. The water works are very extensive and there are several very large ponds. The stables are not to be equaled in the world and are made to contain five hundred horses. Nothing can be said in favor of the apartments of the Prince. The chief beauty of this place is the park, waters, kennels for the dogs, and lodgings for the horses. In approaching the house, you pass a green of about half a mile over, perfectly level. The people here are all aristocrats. I asked a fellow how the roads came to be so very bad, and says he, "We are all republicans, and are governed by rascals who delight in ruin." Lodge at Breteuil.

January 4th. At noon arrive at Amiens, and while the postilion was putting the horses to, take a view of the town. Three branches of the river Somme enter this city, the capital of the department of Somme. The linen and woolen manufactories employed here formerly about twenty-five thousand persons. Entered the cathedral, which has escaped the ravages of revolution, and remains entire, and is well worth the traveler's notice. [It is] truly Gothic and full of images, but much lighter than buildings of that description in general. Halle au Blé [Grain Exchange] is also a fine building. Beggars numerous. Pass through Abbeville and Montreuil in the night. Refused admittance into the last, the gates being shut, but a piece of silver oiled the hinges.

January 5th. Breakfast at the seaport Boulogne, situated at the mouth of the river Liane. [It is] divided into lower and upper towns, and is the cleanest and best built town I have seen in France. All the cities on this road are well fortified. At about two o'clock arrive at Calais, which I am rather pleased with. The towns on this road are cleaner, better built and more pleasant than any others in France. The inns are pretty good and reasonable for French ones. The theatres of Calais very dirty.

January 7th. Leave Calais early in the morning and arrive at Dover at three o'clock. The collector of this dirty hole and den of pickpockets is a good specimen of English pride, brutality and impoliteness. Owing to the Captain, our luggage was not at the custom house until two or three minutes after four, and we could not get it ex[amine]d until Monday Morning, this being Saturday. So we left our trunks and sat off for London on Sunday morning and arrived in the evening. Some handsome scenery on the road. The river Thames crowded with vessels. Seen nothing as yet in England equal to the delightful views in France. And as to climate, France is certainly preferable. If the people of France were honest, good fellows, what a charming country it would be to live in!

January 15th. Have been running about London. Visited the theatres. Saw Mrs. Siddons in Millwood in *George Barnwell*, and Miss Farren [41] in I do not know what. Disappointed in both as well as in Drury Lane Theatre, which is not so handsome as the Opéra or Républic at Paris. Neither is their acting so good as that of the Comédie Française. Saw *Their Majesties' Servants* [a company of actors] at Covent Garden perform the new play of *A Cure for the Heart Ache* by Morton,[42] a very good thing. The Royal family present in the three first boxes from the stage, hung with crimson damask, fringed with gold. The King [George III] looks like the pictures I have seen of him: a vacant countenance and broad laugh. He was plainly dressed and so was the Queen. The girls looked well, and upon the whole they are a handsome family. But so much parade, singing, hurrahing, nonsense and stuff appears very ridiculous to one unaccustomed to it. I prefer this theatre to Drury Lane. I never was in an American or English theatre in my life, when before the evening was half gone, I did not wish myself out. But in Paris one may sit forever.

February 6th. I find myself, my dear S[usan], very incompetent to keeping a journal, at least an entertaining one. I will however proceed. It may serve to call to mind a number of things which may prove satisfactory one day or another.

The first object that attracts a stranger's notice in this city is St. Paul's Cathedral, a building with very little about it that pleases or astonishes you, but its enormous size. This building is encompassed by houses in such a manner that you cannot see it before you come upon it, except from Ludgate Street, where you have a view of about two thirds of the front for some hundred yards. . . . St. Paul's is unquestionably one of the most magnificent buildings in Europe for loftiness, grandeur, beauty, design, and harmony of parts; but certainly falls far short of the Pantheon at Paris in simplicity and elegance.

A few days ago I went to see the Tower, where are shown wild beasts.[43] All these I had seen before, and found very little worth notice except the crowns, scepters, and armor. The Spanish armory consists of lances, pikes, shields &c., which were taken from the Spanish in the reign of Queen Elizabeth, 1588, out of the Armada. The small armory, so called, is well worth seeing. Swords and bayonets curiously displayed in military fans.

These bayonets are the first invention having plug handles which go into the muzzle of the gun instead of over it; so that when the piece is fired it shoots away the bayonet. Their invention was at Bayonne from whence they receive their name. . . .

You are shown the Earl of Mar's fine piece inlaid with mother-of-pearl and curiously wrought. The implements of war here shown are said to be the greatest curiosities of their kind in the world. The mind is struck with horror at using so many inventions of mankind to destroy one another. . . .

London, at this season of the year, is one of the worst places in the world to live in. You are choked with coal dust and enveloped with smoke, and do not see the sun once a week; and in some parts of the city the people use candles [for a] great part of the day. The flat stones are so greasy that it is with difficulty you can walk, and the insolence of the lower class of people and the inconvenience of the Scotch mist are insupportable.

February 26th. Leave London in the evening with the mail coach for Dover in company with Mr. Trist [44] of Philadelphia. Being Sunday night we had no mail with us, and were therefore obliged to put up with the driver's stopping as often as he wanted a dram, which took him from twenty to thirty minutes to swallow.

February 28th. Leave Dover in the morning and arrive in five hours at Calais. One of the sailors in endeavoring to check the vessel had his leg torn to pieces.

March 1st. Depart from Calais about noon with Mr. Whittemore,[45] and before we got far on the first post, our horses ran away with us. The postilion was thrown off, and we were in great danger of having our limbs broke.

March 3rd. Arrived in Paris.

May 15. Leave Paris in company with Hore Browse Trist of Philadelphia for Amsterdam; and after passing through the cities of Compiègne, Ham, and Cambray, we arrive, and lodge on the 17th, at Valenciennes. We have passed over a well cultivated country, full of people who appear more wretched than they really are. The roads execrable and my companion fretful.

Compiègne is a large place. It was here that the famous Maid of Orleans was taken prisoner in 1430. Cambray is much of a commercial and manufacturing city. Its principal branch is that of cambrics.

May 18th. While the municipality are examining our passports, we amuse ourselves by viewing this distressed city, one third of which has been destroyed by the army under the Duke of York, which lay before it [for forty-three days], and the misery occasioned by this siege is perhaps as apparent now as ever. The heart of the traveler is melted with pity to see the ragged, wretched condition of the inhabitants of this once flourishing place. Some houses are without roofs; others without doors and windows; others nothing but a pile of rubbish; and others, being partly destroyed, the remaining half is inhabited. The fortifications are going to ruin, not having had repairs since the siege.

After receiving our passports, we proceed to Jemappes, a village on the junction of the rivers Haine and Trouville, remarkable for a battle fought here the 6th of November 1792.[46] Dumouriez, after having been at Paris to concert measures for entering the Netherlands, returns to his army and opens the campaign by attacking the Austrians on the 4th of November at the village of Boussu about three or four miles from Jemappes. The Austrians had an excellent position, but could not withstand the ardor of the French. They were in so little expectation of an attack that the officers had prepared an elegant entertainment which the French arrived in time to take possession of.

From Boussu Dumouriez proceed[ed] toward Mons, and soon came in sight of the enemy, strongly posted on the heights of Jemappes. Three rows of fortifications were seen one above another, upon which were mounted one hundred mouths of cannon. On the 6th of November at seven o'clock in the morning, a heavy cannonade commenced, and continued without much effect on the part of the French, which determined the General on a close attack. The number of the French who formed for this purpose amounted to 30,000, and the Austrians are computed at 20,000. The infantry formed instantaneously, and the General presenting himself in the front of the line, the music began to play the celebrated Marseillaise song. The soldiers thus encouraged rushed impetuously on with shouts of *Vive la Nation!* The first line of redoubts were instantly carried. Soon after possession was taken of Jemappes and the second line of redoubts; and after a short resistance on the heights, the enemy at two o'clock retreated with confusion to Mons. The loss of killed and wounded on both sides amounted to about five thousand, of which two thirds were Austrians.

Where these brave men fell now grows the finest wheat I ever saw. This is a charming country, rich and cultivated beyond anything I have ever yet seen; produce: timber, corn, fodder, flax, iron and coal; manufactures: cambric, lace, and earthenware.

Pass Mons, a fine large town, containing about 30,000 inhabitants, who have considerable woolen manufactories. The streets are broad and clean. The place has stood several sieges and is of considerable note. It surrendered to Dumouriez the day after the battle of Jemappes, and was taken possession of by Gen'l Beurnonville.[47]

May 18th. Sleep at Brussels, a rich city of Brabant, called the ornament and delight of the Netherlands. The most pleasing city I have seen in Europe. It is situated partly on an eminence and partly on a plain, through which runs the river Senne. The inhabitants are in number about 100,000, who seem industrious and in good circumstances. There are many fine public buildings and very many superb houses which formerly belonged to the nobility. There are also some country seats about B[russels], which surpass anything I have ever seen either in France or England. This city was formerly the residence of the Court. The park, though not very extensive, is very beautiful. The principal square is handsomer than any in Paris or London.

The country about this place is a garden: in short Brussels and its environs is a perfect paradise. It has a communication with Antwerp by means of a canal, which is out to the river Rupel, an extent of about eight miles. There are many parish churches, besides chapels, monasteries and convents. The people are Catholic, full of religion and superstition. The streets of the city are not very clean, and among other things are infested with priests. Here is a cabinet of natural history and an extensive library; fine inns.

May 19th. At noon leave this enchanting city and ride along the canal having on both sides a fine wood and many country seats. The road full of travelers and several boats passing up and down the canal. Stop at Malines, and, while our horses are changing, take a view of the cathedral, a very superb building with a steeple or tower more than four hundred feet high. In this church are yet to be seen many fine paintings. There are also five other churches in this town, besides a great many religious houses both for men and women. What a thirst for religion, and what an unprincipled set of devils withal! This place was formerly the seat of an archbishop, whose jurisdiction extended over seventeen cities and four hundred and fifty villages. The inhabitants amount to about 20,000, and carry on a considerable trade. They are noted for their manufactories of thread bed quilts, and particularly lace which is much celebrated.

The same day we arrive at Antwerp or Anvers, once one of the greatest commercial cities in the world, and now grass grows in the streets. It is situated on the eastern side of the Scheldt, which is here about four hundred and fifty feet broad and twenty-five feet deep at low water; so that the largest ships can unload at the quay or enter the town by eight canals which communicate with the river, some of which are very large.

About two centuries ago this place cont[aine]d more than 200,000 inhabitants. At that time near three thousand foreign vessels entered the river yearly, and it is recorded in the annals of the city that the value of merchandise imported in the year 1550 amounted to 133,000,000 of gold. As of proof of its immense riches, we are told that a merchant named John Dains, having lent the Emperor Charles V a million of gold, invited him to dinner; when, after a royal entertainment, he threw the bond into the fire, which was made of cinnamon.[48]

In the year 1585–6, when the King of Spain took possession of Antwerp, the Protestants, to avoid the government of a Catholic prince, removed with their families to Amsterdam. This was the first stroke to the commerce of Antwerp; and from that time, that of Amsterdam increased. At the Treaty of Münster in 1648, between Philip IV and the United Provinces, which put an end to the religious wars, which had con[tinue]d more than thirty years, Antwerp fell a sacrifice. For by an article in that treaty, it was agreed that no merchant vessel should sail up to Antwerp without first unloading her cargo in one of the ports of Holland, from whence the goods might be sent to Antwerp in boats. This gave a death to its commerce; but it is to be hoped that being now in possession of the French, that they will restore its ancient privileges, and permit a free navigation up the Scheldt, which is fitted by nature for one of the greatest commercial spots in the world. Should this take place, Amsterdam will dwindle away, and even London feel its influence.

The houses are five, six, and eight stories high, and narrow, of a miserable style of building. The streets are broad and clean. There are some superb private houses, and many noble public buildings such as the Cathedral, the Bourse, the Townhouse, and several parish churches. The Cathedral is a magnificent structure with a steeple of stone curiously wrought, four hundred and twenty feet in height. The paintings of Rubens, which were so much celebrated, are removed to Paris. These Frenchmen left nothing standing in the Netherlands which they thought would enrich or ornament their idol, Paris. The altar of this church, and indeed the other decorations of marble and brass, exceed anything I have ever seen. . . . We were lucky enough to see Mass in perfection. Here is as much of *des cultes et des cloches* as any reasonable or unreasonable being can want. Such superstition, trumpery and nonsense! You meet with saints and crucifixes in every street, and Virgins and little Jesuses at every corner.

Near the Cathedral you are shown the iron railing of a well, the workmanship of Quinten Matsys,[49] then a smith, but afterward a painter. He was a native of Antwerp, and fell in love with a painter's daughter. The father refused to give his consent, being determined to give her only to one of his own profession. Love induced him to go to Italy, where he studied the art, and gave such proofs of his abilities that the old man gave his consent to the marriage. Antwerp boasts of many of his works, and the famous picture of the *Misers* in Windsor Castle in England is of this master's painting. Antwerp produced among other great men: Ortelius, the famous geographer, Gramaye, the historiographer of the Netherlands, Rubens, Vandyke, and the two Teniers.[50]

The quay is in a ruinous state, but is about to be repaired, as all the lots round it are purchased up on speculation. An American vessel belonging to a gentleman of Boston entered the river about two years ago; the first that had sailed up it for more than a century. There are here some valuable woolen manufactories. Language Low Dutch and bad French.

An American, who has never visited this country, can have no just idea of its cultivation, population, and picturesque scenes. The road from Paris to this place is very interesting. You ride through large commercial cities, fortified and manufacturing towns, and romantic villages. You have a view of old towers, Gothic churches, decayed fortifications, ancient castles, well situated convents, superb palaces, elegant country seats, horrible prisons, delightful pleasure grounds, and serpentine rivers. In short you see nature throughout all her pleasing varieties, and art, flourishing and decaying.

May 20th. Leave our post chaise and take a coach and four, in which we quit Anvers, and pass over a barren tract of land for fourteen leagues. Not a house nor a shrub to be seen: a devil of a road to be sure. My companion insupportably peevish, cursing the roads and scolding the driver, out of whom he could [get] nothing but "Yaw."

My feelings were very different from his. I was occupied with the pleasing prospects that were before me of my adorable wife and her infant [Susan Palfrey Lee, then two years old], and the affectionate friend I had left in Paris. Pardon me, my S[usan]. What I feel for Madame B[arlow] does not injure you. You must be to her what she has been to me: a dear tender friend. The love of her society has kept me from the busy scenes of the dissipated capital, and she deserves your esteem, as much for having preserved your husband, as from her own merit. O! How I long to make you acquainted with her! When I want a friend, a consoling friend, I will fly to your sex. Their bosoms only possess the healing balm, for:

What is the friendship of menkind but show, mere outward show?
T'is like the harlot's tears, the statesman's promise or French patriot zeal;
    full of fair scenery, but delusion all.[51]

I believe you will smile; but you know my heart. Nature has given me one that causes me to be either supremely blessed or supremely miserable.

In the midst of these ideas, Mynheer would intrude himself. I began to imagine what sort of a being I should find him. I had seen the amphibious animal abroad, and was anxious to view the beaver at home. . . .

In crossing [the islands of] Voorne and Ijsselmonde, we were introduced to Mynheer. The good-natured looks of his Frau, the neatness of his cabin, his large small-clothes [tight-fitting knee breeches], square-sleeved coat, full-bottomed wig, fore-and-aft hat [cocked hat with the peak in front], and copious pipe announce him to be a citizen of Batavi[a].[52]

20th. Sleep at Rotterdam.

May 21st. Leave Rotterdam, and take a delightful road by the side of the canals to The Hague.

May 22nd. Leave my friend Trist at The Hague, and arrive at Amsterdam. . . . The streets are in general broad, with canals in the center, and a row of trees on each side. The bridges over these canals are very numerous and make a pleasing appearance. The canals are mere mud puddles, and serve as receptacles for all the filth of the city. I lived at an inn on one of these canals:

the stench of which was so disagreeable that I could never open my window.

This city contains about 26,000 houses, built upon piles of timber, driven into the earth at an immense expense. 13,659 of these piles were rammed into the ground to support the Stadt House.[53] This magnificent building is of stone. . . . The inside is finished in a superb manner, and every apartment is of some public utility. How very different from buildings of this nature in Paris! Take this pile throughout, and it gives one a great idea of the riches of the city, and of the regular system with which all business is transacted among these truly industrious people.

The Exch[ange] has nothing to recommend it. The persons who attend here have more the appearance of a set of divines than merchants. The Dutch playhouse is now shut, but the French one is open, where I have been much entertained with the comedy of *Tom Jones*.[54]

Tuesday [*May 23*] visited the Rasp House. This is a place for criminals, who are chained to a block of Brazil wood, which they are continually sawing and filing. Went also to the dockyard, where we were politely rec[eive]d by a Mr. Darley, who showed us all the stores and conducted us aboard a seventy-four, fitting for us. Saw here the camels or buoys with which the largest ships are bro[ugh]t up from the Texel [55] to this dock. These camels are about twelve feet deep. When brought alongside of the ship, they are filled with water, and then drawn close together by means of cables, which pass under the keel. The water is then pumped out, by which means the vessel is buoyed up and bro[ugh]t into shoal water.

There are twelve hospitals and many charitable institutions in this city. All of them are noted for their wholesome laws, and have been held up for models to other cities of Europe.

Strolled into the Jews' Synagogue. Such a collection of dirty, ill-looking thieves I never before beheld. Their ceremony was quite new and ludicrous.

The "Spie House" is a place where loose young women are confined and kept continually shining to atone for their follies.

The Speel houses [gambling houses] are licensed bawdy

houses under the direction of the police. Degraded human nature! Here the common people amuse themselves with drinking. There are governors to every house to prevent riots, which very seldom happen. You see very few of these poor, helpless, shivering females in the streets of Amsterdam. They are not permitted to walk out in the evenings.

Amsterdam is certainly one of the most opulent cities in the world. Its commerce suffers much for the present, and perhaps never will again arrive to what it has been. The shutting of the Scheldt in 1648 was the cause of the growth of this city. Should the French open that noble river, Amsterdam will suffer considerably, and Antwerp revive. For twenty-five years back near three thousand vessels have entered this port annually. The East India C[ompan]y can hardly be said to exist, having lost almost all their possessions. They still however hold their charter, and no individual of the United Provinces is allowed to trade to the Indies.

They have a great inland navigation by means of their canals, and the rivers Rhine, Meuse, and Scheldt. Their situation is also advantageous for the trade of the Baltic, which they carried on to great profit.

Almost any town in Holland is remarkable for some particular branch of trade: viz. this city for the trade of the Straits, Spain, E and W Indies, and herring fishing; Rotterdam for the Scotch and English trade, which is even now carried on to great extent through contraband. English manufactures are sent from Rotterdam into France, and under an escort of four hundred men, who have frequent skirmishes with the guards. This is smuggling with a witness. Zaandam is noted for ship building; Delft for porcelain, and Leyden for woolen manufactories. It is indeed wonderful that in this country, without stones, without forests, and without arable land, they have the finest stone bridges and houses in the world, the second navy that swims, and supply half of Europe with corn [i.e., grain]; and that with a tract of country not larger than one of the U. S. of A., they raise men and money enough to make themselves of the greatest importance in the nat[ion]s of Europe.

May 28th. Took a stroll to the flower market. The Dutch are remarkable for their love of flowers. Sherlock [56] says that in his travels he remarked that every nation had a peculiar way of ruining itself. " The Dutch " says he, " ruin themselves by avarice, by lending money at an exorbitant interest on bad security, and by their passion for flowers." A Dutchman, who had a very fine tulip, heard that another person had one as fine as his. He purchased it of him for an enormous sum, and then destroyed it, saying, "Now there is not a man in the world who has such a tulip as mine."

"Every nation," says the same author, " excells in making something. The English, for instance, in making men and women." That the species thrive better in England than in Holland, I believe, is true; though the Dutch certainly make the prettiest children, but the speaking of their horrible language distorts their features and renders them hideous before they grow up.

The avarice of these people and their thirst for gain is to be seen in all their actions. When a stranger arrives in their country, they take good care to find out his character, connections, and property. If he is likely to be a profitable acquaintance, they are seen to cultivate his *Friendship*. My letters to several very respectable merchants mentioned that my plans were extensive, and that I might be relied on. Nothing could equal the civilities I rec[eive]d. When it was known that I wanted to borrow money on *Inscriptions and Nationals Estates*,[57] I no longer rec[eive]d attentions. I might have stayed in Holland a year without an invitation to dinner, unless I had adopted the art of the diamond man.

A gentleman once laid a bet that he could go to Amsterdam and remain there several days without buying or selling anything, and yet dine at the best tables. He goes to Amsterdam and takes his stand on the Excha[nge], where he soon meets with an old acquaintance, who accosts him with, " Yah, well yes, what you milt come for to see once again more? What milt you have us give you? You, what milt you give us? " "Nothing." " Dat is baad," says the Dutchman, and turns on his heel to go off. "Do you know how much," says the stranger instantaneously, "a diamond weighing forty carats will bring?" "O mine God! Forty carats! No! Forty carats! Dat has been a divil for un diman. Un you must come and take a little coffin tea mit me in the morrow morng for breakenfast and we shall see what we shall see. Forty carats! God beware!!" The stranger makes an excuse: he is engaged. "Well, come and dine a little bit." Accordingly he goes to dinner, where he meets with two or three dealers in precious stones, all eager after diamonds. "Dish has been Mr. Moses; dish is Mr. Michael, Mr. Moses' brother, un dish is Mr. Conrad Stumperfunk, un all had been very honest men. Yah! and dealers in diamonds too!"

Moses says, "Well and you milt dine with me on the morrow." "And after to-morrow, you will dine with I," says Michael, "but don't mind what my brother says to you. He is a dam'd rogue." Stumperfunk says, "On Sunday, you will come and stay at my country home at Haarlem, *Rust Lust*. It will cost but little. You can come up in the Trekschuit [horse-drawn canal barges], and take care how does make any business with dese peoples. You have got among dam'd rogues. Why didn't come to me? I be the greatest buyer of diamonds in all Amsterdam." The stranger accepts of all their invitations, and when is about to go, is pressed very much to procure his diamond; when he informs these honest men that he only came to inquire the price of such a diamond in case he should find one.

Their regularity and system in all their concerns is observable to any eye, and in part worthy of imitation. . . . They are truly industrious and in anything husband time.

One of the Sundays I passed in Holland was spent at Broek,[58] a village in North Holland opposite Amsterdam. This is a very singular place. Not a horse is suffered to enter the village. The streets are paved with brick in all manner of figures and sanded. The houses are clean to a fault, and it is with difficulty you can procure entrance. They have a door to each that is never opened but to receive a bride and bridegroom, and to let out a corpse. The courtyards before the houses are all commonly ornamented with shell work, but never entered. The richest families in the

United Provinces reside here. When a man marries his daughter, he gives her so many tons of silver. This is the way of estimating wealth: such a young woman is worth ten tons. I entered this village just as the people were coming from church. The old ones were on one side of the street and the young on the other.

Went from Broek to Zaandam, a large town of ship carpenters; a republic of wind mills. There are, I am told, eight hundred and fifty windmills in this place. They have built here a vessel for every day in the year. Went to see the shop where Peter Czar served his time to a carpenter.[59] Also visited the church, which we entered in time of service. The gestures of the preacher and his articulations were very amusing. An Englishman or American is very apt to laugh at this language. He does not reflect how much it is like his own. . . .

Wednesday, June 15th. Leave Amsterdam in company with Mr. Charles Vancouver,[60] and lodge at Haarlem. From Amsterdam to this place you have a fine road, perfectly straight and level, with Haarlem Lake on one side and a canal and part of the Zuider Zee on the other. Haarlem is a rich walled city, containing about 30,000 inhabitants, who have considerable manufactories in linens, ribands, tapes, and beer. They also carry on a great trade in flowers, some of which sell for astonishing prices. Such is the passion of the Dutch for flowers that a hyacinth has been known to bring 10,000 florins. This place gave birth to Laurenz Coster,[61] the first inventor of printing in 1440. John Faust, who is generally said to be the inventor of this art, was a servant to Coster, and stole from his master, while he and his family were at church, his printing materials, and fled with them to Mainz. The first book Coster ever printed is kept in the Stadt House for the inspection of the curious. . . .

Observe a singular custom: When a woman is put to bed, a piece of lace resembling the back part of a child's cap, is pinned on the outside of the front door of the house. If the child is a boy, the lace is put on a white ground; if a girl, the ground is half pink and half white. This lace remains on the door until the woman is churched [thanksgiving given in church], when it is taken in, which is a sign that the lady is ready to receive company. . . .

June 16th. . . . At sunset we arrive at The Hague, a delightful spot. Lodge here, and in the morning call on Mr. Adams, Pinckney, and Murray: three American ministers.[62] Also on citoyen Noël,[63] the French minister, to whom I had a letter of introduction, which procured me a passport for Paris. After these three visits, we amused ourselves in viewing this place, which certainly deserves all that has been said in its favor.

It is situated about half a league from the sea, and though called a village, not being walled, it contains full 40,000 inhabitants, and is considered as the capital of the United Provinces. It stands something higher than the rest of the country upon a dry soil. The environs are enchanting; the houses are excellent; and the streets broad and long, adorned with rows of trees. There are several squares, and many magnificent public buildings. But the most pleasing thing to be seen is a grove of wood, which has all the wild appearance of an American forest. This wood is very extensive, divided into delightful walks.

Dine with Gen'l Pinckney, and at five leave The Hague for Rotterdam. Pass Delft, a fine large opulent town, noted for its earthenware, pipe, and beer manufactures.

June 17th. Sleep at Rotterdam. This place I prefer to all others that I have seen in Holland. The canals are larger and sweeter; the houses better built and handsomer; and the streets broader than at Amsterdam. This place is built on the river Rotte, where it joins the Meuse. Its harbor is convenient, and so deep that the largest merchantmen can enter it, and by means of the noble canals can unload at the merchant's door. After weighing anchor, one tide will take a vessel to sea. It contains 50,000 inhabitants.

June 18th. Rise at four in the morning, cross the Meuse and take carriage for Willemstad. The road over Ijsselmonde is bad, but the country luxuriant beyond description; having wheat, flax, clover, and mustard; the farm houses neat and clean. After again crossing the Meuse, we arrive at Willemstad, a small walled town on the banks of the river, considered as one of the keys of Holland. The French besieged it for twenty-seven days in 1793, and then retired. A great number of cannon are to be seen sticking in the houses. . . .

June 20th. Part with my friend Mr. Vancouver, and proceed to Ghent, where I remain some hours, my carriage wanting repair. Ghent is situated on the conflux of the rivers Scheldt, Lys, Moere and Lieve, which together with a great many canals, divide the town into twenty-six islands, which are joined by three hundred bridges. On one of these bridges is the figure of a young man in bronze, who was commanded to cut off the head of his father with a sword. When he was about to strike the blow, the blade flew off leaving the haft in his hand, in consequence of which they were both pardoned.[64]

This place, once so commercial and flourishing, is now in a ruinous state. Grass grows in its wide, commodious streets, and its noble houses are decaying. It has some trade in corn, and with cloth, linen, and silk manufactories, and has a communication with Bruges and Ostend by means of a canal.

June 21st. Leave Ghent, and in the morning pass Courtrai, a town situated on the Lys, and famous for its table linen manufactory. Saw much of this linen out bleaching. This town strikes one very agreeably on passing through it. It was taken by the French on the 18th of June, 1792, under Gen'l Luckner. . . .[65]

June 22nd. Sleep at Bapaume and arrive at Paris the 22nd of June in the evening.

1798

March 18th. Depart from Paris in the diligence for Bordeaux in company with Saml. M. Hopkins and I. Kidder.[66]

March 31st. Leave the mouth of river Garonne with Capt. Haff of the snow [67] *William* for Philadelphia.

April 29th. Suppose ourselves to be near the Grand Bank[s] [submarine plateau off S. E. Newfoundland] in the morning of this day. A brig appeared in sight astern at noon. She came up with us, and proved to be the *Witch*, Capt. Brown of Philadelphia, who left Bordeaux seven days after us. He passed us and at sundown was scarcely discernible.

May 10th. Imagined ourselves near Georges.[68] Saw a sail ahead, and hoisted our colors at foretopmasthead, which he answered by heaving down upon us. He proved to be an armed schooner from New Foundland, bound to the West Indies. Inquired our longitude and found to our great mortification that we were only in 51. Tacked ship immediately and stood to the northward.

May 25th. Saw a schooner to windward about four miles. Hoisted out the boat, and dispatched the mate, Mr. Kidder, and four men to endeavor to obtain a supply of provisions and water, of which we were in want. After being caught in a fog, and rowing four hours, they miraculously made the brig, which they never would have done had not the Capt. hove to immediately on losing sight of the boat, and Mr. Kidder had the precaution to stick his tooth brush in a hole on the gunnel of the boat. The shade of this enabled them to reach us very much fatigued, not having boarded the schooner.

May 26th. Very foggy; wind SSW. At seven o'clock P. M. sounded and found only sixteen fathoms of water. Supposed ourselves, from the depth of the water and number of birds, to be near the Isle de Sable.[69] Notwithstanding this, the Capt., being unacquainted with the coast, had the imprudence to lay to and fish for half an hour. Tacked at half past seven and ran off with wind at W into forty-five fathoms of water. At four o'clock tacked ship, and stood to the northward, thinking we might be on Brown Bank, fifteen leagues to the westward of Cape Sable. At twelve sounded and found twenty-five fathoms of water. Imagined we saw the cape, the fog having cleared off. At three sounded and found ten fathoms. We were then convinced it was Sable Island we were running for. Tacked ship and stood off; wind at W.

May 28th. Monday morning the 28th, sounded and found 50 fathoms, fog cleared off. Saw a schooner to windward, standing W and by S; wind SE. We hauled up SW and by W to speak. At two o'clock we spoke him, and found him to be the same schooner we had seen on Saturday. Hoisted out our boat and the Capt. and myself board him, and found he was bound for Marblehead. The Capt. having got a supply of provisions sufficient to take him to Philadelphia, I thought best to shift vessels, and accordingly took out my luggage, which I sent on board the schooner and followed myself, accompanied by Mr. Hopkins for Marblehead.

Monday evening lost sight of the snow *William* and found ourselves among an honest set of people, who showed us all the civility in their power. The skipper informed us that he saw us on Sunday, standing in for Sable, and that when we tacked the NW breaker was under our lee. The schooner was then in shore of us, and saw a schooner on shore. The people had a tent put up. The surf ran so high that the skipper could not assist him.

June 2nd. Arrived at Marblehead and proceed to Boston.

After the diary entry of the date of William Lee's arrival in America, the entries are few and brief. Minor entries for the years 1798 to 1801 recount primarily dates of Lee's departure for and arrival at Halifax, New York, and Philadelphia. We do know from James Spear Loring [70] that Lee visited President John Adams in 1798. And Lee himself wrote that on January 21, 1799, while in Philadelphia, Mr. Thomas Adams [71] called and, "by the President's desire, invited me to dinner in a family way." For this period of Lee's stay in his own country there is a dearth of material, in marked contrast to other periods of his life, but two final entries in the diary are worth noting. On July 26, 1801, Lee wrote: "Leave Boston with Mrs. Lee and two children in the *Paragon*, Capt. Appleton, for Bordeaux," and on Monday, September 7, six weeks and one day later, he writes, "Landed with Mrs. Lee and family at La Rochelle. Arrived at Bordeaux Friday evening the 11th of September." His fifteen-year stay in France had begun.

II

"CONSUL" AT BORDEAUX

1801 – 1808

After Lee returned to the United States in 1798, he sought earnestly to be appointed consul at the busy port of Bordeaux. Since that office carried no salary and the commissions (as specified in the Act of April 15, 1792) were rather small, consuls by general agreement could and did engage in other commerce to supplement their incomes. Finally, on June 3, 1801, through the influence of Elbridge Gerry, George William Erving, and James Monroe, Lee was appointed by President Thomas Jefferson as commercial agent [1] at Bordeaux, an appointment that was confirmed by the Senate in 1802 and again in 1805.

Lee left Boston on July 21, 1801, with Mrs. Lee and the two children (a second girl, Mary Elizabeth Lee, had been born in May 1799) aboard the *Paragon*. The Lees arrived at Bordeaux early in September for a residence that was to last for fifteen years. The period from 1801 to 1806 is represented by very few letters from William Lee, since during these years the growing family — a third child, William Barlow Lee, was born in January 1805 — was living together at Bordeaux.

In addition to his consular duties, Lee engaged in import and export business for the house of Perrot and Lee. An illness of seventeen months prevented him from attending to these affairs, and as a result he suffered much from what he called " dishonorable conduct " on the part of M. Perrot. The business of this house was terminated on May 12, 1805, and by exercising great economy, Lee was able to pay off all his debts.

Most of the letters from Lee during this period were addressed to the Secretary of State, James Madison, and described frauds practiced upon American citizens by the French. Typical is a letter included here recounting the hardships of American seamen who had been discharged from ships with no means of returning to the United States. During the Napoleonic Wars of 1803 to 1815 the position of Americans in France grew increasingly uncomfortable. France was openly at war with England, and by 1804 American ships were being seized outright and taken into English ports. By Napoleon's Berlin Decree of November 21, 1806, France imposed an official blockade upon Britain, which could not be made to work because the British were supreme on the seas.

Although Lee remained at his post in Bordeaux, Mrs. Lee and the children left for Paris in October 1806. The Lees suffered many anxious moments because of the difficulties in receiving and sending letters written in English. Susan, now eleven and one half, and Mary, four years younger, were entered at the famous school of Mme. Campan in St. Germain. Their schoolmates were mostly young women of French society, among them Caroline Bonaparte, sister of Napoleon and later Queen of Naples, and Hortense Beauharnais, daughter of the Empress Josephine, and afterwards wife of Louis Bonaparte, King of Holland. During her seven-month sojourn in Paris, Mrs. Lee saw much of her old friends from Boston, Mr. and Mrs. William Tudor and their daughter Delia. At the end of the school year, in May, 1807, William welcomed his family back to Bordeaux. The Lee's second son, Thomas Jefferson Lee, was born in August of 1808.

With the family reunited, there were few letters during the following two years, except for some to the Secretary of State. These "reports," several of which have been included, are filled with rumors about the progress of the Grand Army and the division of Europe between Napoleon and Alexander of Russia. In the midst of treaties and toppling thrones, the United States in 1807 imposed an embargo on all vessels at American ports; but this was found self-defeating and was repealed in 1809.

To the Secretary of State [James Madison]

United States Agency
Bordeaux, January 20, 1802.

Sir:

I take the liberty to enclose you a list of the vessels which have entered and cleared at this port from the 26 Oct. [1801] (the day on which I took charge of the agency) to the 31 December. I wish it was more perfect, but such is the unaccommodating disposition of our American Captains, that there is no persuading them into any measure of public utility not enforced by the Government. Were they obliged by laws to exhibit their manifest and other papers to me, it would then be in my power to give a correct state of the supplies received at this market by which means our merchants would be enabled to make accurate calculations.

I am much harassed with the complaints and sufferings of American seamen, twenty of whom I have now in the hospitals, and there are at least one hundred and fifty strolling about the streets of this city in the greatest distress. Some of these men have been turned on shore from their respective vessels upon the most frivolous pretences. Many have been discharged from ships which have been sold; but most of them have collected here from Spain and different ports of the Republic; and they conduct in general in so unruly a manner, that the Commissary of Police has written me the following letter respecting them.

Copy by translation

Liberty   Equality

No. 3625   Police of Bordeaux

——————

Bordeaux 25 Nivose 10th Year of the French Republic One & indivisible

The Commissary General of Police
        To the Agent of the United States of America

Citizen

I am informed that a great many foreign sailors, most of whom call themselves Americans are strolling about the streets of this city, and that not belonging to any vessels, have no place of residence, and therefore very easily escape the inspections of the police, and the research of the citizens who feed and furnish them with necessaries. Their conduct authorizes me to consider them as vagabonds, and it is to be feared that they will disturb the public tranquility.

It is therefore with a view of preventing such consequences as well as for the sake of your nation that it appears to me an object of the first moment to compel these American seamen to repair to their respective ports. If you are of my opinion, as I am sure you must be, I invite you to take such steps as you think necessary to hasten their departure from Bordeaux; and in case you need my interference to put this plan into execution, I will cooperate with you in the most efficacious manner.

Salut
For the Commissary General
    The Secretary General
(signed)   BABUT

On receiving this letter, I assured the Commissary that I would do everything in my power to remedy the evil he complained of, and accordingly I have been for some days past occupied in distributing among the American vessels now in port all the idle sailors to be found; and I have been so successful that in a few days I hope to have only to provide for the invalids and those who are in the hospitals, which I shall do by furnishing them with provisions, and procuring them a passage in some vessel bound to the United States, the Captain of which I shall take the liberty to refer to you for such compensation as you may judge fit to make.

The ports of Europe are at this moment full of this valuable class of our citizens, and it appears to me that if one of our national ships, now in the Mediterranean, was ordered to visit on her return home some of the principal places, and to take on board all those seamen who may be found in distress, or even if a ship was ordered out from America for that purpose, it would be attended with much less expense to the United States than the present mode of providing for these fugitives.

In venturing this hint, permit me to go further and suggest the necessity of a revisal of the law for the protection of seamen, which in its present state is quite inadequate for the purposes intended. If Captains were not allowed to discharge their crews in foreign ports upon any pretext whatever, it would put an end to the cruel treatment which seamen frequently experience from them, in order that they may be forced to ask for their discharge. When a vessel is sold abroad, the Captain should be obliged to procure his crew a passage home, and to support them until they arrive there. As the law at present stands, it is optional with the master whether to find them a passage or to furnish them with a certain sum of money for that purpose, which has generally been fixed at two months advance; but the Captain has it always in his power to bring the sailors in debt, and of their two months advance there ever remains but a trifle. These alterations would go a great way toward preventing our seamen from becoming a charge to Government, and from entering into foreign service to the prejudice of the commerce of the United States.

Among the many frauds practised upon our citizens is one which I beg leave to mention to you, as I fear it is not in my power at present to remedy it: the Consular Convention not being in force nor any law defining clearly the powers and duties of Consular Agents.

Foreign merchants settled within the United States, and particularly Frenchmen, are in the habit of purchasing damaged tobacco, cotton, rice &c at public auction, which articles they invoice at the highest market price, and then ship them, taking care to be well covered by insurance. When arrived at this port, the Captain as is usual makes his declaration and enters his protest of which the consignee procures a copy, being well instructed to cause a survey on the goods. This is usually done by a broker in the presence of two Justices of the Peace, who create such an average, of which they draw up a *procès-verbal* [official report] (for which they are well paid) as suits the factor and his friend, who after disposing of the goods at public sale come upon the underwriters for loss on sales, damages, &c. There are several French houses in New York and Philadelphia who have made large fortunes by this nefarious practice. In addition to the losses which our underwriters sustain by this means, the staple articles of the United States are lowered in estimation by the sale of this trash; and if the abuse is not corrected, our commerce will suffer greatly therefrom. I am now contending with the Chamber of Commerce for my right to appoint in behalf of the underwriters a person on each of their surveys, and I hope I shall succeed to my wishes.

I shall occasionally trouble you with such occurrences as I think worthy your notice, and have the

> honor to remain with great respect
> Your obedient Servant
> William Lee

To Miss Susan Palfrey Lee at Paris

Bordeaux, October 14, 1806

My dear Child.

This is the first letter I have ever written you. I hope you will experience the same pleasure in reading of it as I do in writing it. Since you all left me I have been very dull. The house appears like a wilderness in the evening, and during the day time the workmen's trowels and hammers make such a confounded noise, and form such a distressing contrast to the voices of my charming children, which used so often to ring through the corridor, that I feel relieved when the time comes to shut up the office, and go to change or to my dinner.

This dining at a restaurateur's I do not like; though, tell your dear mother, it costs me but little. Mouton's [Lee's valet] and my dinner together runs from fifty to sixty sous per day. I hope you will all study the same economy. But William must have his belly full *coute que coute.* I hope my little Mary, now that she has visited the great capital, will become a little woman, and check her propensity to crying on all occasions. She began to be very fond of reading before she left me, and I hope her taste for it will increase. You must both be very kind and attentive to your affectionate mother, and study to make her time pass off without inquietude. There are few little girls who can boast of so sweet, so dear a parent. Her whole happiness depends on your dutifulness.

I have had nothing to amuse me since your departure, if I except a frolic we have had with a bear, which a Captain made me a present of. I tied him in the wood shed; and the night before last, while Mr. Loring,[2] Stackpole, Lovell and myself were sitting in the library, he broke his rope and came in among us, and such confusion you never saw or heard of! I seized him by the ears and carried him back to his hole and fastened him anew, where he has remained ever since; and he has done no mischief, except killing a strange cat that frequents the house, and catching poor *La Rivière* by the tail, and frightening him half to

from Boston are 110 R. Cotman
J Williams & J Wyprimm Wolcot
J Robinson ...

The Snow has fallen barefoot
and the weather so as cold as we
commonly have it in Boston in
mid winter. —

March 6th Dined with the american
Minister Mr Munroe — g on the 9th with
Fulwar Skipwith american consul at
his house at Journee distant about
3 miles from Paris agoing to at Stepaad
a bridge called Neuilly the most
beautiful one I have yet seen — it is
perfectly level of white stone and surry
got an eight span across on the water — the
arches arelliptical and an
number of about feet wide I
measured several of the stones upon

the edge and found them from 17th
32 feet long and from 32 to 16 inches
square —

March 18th Having no business
to me I have employed myself in
reading writing my friends and ramling
about the city —

I have been in the Library
lately called the Kings this is said
now to contain 350,000 Vol. it is
open to citizens every day in the week
there are tables and chairs for their
use any one is admitted but you
must observe a profound silence — there
are a number of curiosities here are
cases full of agates upon which the
heads of all the roman Emperors of
the Kings & Queens of France wrought
and other curiosities and of their

Au nom du Peuple Français.

Le premier Consul de la République, ayant vu et examiné la Patente de M. William Lee, en vertu de laquelle il a été nommé par le Président des États-unis d'Amérique, Agent Commercial des États-unis d'Amérique dans le port de Bordeaux, et autres ports voisins, et que ce Gouvernement a jugé convenable d'établir ——

Autorise conformément à l'article 8 de la convention, en l'office du contenu en ladite Patente, Ordonne à tous les Corps administratifs, Tribunaux et autres cet Agent commercial jouisse de l'entier effet, du contenu en ladite Patente, & de le reconnaître en sa qualité d'Agent commercial des États-unis d'Amérique dans le Département de la Gironde —— afin qu'il puisse exercer librement les fonctions qui y sont attachées, & la charge néanmoins, qu'au cas qu'il fasse quelque commerce pour lequel il entre dans des engagements, il sera soumis aux Loix de la République, dans le Département de la Gironde ——

Donné à Paris au Palais national des Consuls, sous le sceau de la République française, le dix huitième ...

Le premier Consul de la République,

Bonaparte

Par le premier Consul.
Le Secrétaire d'État.

Hugues B. Maret

Le Ministre des Relations extérieures,

Vu et Enregistré au Secrétariat de la Préfecture du Département de la Gironde.
Bordeaux le 29 Vendémiaire an 10 de la République française
Le Secrétaire Général

J. Dulaurens

death. I have given him to Mons. Rabas, who I expect will send for him in a day or two.

Poor Mariette! [3] You cannot imagine how much she cried when you left her. The cook was quite concerned about it. This jade stole all your little pigeons, as Mouton thinks. They would steal everything from me, if your mother was to leave me for a long time; and then, if I was to die, my will would be somewhat like father abbé's, which I here enclose, to make you laugh. Copy it into your book, for it is the production of old parson Secombe,[4] the first teacher I ever had, and I set great store by it. My paper scarcely allows me place enough to say how much I love you all, my dear children, and you, their blessed mother.

W. Lee

Parson Secombe's Will

In my own name I constitute
This my last will to prevent dispute
Knowing the frailty of this state
That all must leave it soon or late
And be reborn again in heaven
With all their deeds and sins forgiven
In perfect mind tho' weak in health
I now bestow my store of wealth
My Soul of course I leave to heaven
And God by whom to me 'twas given
My body to the dust allied
I freely to the dust confide
Imprimis let not debts be paid
But all my creditors persuade
That orders drawn on me above
Will answer'd be with purest love
That is to say my trusting friends
Must take their labor for their pains
Item the Gin now on my hands
That on my Walnitt Table stands
I give to him whom cholicks haunt
And such warm medicines may want
Isaac my friend being sometimes prest
With such rude pangs as peirce my breast
I recommend to my right heirs

When they have settled my affairs
The Gin and bottle him to give
(If at that period he should live)
To ease the throbbing of his breast
And soothe his raging pains to rest
Item if lands I now possess
The're seated in a wilderness
Where human footsteps never press'd
A lonesome haunt to preying beast
This situation I devise
To woman-kind of every size
Where to each gently passing gale
They may unfold sweet slander's tale
And green-ey'd envy holds a seat
In Chair of State when e'er they meet
Item to my dear sister Tye
If she be living when I die
I give my Table and my Chairs
My prudence in my small affairs
Consisting of my Cottage Tongs
With rust and what to them belongs
My Shovel and my iron Logs
With all my bottles and my jugs
Item my books I leave to Pat
With my new purchas'd Silk-lin'd Hatt
Item to my dear sister Nance
Her merit here on earth t'enhance
I give my yellow worsted Hose
And especially to them repose
In trust to her until the day
When Hymen shall emit a ray
To melt the cement on two hearts
And join in one the seperate parts
Them on her Spouse she may confer
The Hose were ne'er designed for her
Item the taxes on my Pen
Are any taxes on it due
I grant them all to Elder Wright
To have and hold in his own right
And further do to him convey
My claim and Rights said rates to pay
Item to Capt. Otis Crew
I grant them all thats to me due

But humbly recommend to all
Not into this my scheme to fall
For 'tis from pure necessity
I to their terms do now agree
For should I wait till end of time
I ne'er should hear the Dollars chime
Item my Phials full of air
My Gally Pots [5] and such like ware
I leave to Lorenz my good friend
Upon condition he them lend
To all poor Devils in my case
For six whole weeks no longer space
Item my notes and all the Bonds
That to my great Estate belongs
I give in lease to Sons of Cake
Together with my minute Book
Item on Cooper I bestow
My Guater [guitar?] and my Gun brush too.

To Mrs. Susan Palfrey Lee at Paris

Bordeaux, October 21, 1806

My dear Girl: I received your letter of the —— yesterday.
That by the conductor has not yet reached me.

I am sorry to hear Mrs. P[reble] [6] is at St. Germain, as she is
an acquaintance I do not wish you to make. You know, I suppose, that she is the daughter of Mrs. W[right], P[arker]'s mistress, and that they have both longer lived with that gentleman
to the great injury of both their reputations. Do for God's sake
keep such people at a distance. I know a great deal which will
not do to commit to paper which I never told you of, because
a virtuous woman is much happier when she is kept ignorant of
the wickedness which surrounds her. Parker has kept Preble
roving round the world in the strangest manner, and I believe
the house she lives in at St. Germain is Parker's, or if she is at
lodgings, her mother lives at the estate purchased for them there
by Parker. Mrs. Tudor must be more circumspect on account of
that angel Delia. [7]

Mrs. Leavenworth is a very good hearted woman and her husband one of the best informed men in Paris, but an odd one. I

have a regard for them on account of their kind attentions to me when in Paris, and if an opportunity offers, tell them so. I did not call on them when I was last in Paris, as I passed thro' in a hurry, and was told they did not wish to see me on account of my law suit &c with their son-in-law Phelps.

Have you seen Mme. La Croix [8] and Mme. Vernenac? They live in rue Giemelle in your faubourg, and I believe not very far from Talleyrand's office. Those are the sort of people I wish you to be acquainted with, after your own ambassadors' and consuls' families. But if I hear you are with Mrs. P. and Mrs. W., I shall come and bring you home directly; for reputation is all we have, my dear Susan, and we cannot be too tender of it.

Mr. Johnston [9] is to give you to-morrow a letter of credit on Paris, which will answer your purposes. I shall send it to May, as I do not wish to trouble Judge Tudor, and by Stackpole, who goes to-morrow or next day, I will send you some loose cash. Tell Susan to answer my letter. I have got into the other house, tho' Vears has not moved all his furniture out, and expect to move my office in all this week. I shall do nothing to the house until Spring, as the weather is now too damp, and it will be an amusement to you to fit it up when you come home in May, for I shall not consent to your staying longer — the sacrifice is too great for me. I have no acquaintances here and feel at times very dull. You know I hate cards and the theatre.

Adieu my dear good wife. I love you tenderly. Kiss the dear children for me.

W Lee

To Mrs. Susan Palfrey Lee at St. Germain

Bordeaux, November 21, 1806

I write you, my dear adorable Girl, in bed, where I must remain eight or ten days, having dislocated my ankle and fractured perhaps one of the small bones of the foot. I am in excruciating pain but the surgeons assure me I shall be up in the course of a few days, but that it will take five or six weeks to restore everything.

I was coming home last evening from Mr. Forster's at 10 o'clock, the weather was drizzling and the walking of course slippery. In crossing over from the alley to the house, I slipped into one of those holes, which are perfect traps, and I turned out my left ankle with such force that it made a noise like a pistol. I thought not to tell you this, but Meyer [10] says they have got it out of doors that I have broke my leg, and if such a report was to reach you it might give uneasiness. I will write you every post and I desire you will not be unhappy on my account and that you do not think of quitting the children for such a trifle as this. It will keep me at home and prevent my rocking.

Adieu my dear girl. Kiss my children for me.
Your affectionate

Wm Lee

P.S. I open the letter to say that the surgeons have just examined my leg and foot and find no fractures but only a severe strain and dislocation of the ankle, which cold water, bandages and patience will cure. Mrs. Forster has sent me some nice bandages and I have every attention I could wish. The pain is almost unsupportable.

W. L.

To Mrs. Susan Palfrey Lee at St. Germain

Bordeaux, December 7, 1806

My dear Girl:

I wrote you yesterday and the day before two letters addressed to you at St. Germain, and enclosed one from brother Thomas, another from Appleton, and another from Nancy Lowell.[11] I wrote also Stackpole, and ordered him to pay you 1000 fr. out of the 2000 fr. he wrote me he was about receiving from Mr. May.

All these letters I am afraid will not go safe, as by the *décrit* of the Emperor I find all letters addressed or written in English are not to be suffered to go on in the post. As I cannot write French, we shall be put to great inconvenience. If your letters do not arrive, write a letter to the *Directeur-Général des Postes à Paris* and demand them, stating they left Bordeaux before the decree was known, that you are an American, and perhaps he will suffer them to proceed to you. I write you again to-morrow.

Your affectionate
Wm Lee

To Mrs. Susan Palfrey Lee in Paris

Bordeaux, December 9, 1806

Your letter of the 3rd has reached me, my dear S., but this day. I hope you did not entrust it to any one to put in the office, who may have looked into it, as it contains opinions respecting some of your new acquaintances. Your letter enclosing the bill of furniture came to me yesterday. But we must now lay aside all ideas of buying furniture, and I have stopped all the workmen on the house, who were doing anything on my account. This decree of the Emperor has thrown everything into the greatest confusion, and privateers are now fitting out here to attack American commerce.

The first article declares the British Islands in a state of blockade. Therefore all vessels bound to England, or that may have cleared out for England, and a market, will be taken and brought into France, if Gen. Armstrong [12] does not procure some modification of this decree, which it is not probable he will be able to do. All letters written in English are not to be permitted to pass in the post office. Write me therefore in French, and as I cannot write French, I will get my letters to you as well as I can. All British goods coming from their colonies or manufactures are to be a good prize wherever they are found. Therefore all American vessels with British goods or produce on board will be considered a good prize, and I expect to see the river full of our ships as enemies. The Minister of Marine is charged with the execution of this decree. Therefore there can be no doubt but that it is aimed at us.

This stroke puts a final end to our commerce to this city and renders, my dear Girl, our situation peculiarly uncertain. I hope it will not be distressing. We shall get no news from America; for the moment a vessel arrives, her letters will be taken by the boarding officers, and those in English will not be permitted to circulate.

See all you can of Paris, and let me know when your quarter for the children is up, as I expect I shall be obliged to send for you or come for you; for in times like these we had better be together, for who knows now what will happen? Our ministers in England,[13] it is said, have made a treaty with that infernal nation. If it be a favorable one, our Government will have their hands full. One party will be for declaring in favor of France, another in favor of England; and if France captures many of our vessels, they may possibly adhere to England, in which case we should all be taken up here and put in prison or sent to Verdun. We should have less favor shown to us than English-men receive, and that nation would be exasperated against us. The friendship you and I have shown to the individuals of this nation both in America and here would avail us nothing. My attachment to France would be a curse to me were I, in case of such an unfortunate event, to return to America, and it would be worth nothing to me here, particularly at Bordeaux, where you know I am not generally liked by the merchants, because I never would consent to do dishonorable things to gratify their views.

The crisis is really alarming. I have written Gen'l Armstrong on the subject, and wish he would write me on the business, but I presume he has too much to do. If you see Judge Tudor, ask him what our ministers' opinions of things appear to be. How unfortunate it is that they come to France just at this moment! Husband all your money! Had I foreseen all this, I should not have expended 1000 fr. or thereabouts on this house. And as it is, I do not intend to take a lease of it for the present, until I see how the storm breaks. My bills on England, which I took for the ship, cannot now be sold here, and I shall be in want of money.

I sent you this morning an order on Stackpole for 1000 fr.

which he has received of May. The other 1000 fr. from the same quarter shall also go to you. Tell me from time to time how it lasts. Pay up all your bills daily, that if necessary you can quit at a moment's warning. It will be four or five months before the dispositions of our Government relating to this decree will be known here, and before that period we shall remain unmolested. But, should the President's answer to the communications that will doubtless be made to him from this country not suit the Emperor, we must then look out, and I mean to be prepared to fly with you all to our native country. Do not think I am exaggerating things! Our Government has but three things to do: 1st to declare in favor of France: 2nd to declare in favor of England; or 3rd to put on an embargo. This latter is probably what they will do to avoid a war and such a measure would put an end to our resources. I shall keep a good heart and worry through whatever may be our destiny. There are so many persons more distressed than we are that I will not repine. If I can find support for you and the children and keep with you, it is all I shall ask for. Write me all you hear, and tell me what say Skipwith and Tudor to all these things.

God bless you. I wrote my darling this morning. I hope it will go safe.

To Mrs. Susan Palfrey Lee at St. Germain

Bordeaux, Sunday morning, February 1, 1807

My dear S.

I received your letter mentioning your determination to remain another quarter at St. Germain. As you have concluded, I shall not disapprove. Though I think you would have been better pleased at Paris a month or six weeks, and then you would have joined me; for this sort of life is not pleasing to me. I never passed such a dull winter in my life. Whole weeks I have been confined to a room with my leg on a chair and in the evenings not a soul to converse with.

Yesterday I went through a very painful operation and expect now to be on my legs as well as ever in the course of ten days. I had employed first and last four different surgeons, and found of late that my ankle grew worse instead of better. At length I consulted a Dr. Roberts, who, on examining the ankle, said the small bone of the leg had been badly set, and that it must be broke again before I could walk. This opinion was distressing, and being that day engaged to dine with Fenwick,[14] I mentioned the affair to Mr. Abbiot who sat next to me at table. He advised me to send to Eysines, about two leagues from this, for a bonesetter, who was very celebrated, and whose family had been possessed of the art of setting bones for three or four hundred years from father to son.

I sent for this man — an ill looking peasant of few words and no magic tricks. He looked at my ankle, made me hobble across the room, put his finger immediately on the place which caused me to suffer, and told me my surgeons were asses. " Ils sont des ânes." And said he could cure me in five minutes. I had no confidence in him and told him so. He then referred me to Dan'l Lacombe, a rich merchant, who had some time ago met with the same accident. I called to see Lacombe, who told me he was three months without walking when he was advised to send for this man, who operated upon his foot, and that very day he walked to 'change. He sent me to our neighbor Martin, who told me he was six weeks without walking; that the surgeons could do nothing for him, when he sent for this man, who put him on his legs in two days.

After these assurances, I sent again for the man, and he made his appearance yesterday about ten o'clock. My heart failed me; but there being four or five persons present, they laughed me into confidence, and I gave the fellow my foot. He instantly dislocated every toe beginning at the small one, extended all the sinews with all his force. He then turned my foot out as far as his force could get it; then turned it in towards the other; and lastly pressing his hand on the ankle joint, he pressed with his other hand the toes and foot toward the shin bone, and the bones all went into their places. The pain was excrutiating beyond all you can have an idea of. But I can walk as well as ever, except that the parts are weak and require a few days rest. I have thrown aside my stick, and shall walk without one to dinner at Mr. Forster's to-day. I expected to be lame all my life.

Meyer has been with me all the week helping me get up my " annual returns " to Government, and I expect will remain three or four days longer. The work of the office will fag me, but I am determined to go through it. Delplu and myself leave our dispute to Lacombe and Gernon.[15] He is a poor miserable devil. I paid Coste 700 fr. for the time he tended the children. Am interrupted ———

Yr. W

To Mrs. Susan Palfrey Lee at St. Germain

Bordeaux, Saturday, March 14, 1807

My soul is full of my S., full of her virtues, of her lovely mien and her dear offspring. What a delicious thing is this love! It is a charm: a *"véritable délice."* Loveliest of mortals; there is nothing that can compensate for the loss of your society —*" absolument rien qui puisse remplir le vide affreux que ton absence fuit dans ma vie."* Do hurry back that I may again commence to live and feel my existence.

Tell Susan it is my desire that she does not lace herself tight and that she takes out every bone in the new made stays. Do not sacrifice the health of your children to the whims of dancing masters. Look at the black mulattoes and other women of the West Indies. They have the finest forms in the world and do not know the use of whalebone. Read Buffon[16] on that subject and he will frighten you. Do, my dear Girl, attend to this. Susan is straight by nature and always will be, unless you create a deformity by lacing her up. Some of these evenings I will consult some experienced authors on this subject and give you some extracts, for I think, my dear, it is a point on which you have erred very much. I am interrupted. My love to my darlings from

W.

To Mrs. Susan Palfrey Lee at St. Germain

Bordeaux, April 18 [*1807*]

After writing you yesterday, my dear Girl, I received your letter. It gave me pleasure and cured me of a night of anxiety. I sent you by yesterday's post a letter of credit from Blanchard and Hardy on their banker *Rougemont de Lowenberg* for 2000 fr. This banker lives rue Bergère No. 9 à Paris. Your signature I have cut off from one of your letters and sent to this banker, so that you will have nothing to do but to draw on him or call on him as our friend Skipwith shall think best.

If my arrangement with Johnston takes place, I will come for you, provided I can suspend the sittings of the arbitrators on my affair with that pitiful wretch Delplu. If not, I will meet you at Tours. But had you not better hire a carriage and take in Harris or Capt. Silliman and come on in easy stages, stopping at the towns of Orléans, Tours, Blois, Poitiers, Angoulême &c? Riding at nights is fatiguing and dangerous on account of colds, which create at this season the tertian fever. Silliman speaks French very well, is accustomed to traveling, and is certainly the most respectable captain who frequents this port. I will see the conductor and make a conditional arrangement with him and leave it all to your own choice, provided I do not come for you, which I certainly will strain a point to do.

John [17] is certainly to be married to a Miss Phillips of New Orleans, a young handsome woman. What a fool! He gave Hackly who has just arrived liberty to tell me so. He has been appointed Colonel: so in future you must direct to Colonel Palfrey.

I wrote Susan a few days since. I expect you are spoiling William. God bless you sweet creature. I long to see you and to make you happy. Your neighbors here are all much attached to you. You are as much liked at Bordeaux as I am disliked.

Your affectionate

W.

Take an opportunity and do away to Skipwith the idea of my office being profitable. Even if it was so, I should try to make people believe otherwise. But the fact is, my dear, it will not support us without great frugality, and if I do not make my arrangement with J[ohnston], Meyer must go. When Fenwick had the office, 400, 500, even to 633 vessels entered per year. Now last year 180 vessels entered only and this year by appearance only 150 will enter. Thus, if the office was then worth 30,000 francs, it cannot be worth half that now. I have only bills of lading and certificates of drawback. In short 15,000 francs, my dear, is the very extent of the produce of the office.

To James Madison at Washington

Bordeaux, July 23, 1807.

Sir:

By the enclosed article, which I have cut out of the paper of this morning, and the ringing of bells, which are now sounding in my ears, peace it appears is concluded on. The treaty it is reported is not to be promulgated until the 16 August.

It is said that the two Emperors have divided Europe. Alexander is Emperor of the East and Napoleon of the West. The old family of Naples is to be reinstated. Joseph, the present King of Naples, is to be King of Holland, his brother Louis having abdicated his throne in his favor. Eugene the Vice-Roy of Italy to be King of Italy; though some accounts say Joseph is to be King of Italy and Eugene of Holland. The Emperor of Austria to be King of Austria and Bohemia. The Archduke Charles King of Hungary. The Grand Duke of Berg to be King of Poland. The Grand Duke Constantine to be King of the Greeks, to reside at Constantinople. Bernadotte Duke of Hanover, and Jerome King of Saxony.[18]

This, Sir, is the news of the day. Full credit is not to be given to all of it, but there is no doubt but great changes are to take place. England it appears is out of the question in this arrangement.

With great respect I am, Sir,
Your obedient Servant
Wm Lee

To James Madison at Washington

Bordeaux, Dec. 10, 1807.

Sir:

I have just received intelligence from Mr. Lanne, my agent at Bayonne, that the brig *Hypsa and James* of Salem bound to this port has arrived there after having been visited by the British squadron at the mouth of this river, who made the following endorsement on her papers: "Warned from entering any port in France and all her dependencies, Portugal, Spain, Italian and Mediterranean ports, and the Colonies of Spain and Portugal.

> Given under our hands on board his
> Majesty's ship Tribune off Cordouan Light
> House this 3 Decr. 1807.
> > signed J. Baker Capt.
> > S Hood Capt."

It appears by this that the blockade is to take immediate effect, which much alarms us here for the fate of the sixteen vessels that left this last week for the United States. The measure is considered as very hostile to the United States, and it is believed the English intend carrying in as much American property as they can capture under the persuasion that they will be able to make better terms by this means with us. Under this impression I have advised all the American masters now in port to remain here, which, however, they do not incline to listen to.

We have had two arrivals at Rochelle, one of them, the brig *Elias*, Capt. Dandelot, in attempting to come round here, has been captured by the English. The other, a three-masted schooner from Baltimore, has been refused a pilot at Rochelle under the suspicion of her having been in England. The consignee, Mr. Andrews, has gone on to Rochelle and will I hope be able to procure a pilot or an entry. I mention these circumstances to show you that this Government appears determined not to admit any vessel to an entry that may have touched in England.

Our city is crowded with troops. Part of the Imperial Guards have arrived, and the Emperor is expected on the 28th. Much is said of the dismemberment of Turkey; of the new Kingdom of Navarre; the siege of Gibraltar; and other vast designs, which it is impossible to fathom. The Queen of Etruria [19] is to reign in Portugal. Rumors of peace are on float; but it is said they originated in England, where it is probable they have been fabricated in order to serve the purpose of that Government in America.

> With great respect,
> I have the honor to remain
> Your obedient Servant
> Wm. Lee

Written on the outside
This letter opened by the agents
of the British Privateer Mars
of Falmouth Eng.
> Sealed by Your
> obdt Svt. Sir
> J. Silliman

To James Madison at Washington.
Private.

Bordeaux, Nov. 1, 1808.

Sir:

A severe indisposition, which has confined me to my bed for several days, scarcely leaves me strength enough to apologize to you for the confused style of my letter of this morning and to say a few words on other subjects.

The things Mr. Baker purchased for you, with the hogshead of white wine and brandy I hold in readiness to send, the consignee and Captain of this vessel have refused to let me put on board. I tried to pass the small articles as stores for the passengers, but could not succeed, the Captain, consignee, and

Custom House have been so very strict. If I do not meet an opp[ortuni]ty before the spring I will bring them with me, as it is my full intention to leave this on the beginning of March for the United States.

The Emperor is now in this city on his way to join the army. The quantity of troops, artillery, wagons &c which are continually passing is incredible. He will head an army, it is said, of 300,000 men, composed chiefly of veteran troops. The Spanish have been so very inactive in allowing the French to concentrate their forces (which they incautiously had distributed in small detachments all over the kingdom), and to throw in this great reinforcement before they struck a decisive blow, that there is now scarcely a judicious man to be found who is not of the opinion that the conquest of that country and Portugal will very shortly be achieved.

The troops composing the army of Gen'l Junot [20] have but just been landed, and are, it is said, to be marched into Spain. All that has as yet transpired of the meeting of the two Emperors is their expediting two couriers for London (which however does not appear very certain) and what his Majesty thinks proper to communicate to the legislative body in his speech which I have the honor to inclose.

I am not without apprehensions for the safety of Mr. Erving. [21] The last letter he wrote me was from Madrid mentioning an attempt had been made to assassinate him.

With great respect,
I have the honor to remain
Your devoted Servant
Wm. Lee.

By Capt. Marriner, the bearer of this, I have the honor to forward you two letters from Gen'l A[rmstrong].

To show something of the life of William Lee and his family in Bordeaux during the years 1807 and 1808, some extracts from Lee's " Memorandum Book " have been inserted. As the highest ranking official representative from America at Bordeaux, Lee naturally exercised his ingenuity to extend courtesies to all the important visitors to that city, such as Cambacérès, Champagny, and the Em-

73

press Josephine. He may have had contacts with these ministers while he was in Paris in 1796 and 1797, but this was probably his first introduction to Josephine.

1 8 0 7

Memorandum Book

November 18. Cambacérès,[22] Prince and Archchancellor of the Empire, arrived here this day.

November 19. I was presented to the Prince.

November 20. Dined with him.

November 23. Assisted at the ball of the city given to the Prince.

November 24. Mrs. Lee and myself passed the evening and supped at the Prince's.

November 25. I accompanied the Prince in the city yacht to view the harbor &c. of Bordeaux — manned the yards of an American ship and prepared a collation on board for the Prince, which the tide prevented him partaking of.

November 26. Mrs. Lee and myself assisted at the ball the commerce gave the Prince.

November 20th. omitted. All American vessels were arrested at Bordeaux. Their log books, rolls, and equipage &c. examined and interrogated. The object not known.

December 12. We received at Bordeaux the intelligence that the Count of Portugal [23] embarked on the 28 Nov. for Brazil, accompanied with an English fleet under the command of Sir Sidney Smith.

1 8 0 8

Monday, April 4. Napoleon, Emperor of France and King of Italy, arrived at Bordeaux.

Friday, April 8. Paid a visit to M. Champagny,[24] Minister of Foreign Affairs.

April 9. Lent my barge to the Commissary of Marine with eight sailors to go to St.-André-de-Cubzac to bring the Empress across that ferry of the Dordogne.

April 13. The Emperor left Bordeaux for Bayonne.

Sunday, April 24. Mrs. Lee and myself were introduced to the Empress by the *chambellan* M. Beaumont [25] Present only two maids of honor. She received us with great kindness, made Mrs. Lee sit down by her, and conversed with her in the most familiar manner for half an hour.

III

GOSSIP FROM PARIS

1809–1810

In November, 1809, William Lee set out for Paris, taking the model of a bridge that he had designed to be constructed over the Garonne River. During the five months he spent in the capital discussing this project and others, Lee watched the international situation grow increasingly tense. Following the repeal of her embargo in 1809, the United States proposed a Non-Intercourse Act aimed at stopping all trade with England and France. Until this act was repealed in 1810, the French continued to seize all American ships in French ports as "enemy prize." Typical of the confusion and intrigue in Franco-American relations at this time was an incident involving General John Armstrong, U.S. minister to France. By a dishonest note, delivered to him by Cadore, the French foreign minister, Armstrong was led to believe that France had revoked her punitive edicts of Berlin and Milan. Armstrong returned home in September, 1810, confident that he had accomplished a great deal for his country.

The letters that Lee wrote to his family in Bordeaux during these exciting days — accounts of sightseeing trips and visits to the various ministers — make no attempt to conceal his distaste for the scandals of Napoleon's court. Lee was received and entertained by a number of famous — and even notorious — people in the capital. Among the latter were Messrs. Hauteval and Hottinguer, who had been Talleyrand's two Swiss agents in the XYZ Affair of 1797. These men apparently found it politic to treat Lee, as well as other Americans in Paris, with great civility;[1] and Lee, in fact, mentioned M. and Mme. Hottinguer often and favorably in his letters. Aside from social and business engagements, Lee was, as always, occupied with the affairs of his family. He described with some interest the Parisian outfits he had bought for his wife and daughters and continued to express his concern for the education and deportment as well as the health of his children. After five months in the French capital he returned to Bordeaux in March, 1810, apparently having made no progress on the projected bridge.

To Mrs. Susan Palfrey Lee at Bordeaux

Paris, November 23, 1809.

My much loved wife — My time has been so taken up since my arrival in this city, the days are so short and the distances so great that really the hours fly off without note, without even carrying an offering to the best of friends, unless zephyrs should have wafted to you some of those sighs which the thought of you and our dear children so frequently draw from me. To-morrow, however, I shall dedicate to the purchase of a few things for you and the children, which I shall send by Mr. Cramer who lives in the same hotel with me and goes off in a day or two for Bordeaux.

I have really been feasted beyond all calculation since my arrival. To-night I am going to the Theatre of the Court in the Tuileries and my day is to be taken up in a visit to the Minister of the Interior by appointment and to Mons. le Sénateur Monbadon,[2] who writes me in this style this morning: "Mons. le Sénateur, comte de Monbadon a l'honneur de se rapeller au souvenir de Monsieur Lee et de lui témoigner le désir de l'entretenir le plus-tot possible d'une chose qui l'intéresse. Il sera chez lui jusqu'à 4 h. de soir." signé Monbadon. This senator must have got my address of the Minister of the Interior or some of the great folks I have been dancing after, and perhaps he is on the bridge scent, which is but a secondary object with me: as we say in New England — a tub to catch a whale with.

Yesterday I dined at Mde. La Croix, who lives in a pretty dignified style. I always liked that family. There is something very *distingué* in their manners. Mr. and Mrs. Hoskins are here in a dirty hotel as much like her ladyship's boudoir at Bordeaux as possible. Flowers and feathers are really very dear as Miss P. F. says and their price will be enhanced by the arrival of this lady in the capital, unless she should content herself with second hand ones, which is not impossible.

Send for M. Ducourneau and tell him that I have every reason to expect success, and that I should have written him on the subject, but it is a subject which it is not proper to write on by ordinary conveyances. Tell him I thank him for his attention to my house concern and I am happy in the decision of the Tribunal. Among other things, my dear,* I have written Barlow to apply for the General Consulate for me. The salary is 10,000 francs per annum and the perquisites will amount to as much more if well managed. This I have done to assure as a sort of *dernier* resort and on account of our children. For if I am at last obliged to take a place, one here is preferable on the account of their education, than one at home, at least for two or three years.

I will write Meyer to-morrow. My love to the children. Get Susan's writing master back if possible.

Your devoted
W.

*Not a word of this to any one for your life. The place you know is vacant. Warden [3] only acts.

To Miss Susan Palfrey Lee at Bordeaux

Paris, November 26, 1809

My dear daughter:

I intended, when I set out, to have given you an account of my journey; but we were so continually on the move, and so few incidents occurred that would entertain you, that I postponed writing you until I should have seen something of Paris. I have been here more than a fortnight, and strange to tell, I have seen nothing except crowded midnight halls and full tables. Here, as Addison says, " The gout, the dropsy, and all their attendants lay in ambuscade." . . .[4]

The first evening we left Bordeaux, we stopped at Carbon-Blanc, where we were arrested by two *gens d'armes* for English prisoners, who would not suffer us to leave our room to go in search of our passports, which we had left in our carriage. The *brusque et malhonnête* manner in which this arrest was con-

ducted was so extremely improper, even had we been English-
men, that I flew into one of my violent fits and treated the *gens
d'armes* with such contempt, that *Monsieur le Maire* and his
Adjoint were called in, who recognized me and adjusted the
affair. How ridiculous are some men apt to appear when armed
with a little brief authority, and how necessary are kind words
and gentle manners to our own happiness! Your character is too
much like mine. You must endeavor to mold it more after your
mother's, whose sweetness of disposition makes her adored by all
who know her.

We left Carbon-Blanc at three in the morning and passed the
Dordogne at daybreak at St. Pardon. Between this place and
Libourne, near the latter, we left our cabriolet to ascend the hill
of Fronsac, from which we had a most enchanting view of Libourne and all the adjacent country, with the rivers Dordogne
and Isle meandering through a plain luxuriant beyond anything
I ever met with. Sawney [5] was astonished, and made some interesting reflections occasioned by the beauty of the scene contrasted with the wretched remains of the duc de Richelieu's
palace, which crowns the summit of the mountain, and is now
inhabited by a poor peasant family. How futile and transitory
are the schemes men generally form in the pursuit of happiness!
The life of Richelieu [6] was one continued round of dissipation,
and this one of his seats of riot. Time's cold breath has long since
destroyed his gay beautiful dream of ambition and luxury. . . .

At Palissoux, a small town three or four posts distant from
Périgeux, we halted for breakfast. It being market day, several
peasants presented themselves with sacs of truffles, for which
they asked us twenty sous per pound. We told them to come
after breakfast and we would buy of them (intending them as a
present to Gen'l Armstrong). The woman of the house, hearing
this, went into the market and bought up all the truffles, in order
to make a speculation out of us, and then modestly asked us
fifty sous per pound. But the trick displeased us so much that
we declined to buy any, which enraged her ladyship to such a
degree, that she told me she took me for the Emperor's cook,
who had passed that road with his Majesty, and bought a great

many truffles. This she meant as a terrible insult, as she had just before called me *My Lord Anglais*. As we had bargained for our breakfast (which is the only way in traveling through this country), we paid our bill and left Madame *en trés mauvaise compagnie,* bad humor and bad business. . . .

On Saturday night we arrived at Limoges, after having rode through a picturesque country, whose valleys are finely cultivated and whose hill tops are covered with forests of chestnut trees. Périgueux is the capital of the department of Dordogne, and Limoges of Haute-Vienne. The latter town contains about 25,000 inhabitants, who are very commercial from their position; five of the principal roads of the Empire meeting here and the river Vienne running through it, giving birth to many manufactures, such as cloth and cotton, paper and iron mills, all of which we visited. It being also situated on the declivity of two or three little hills, the principal streets are kept very clean by means of a reservoir of water, which is filled over night, and in the morning thrown into them to wash the mud into the river. . . .

Mr. Alluaud, to whom my companion was particularly recommended, being from home, we hired an old cabriolet and two horses, to take us to St. Yrieix, about thirty miles off, in order to meet him. Such roads I never passed before! The cabriolet upset twice, but luckily we were not in it, for I insisted in both spots on getting out. Having left Limoges rather late in the morning, night overtook us, and we lost ourselves in a forest of chestnut trees, from which we were extricated by a tinker and a mason, who were traveling to St. Yrieix to mend the pots and kettles and Rumfordize [7] the fire places of Mons. Le Sous-Préfet.

While in this forest, incredible as it may appear to your mother (who never deals in the marvelous), the wolves were howling round us in every direction, and our fellow travelers were so much afraid of encountering wild boars, that they requested me to let them get up, one behind and the other before the carriage. I began to imagine myself in the wilds of Labrador. We entered St. Yrieix at about nine in the morning. It being very cold and dark, I had left the carriage, and was walking on foot in my white coat and pantaloons, which terrified many young men and women, whom we met returning from the little balls in the neighborhood. Some of them took me in good earnest to be a hobgoblin, which gave us much amusement.

The gentleman whom we were in search of, we were told, put up at the *Graces* (a very pretty name for a country tavern). To the Graces, therefore, we bent our way, and entered a most excellent inn. Two fine healthy, youthful, well-dressed girls, daughters of the hostess, ushered us in with, " Mons. l'Anglais par ici." " I am no Englishman, Mesdames." " De quel pays êtes-vous donc, Mons? " " I am an American savage." " Sauvage! Ma foi! Vous êtes un beau sauvage." There was a sprightliness and good humor about these girls, and a bloom of health which marked a contented mind.

> *Content*, mild maid! delights in *simple* things,
> And envies not the state of queens or kings;
> Can dine on sheep's head, or a dish of broth,
> Without a table or a tablecloth;
> Can use a bit of packthread for a jack,
> And sit upon a chair without a back:
> Nay; wanting knives, can make her fingers work,
> And use a wooden skewer for a fork.
> Sweet maid! who thinks not shoes of leather shocking,
> Nor feels the horrors in a worsted stocking;
> Pleas'd with that nat'ral curls her face that shade,
> No graves are robb'd for hair to form a braid:
> Her breast of native plumpness n'er aspires
> To swelling *merry thoughts* of gauze and wires.
> With nature's hips, she sighs not for *cork rumps*,
> *And scorns the pride of pinching stays or jumps;*
> *But, pleased from whalebone prisons to escape,*
> *She trusts to simple nature for a shape;*
> Without a warming-pan can go to bed,
> And wrap her petticoat about her head;
> Nor sigh for cobweb caps of Mechlin lace,
> That shade of quality the varnish'd face.
> Sweet nymph; like doves, she seeks her straw-built nest,
> And in a pair of minutes is undrest;
> Whilst all the fashionable female clans
> Undressing, seem unloading caravans.   PINDAR.[8]

So much for content. My letter will be as long as my journey, if I go on at this rate, and I shall end by causing a gape instead of a smile.

Mr. Alluaud, whom we came in search of, had left the Graces the day before to visit his mines of antimony and kaolin, [pure white clay, used to form paste of porcelain] and to hunt wild boars. These Frenchmen are the strangest compounds in nature. They mix business and pleasure and jumble everything together — but more of this hereafter. We took our horses from the cabriolet, mounted them, and with a guide left the Graces to hunt Mr. Alluaud. After riding three leagues through the wildest country imaginable, presenting nothing but groves of chestnut trees, huge clumps of rocks, small rivulets, and some pretty lakes, we arrived through a fine row of lofty elms at the château of Monsieur de Chaufaille, a very rich *cidevant* [ex-noble]. Here we met my companion's friend, who introduced us, fatigued and dirty as we were, into an elegant saloon, where we beheld, to our great surprise, four beautiful women, of accomplished manners and fashionable appearance. " Faith mun," says Sawney, " we ha been wandering to and frow long enow. Let us ene tak up our abode in this bonny house. I dunna care to go farther for one week." Poor fellow! Before he got half way to this castle he was obliged to stoop down, " as he must needs, who cannot sit upright," and the transition was so great that it operated like enchantment.

The bursting in upon this scene, after passing through such a dreary country, appeared to me something like the stories in the *Arabian Nights' Entertainments,* and while my friend was admiring living beauties, I was examining the details of the mansion. The family pictures and other drawings, with which the room was decorated, were from the pencil of the lady of the house, and remarkably well executed. The room if anything was too richly furnished for a country residence. The library appeared extensive, and some philosophical apparatus, relating mostly to mine[r]alogy, indicated a taste for the useful (which our neighbor Hoskins is searching after).

These you will say were sufficient of themselves to charm

the way-worn traveler, and compensate for the howling of the wolves; but when you cast your eyes on the prospect before the house, your admiration broke silence. In front was a fine lawn, terminated by a lake of considerable magnitude, whose opposite sides were crowned with clumps of chestnut trees and elms. On the left were ornamental and useful gardens, and on the right, at a proper distance, two mills, whose music, with the noise of the fall of water, completed the scenery.

When dinner was served, we were shown into a large hall, whose rude ancient appearance put me in mind of some of Miss [Mrs.] Radcliffe's [9] descriptions. I was pleased to see the respectable owner of this mansion sit down to dinner with his *homme d'affaires,* and overseers of his mines, mills &c, who with a ruddy-faced priest, two neighboring gentlemen, the ladies, an old *militaire* who fought in the American war, and, as Goldsmith says, at every interval was for " shouldering his crutch to tell how fields were won," [10] Sawney, myself, and his amiable friend made up the society. We regretted much the absence of the father of the lady of the house, who was long colonel of a regiment, in which Napoleon served as lieutenant and captain. It would have been gratifying to have questioned him respecting the character and genius of this wonderful man at that time. He has offered this old soldier several places, none of which he would accept.

After dinner we visited the mines and iron works, and then took our leave of these respectable and amiable people, who pressed us to stay to the hunt of the wild boars; but as Sawney was already sore from hunting Mr. Alluaud, and I was anxious to reach Paris, before Gen'l Armstrong left it, we declined the invitation and sat off for St. Yrieix. On our way night overtook us, accompanied by a brisk shower. We again wandered wild in the chestnut forest; but after many windings and turnings, reached the Graces, as thoroughly tired, galled and jaded as ever I remember to have been.

The next evening we arrived at Limoges, and visited a pretty little theatre, where I was much diverted with a small piece representing Voltaire, when a young man, on a visit to the celebrated Ninon.[11] It was replete with delicate wit and satire. On this second visit to Limoges we learned that a disease something like the yellow fever raged there the last summer, destroying ten, fifteen, and twenty people every day, and driving the inhabitants into the country. It was brought to Limoges by the Spanish prisoners, who were removed from Château Trompette there. What a narrow escape we had at Bordeaux! The police of the country prevented this from being known. . . .

On our arrival at Orléans, we took a view of the Gothic cathedral, which is one of the finest in France, and of the newly erected statue of the maid of Orléans, who was so celebrated in the war of 1428. This city contains about 50,000 souls and many manufactories. . . .

From Orléans you have one continued pavement to Paris, and you ride over the plains of the Beauce, which is one continued wheat field for thirty miles, without an enclosure and scarcely a tree to be seen. It has the appearance of the ocean and the villages look like rocks rising out of the water.

On the 11th November we arrived in Paris, from whence I will again write you, my dear girl, upon condition you will stand straight and continue to love and make happy your best of mothers. To Mary, William and my little Tom I send a thousand kisses. God bless you all. Let your mother decipher this for it is too long for me to copy.

Wm. Lee.

To Mrs. Susan Palfrey Lee at Bordeaux

Paris, November 27, 1809

The note of the Senator Monbadon, my dear Girl, related to nothing but my bridge, which it appears his Majesty is determined to have constructed in some way or another. Tell Susan I have written her a very long letter of twenty pages, which I shall send by Mr. Cramer, my Inn mate, as the postage would cost more than it is worth.

Go to my tailor and desire him to make you a coat. The silk &c I shall send you will be for gowns perhaps. I shall send you a pelisse, but everything is so excessively dear here, particularly at this time, that money goes but a little way. I have great hopes of succeeding in my business. The Americans are much astonished to see me noticed by these great men. There certainly has never been an American here more noticed. To-day I am engaged with the Comte de Molé;[12] on Wednesday I dine with the Minister of the Interior. I have billets for all the fêtes, but in the midst of all this round, I never cease one moment to thinking I love my best of wives. If I get through my plans, which do not do to write about, I shall be happy. My love to the children.

Yr. W.

Vidal will make your coats, because I paid him 200 fr. on leaving Bordeaux. Capes are generally worn to them. I will send a trimming for Susan's old one, which will enlarge it and suit her shoulders.

To Miss Susan Palfrey Lee at Bordeaux

Paris, November 29 1809

My dear daughter:

I ended my letter which I sent you by Mr. Cramer with my arrival at Paris. The first ten days of my residence was taken up in visiting old and new acquaintances, Gen'l Armstrong, and such of the authorities as I had business with. On my alighting at the *Hôtel des Etrangères* I was shown into the old rooms which I formerly occupied, and though twelve years have elapsed, I find no alteration in them. Even the paper, paint and gilding are the same.

In calling for a *valet de place*, an old acquaintance presented himself. The wainscots of the house have stood the siege of the enemy of us all much better than this poor devil, on whose cheeks his furrows begin to lengthen. I engaged him out of consideration for former services; and, as there appears a small mixture of gratitude in his composition, I trust we shall both be satisfied. Besides, as he speaks English, my friend Ronaldson will find him useful.

Indeed there is no getting along in Paris without these sort of people, particularly if one does not speak the language. They prevent more impositions than they practice themselves. And a stranger with one of them at his heels escapes ridicule by listening to his advice. Being myself engaged to dine out the other day, Ronaldson went to the *Restaurateur* to get his dinner without his valet, and, in taking up the bill of fare, called for turbot. But unfortunately, instead of pronouncing it turbot, he called it *tire-botte*. The waiter, who thought he wished to pull off his boots to get them cleaned while he was dining, brought him a *boot-jack*. " Why man," says Sawney, " de ye think I can eat that? "

Yesterday we went to see the *Pantheon*, one of the finest pieces of modern architecture which Europe has to boast of. Louis XV, when sick at Metz, made a vow if he recovered to build up a new church, and in 1757 this edifice, which took the name of the *Church of St. Genevieve*, was commenced by G. Soufflot, a celebrated architect. The form and shape of the building describes a Grecian cross with a splendid dome rising in the center. The front of the building is ornamented with columns in the style of the theatre at Bordeaux, though infinitely more noble. In 1791 the National Assembly changed the destination of this monument from a church to a pantheon, and decreed that the names of all great men should be deposited here. This alteration required also a change in all the ornaments, bas-reliefs &c, which were analogous to that system of religion, which the reign of liberty had destroyed. . . . But this is contrary to the present order of things. The Pantheon is therefore to be again metamorphosed into a church, where public and private vices are to be washed away by livid confessions.

In the vaults are deposited the remains of Voltaire and Rousseau — another inconsistency; for no two men have done more towards destroying the baneful influence of the Catholic system than they. It is therefore to be presumed their bones will not rest in peace. We mounted to the dome of this building by 463 stone steps, and had a fine view of Paris and its busy scenes.

Adieu, my much loved daughter! Continue to improve, and recollect that it is not a fortune that will make you happy, and that you have to depend for your success in life on your virtues and talents. My love to Mary, to William, and little Tom.

Your affectionate father,
W. L.

To Mrs. Susan Palfrey Lee at Bordeaux

Paris, November 30, 1809

My dear adored wife:

Your kind letter of the 24th Nov. reached me this evening. I am glad you are pleased with the hats, though I did not expect you would have been, as I was not satisfied altogether with them. The one you made after Madame Gernon's would be quite the *ton* here. Green, yellow and crimson are the raging colors in every thing.

I have purchased you a thick pink Florentine piqué, which Mrs. Haslin has given to your mantua maker, who I was obliged to employ because she has your measure. I have purchased you a scarlet merino *décolleté* with sleeves that ship and on ship,[13] so that it may become a dress gown for our evening or dinner parties, not for a ball. The trimmings will be of velvet, imitating cashmere borders or ermine.

I have purchased you a pelerine of fur, very handsome, and two pretty ones for Susan and Mary. They will be a sort of cape for their blue coats or they can be worn with any other dress. The cloth great coats worn are either green, blue or orange. The orange is trimmed with fur or plush; the blue and green with black velvet running down before two inches wide; collar and cuffs of the same. Some capes are worn but not many.

I have also purchased four yards of black silk for *tabliers* [aprons] for Susan and Mary. I propose now to buy twelve or fifteen yards of handsome printed muslin or rather cotton to make a gown apiece for you, and if I thought you had not ordered your great coat, I would buy another merino of a claret color and send it to you to make up. It would not cost me but 56 fr. This would make you a modest, elegant dress and bonnet of the same.

8 7

Shall I buy you one of these velvet trimmings which look like leopard's skin to trim your velvet flesh colored dress? Let me know if you have ordered the coat.

Fenwick and M. Guilliot, who leave this to-morrow, will deliver you the pelerines and the silk (black), but the dresses I keep to send by another person who goes on Saturday.

There is some appearance of my getting something of Meyer, but not in money. I have tickets for all the fêtes, such as at Notre Dame, both of the city-opening of the *Corps Législative,* and Theatre of the Court in the Tuileries. I have given them to Ronaldson, because it costs too much money and time to attend to these things. The very hire of a carriage would come to 30 fr. per day. Thus far I have made a hackney coach answer my purpose. I drive up to within a door or two of the hotels of these ministers, and then get out and walk into the court.

If my thing does not succeed, it will be because I am an American. If the *Wasp* now would only arrive and say that our Government had sent off Copenhagen Jackson,[14] my fortune would be made; but, as it is, all depends on the humor the Emperor may be in when the project is presented to him.

My complete success in the bridge project depends altogether with myself; but the new Minister of the Ponts and Chausées, the Comte de Molé, and the Minister of the Interior, Comte de Montalivet, are warmly in favor of my executing of it, and have stated it to the Emperor, who approves and wishes it. I also find some capitalists here who will get a slice of it with me; but all this I shall avoid unless it is presented to me in a very advantageous light, and the Emperor permits me to bring my funds, which I have locked up in the United States in cottons, indigo and dye woods, which, while they seriously keep alive the germ of manufacture in France, enable me to execute the bridge. " The request is reasonable, Mons. le Consul, et je n'en doute pas de votre succès."

Tell Susan I have another letter for her on the carpet, but have not time to finish it. Tell me how she likes the otter. Adieu! best of beings. You are the loveliest, sweetest, dearest wife ever man was blest with. Write me what you want, for if I succeed, I shall lay out two or three hundred livres more for you. What shall I bring my little Mary and William?

It is three o'clock after midnight. Send for Martini to call on you as he goes to the Exchange. Apprise him of my friendship; tell him my business does not permit my writing on it, and read to him the lines I have marked. If he has anything to do here, I will attend to it with the greatest pleasure. Tell him to say to Ducourneau that there has been a question about him in one of the bureaus here and that I have done him some good with much good will.

To Mrs. Susan Palfrey Lee at Bordeaux

Paris, December 3, 1809

My much loved S.

Your silk gown and the two merino ones (for I have bought the other) will leave this about Friday or Saturday for Bordeaux. Such has been the hurry of mantua makers for these fêtes that it was impossible to get them done before. Fenwick I trust will have delivered you all sent by him before this.

The Prince of Bénévent,[15] hearing that I was in Paris, wrote me a most polite note to come and see him, when he received me in the most amiable manner you can imagine. Mde. Vernenac and Mde. La Croix have been very attentive and kind, and your Madame Haslin is an excellent woman. I go very frequently to Gen'l Armstrong's and find him very uncommunicative. The fêtes have retarded my affairs, but I hope a few days will terminate them.

I have been to none of the balls &c given in honor of the Emperor. I had tickets sent me by the Minister of the Interior and [by] M. Monbadon, but the expense of hiring a carriage (say 100 fr. for the night), and that of hiring a dress (for *des uniformes étrangers* are not received) deterred me from going. Besides, by thus economizing, I have been able to buy you an additional robe, and is it not better to gratify so lovely, so charming, so good a wife as mine than to gratify one's own vanity? There is no sacrifice you are not deserving of. You merit all the affection the heart of man is capable of, for surely no sweeter wife and mother ever lived. I love you, best of beings, with all possible tenderness, and long to press you to a bosom continually warmed by the affection your virtues inspire. Kiss our little ones for me. Tell my dear S[usan] that I shall write her again. My letters to her are so long that they cannot be sent by the post. She will find one or two among your gowns.

Your devoted
W.

P. S. Ronaldson desires to be remembered. He is an uncommon fine fellow. The old Princess of Rohan has fallen in love with me, but you have nothing to fear! She is about 75.

To Miss Susan Palfrey Lee at Bordeaux

Paris, December 6, 1809

My dear daughter:

Your letter of the 30th ulto reached me last evening, and gave me infinite pleasure. Your orthography and syntax are both very correct and I now flatter myself you will, before you are eighteen years of age, write both the French and English languages perfectly. This, with your drawing, some music, a good knowledge of history and geography, together with a competent taste for the *belles-lettres* will render you quite an accomplished woman. Your mind is now developing, and your person, if taken care of (and the greatest care must be taken if you mean to correct that *tournure* [shape], which caused me so much pain), will become graceful and elegant. In short, my Susan, I begin to imagine you everything a father could wish, and how could it be otherwise while you have such an example of everything lovely, amiable, and good which your best of mothers constantly offers you? Read Miss [Nancy] Lowell's sketch of her character, and let your constant endeavor be to emulate her virtues.

Since my last I have done little or nothing towards the accomplishment of the object which brought me here. These confounded fêtes have put me behindhand a whole week. We have heard of nothing but processions, balls, fire works, and parades for ten days past. I assisted at none of them, for I detest crowds, though I regret not having gone to the ball the city gave the Emperor, where the Kings and Queens exhibited *en contre-danse.* You know, perhaps, that we have as many kings in Paris as can be found in two packs of cards. And perhaps you will add as many knaves. There is the

King of Saxony
      of Holland
      of Westphalia
      of Naples
      of Württemberg
      of Italy (vice Roi) and the new Spanish monarch is

on his way here. What Napoleon is going to do with them all I cannot imagine. I expect, before he has finished with them, he will make one of them his coachman to drive him to the senate, legislative body &c. If Gen'l Armstrong had been in vogue at Court, I would have followed him there just to have seen some of this pageantry. Though, as it is, I have had a taste of it, having dined at the *Prince Archi-Chancelier's* [Cambacérès]; at the Prince of Bénévent's, with the Comte de Montalivet, Minister of the Interior, and with Comte Molé, *Directeur-Général* of *Ponts et Chausées.* This latter gentleman has been uncommonly civil, and, among other things, gave me a free access to the Hall of Models, where all projects relating to roads, bridges, &c. are deposited. I was pleased to find my model of the Bridge of Bordeaux placed here with " *honorable mention.*"

From viewing bridges, canals, &c in miniature we trudged to the *Musée des Monuments Français* [16] and there spent the remainder of the day. Here are placed all the monuments which escaped the fury of the revolution, and they are so arranged as to show the progress of the arts from the *Celtique* to the Middle Ages and from thence to the 13th, 14th, 15th up to the 17th and 18th centuries. Each age has its apartment, and over the passage leading thereto is marked the *Siècle.* A particular description of this collection of tombs, sepulchres, sarcophagi, altars, chapels, crosses, statues, busts, hieroglyphics, bas-reliefs, mausoleums, columns, cenotaphs, and mosaics, had I time to make it, would not amuse you much. They are things to be seen, not to be described. The whole fills one with awe.

Almost the first thing that meets your eyes on entering are these lines on the statue of a Duchess of Orleans,[17] who died in 1408 of grief for the loss of her husband (what very few French wives die of in our days):

> Rien ne m'est plus
> Plus ne m'est rien. . . .

We returned from these tombs half frozen to death and hungry as bears to dress for dinner and Mrs. [Charles] Haslin's ball. At this entertainment I could hardly believe myself in Paris — there was such a collection of ugly, ill-dressed young and old women. The dancing, however, I must confess was infinitely more to my taste than that of Bordeaux. Mrs. Haslin is an excellent woman, and is always chanting the praises of your mother which delights me.

Tell me what Miss Mary is about; if William continues his school. Adieu! my dear Susan. I shall hurry home to embrace you all as fast as I can.

Your affectionate father,
Wm. Lee.

To Mrs. Susan Palfrey Lee at Bordeaux

Paris, December 10, 1809

I had just returned, best of wives, from giving your mantua maker a good set down for not finishing your things, when yours of the 4th was put into my hands. You say nothing of the things I sent you by Fenwick and M. Guilliot, and yet they must have arrived, as they left this long before Cramer. Mrs. Haslin has undertaken to get your two gowns and *douillette* [wadded dress] done to go by Mr. Phelan, who leaves this on Tuesday. The trimmings you wish shall be sent you, if I find nothing I like better. I am glad you have got your great coat. They make them here with black velvet capes, but mostly with capes of the same. Susan's old coat, with a black velvet trimming up before and a cape, will do for her all this winter, and would, if properly adjusted, make it larger.

I am very sorry to learn she has a cold. Her heart is so weak that I fear she will always be feeble. I wish she would make a practice of leaning and laying always on the left side. A child like a tree or plant may be made to grow into any form; it only requires attention. When a boy, I was so knock-kneed that when I put my knees together, my feet were six inches apart. My father used to tie my feet together and thrust things between my knees, and when I got a little older used to make me ride on horseback. By this and other means I became straight, and so it would be with Susan. Suppose you were to engage her *maître de danse* to give her lessons every day. This would help her greatly.

General Armstrong in my opinion does very wrong in not going to court, and I am also of opinion that if he would use a little address that our affairs with this Government would be in a much better train. He has been invited to all the fêtes, but gives for answer that he is sick or that he is going a journey. I like him as a man very much, but he is not made for a minister to a court like this. As he does not go to court, I cannot be introduced, as it would be improper for me to accept those offers of presenting me which have been made, whilst he is here. I have not been able to see Mrs. Gernon. She gave me her address at Bordeaux, but I could not find her, although I went into every house in the street, and then sent my servant on the same errand. Not content with this, I wrote her a note, and put it into the post office, saying that I was *au désespoir* at my ill success and supplicating her to give me her address. I have received no answer, which leads me to suppose she does not desire to see me. *Tant mieux!* My gentle spirits are becoming boisterous.

You had better call on Madame le Préfet and on Mde. Pierre. Today I am going to mess at the court and I dine with the Archi-Chancelier. He has given me a dinner already as he dines every one, but today is his set day for his friends and the invitation is quite a flattering one. The other *three Consuls* who are here and the rest of our countrymen think it very strange that I am so noticed here. I endeavored to keep it a secret, but it has got out some how or another, and you know what our countrymen are.

As you have mentioned Count Morton,[18] it will not be amiss to say that Armstrong dislikes him much. I sent you last post two letters for Mrs. Train. She is crazy if she does not leave Bordeaux as soon as possible for London. By following that business up she will, it is highly probable, get 40 or 50 thousand francs; but, if she leaves it where it is, not a sou. I know a person who is on the alert and who may set off for St. Petersburg without going to Bordeaux, where his family resides!! He says Irwin had 5000 pound sterling belonging to the house with him. Mr. Ceresir the broker, who is on his way to Bordeaux, can give Mrs. Irwin some information on this business.

The Emperor has ordered all our vessels in the north sequestered. This is not so alarming a measure, because out of 100 it is proved 80 are English with American forged papers &c. &c. Orders have gone on to Spain to examine into the state of those arrived there. Send for Ducourneau or Martini and tell them this and tell them as well as Meyer that a certain General has left this on that business and that he has taken a mercantile man with him to make some operations.* My affairs progress and will succeed in part if not in whole. My love to the children. Adieu best of beings. I begin to long to see you and to embrace you all.

Yr. W.

* You need not mention this to either of them, I have written.

To Mrs. Susan Palfrey Lee at Bordeaux

Paris, December 15, 1809

You must not be angry with me, my dear good Wife, because I do not write you more frequently. The fact is that the General has charged me with some important business, and I have also been excessively occupied this week past in writing two *mémoires* on our liaisons with France: one for the Prince of Neuchâtel,[19] the other for the Minister of the Interior. They cost me a great deal of labor, for after having thrown all my ideas together on the subject, it was necessary to condense them, and render the whole short and pithy that the Emperor might seize the facts without wading through an ocean of reasoning, which his time will not permit him to digest. I expect much good will come of this. Indeed much has already been produced. Vernenac has been my translator, and I am gaining credit if not interest by the exertions I am making for our country, whom a mistaken policy on the part of the Emperor was every day placing at a greater distance from the desired object.

The divorce is concluded on. The happiness and welfare of France demands a Queen who can fulfill the scriptures: increase and multiply. She presides the last time this evening at the Circle of the Court, and to-morrow she goes to Malmaison. She is to have that château and the Petit Palais Bourbon [20] on Champs Élysées, with 5,000,000 of money. She will also reside some time with her son in Italy. This has been the talk in Paris ever since my arrival here, but I have not believed it until yesterday. Yesterday the Empress told it to the Duchess of Raguse. She told it to Mde. Portalis. She told it to Mde. Hottinguer,[21] and she told it to me yesterday at dinner at her own house.

I sent your things by the courier yesterday, and the trimming for your velvet you shall have in a day or two. In haste and with all the affection you inspire and with all the pride the continual praises I hear of you here create in me,

Your devoted
Wm.

Tell Mrs. Johnston I will execute any commission she will give me here; that I have seen many pretty things I thought would suit her graceful form, but that without orders I dare not act. You know I have always been half in love with her.

To Miss Susan Palfrey Lee at Bordeaux

Paris, December 17, 1809

My dear daughter:

I have not written you so often as I wished or intended. The truth is my days are taken up in dancing attendance on men in office, and my evenings in paying a few necessary visits, and in composing some short *mémoires* on American affairs.

I went to a ball a few evenings ago given by a Mr. de Rougemont, a considerable banker, who lives in very great style. The company was composed of foreign nobility and men of distinction; the ladies, particularly the Polish ones, were generally well dressed and handsome, but their dancing I found very inferior to that of the Bordelaises. I met here with some old acquaintances, who told me I am not in the least altered, but this cannot be true. Ten or twelve years makes a difference in the appearance of every one and at every age.

Tell your dear mother that I have been treated very kindly by Mr. and Mrs. Hottinguer, and that I find her an agreeable woman and good mother. She gave me some interesting anecdotes of Mr. Cazenove [22] of Geneva, whom she saw there last summer at the celebrated Madame de Staël's who encourages her visits on account of her natural wit, the very thing for which other people shun her. There is nothing so disagreeable in a woman as wit and satire. Dr. Gregory says in his *Legacy to his Daughters*, " Wit is the most dangerous talent you can possess. It must be guarded with great discretion and good nature, otherwise it will create you many enemies. It is perfectly consistent with softness and delicacy; yet they are found seldom united. Wit is so flattering to vanity, that those who possess it become intoxicated, and lose all self command." [23] At Mr. Hottinguer's I met with a M. Desbessaigne, whom I knew in 1798. I was the cause of his making his fortune and marrying one of the prettiest women in France, Miss Mourque. I have not yet seen her; but she is said to be more beautiful than ever, and I am to pay them a visit in a day or two on the top of Mont Calvaire,[24] where they at present reside.

I wrote your mother yesterday and I believe I mentioned to her that the Emperor has separated from Josephine, who retires with a handsome establishment from the busy scenes of the Court, to make room, it is said for a Princess of Russia. This is a dreadful example of morals for the nation. The Empress left the Palace of the Tuileries this morning for Malmaison, where she will chiefly reside, with the title of Crowned Empress and Queen. Miss Patterson [25] is to be established in Italy with the title of Duchess, and her son, young Jerome, is to be heir to the crown of Westphalia. This has been communicated officially to General Armstrong.

The Parisians think all this is right; give them fêtes, luxury and *calembours* [puns], and they are contented. When I reflect on what they appeared to be in 1796 and 1797, and what they now are: in one case violent republicans, spurning at everything like royalty, and raising altars to reason and liberty; in the other pulling down those altars, creating and supporting a new dynasty and huzzaing to all its pageantry, it brings always to my mind Voltaire's description of the nation, or rather his translation of what an old English author [26] said of them:

Tel est l'esprit français; je l'admire et le plains.
Dans son *abaissement* quel excès de *courage*
La *tête* sous le *joug*, les *lauriers* dans les *mains*,
Il chérit à la fois la gloire et l'esclavage.
Ses *exploits et sa honte ont rempli l'univers.*
Vainqueur dans les combats, enchaîné par ses maîtres,
Pillé par des traîtants, aveuglé par des prêtres;
Dans la *disette* il *chante;* il *danse* avec ses *fers.*
Fier dans la servitude, heureux dans sa folie,
De l'Anglais libre et sage il est encor l'envie.

What a correct and admirable picture even at this day!

Since I wrote you last, I have seen nothing that would very much amuse you by description. The National Library occupied me a few moments the other day, as it is in my neighborhood. This is a collection of about 350,000 volumes of books in all languages; of *Médailles* and antiques; of 80,000 manuscripts and about 40,000 volumes of engravings. In the middle of the rooms are tables where the public sit and read, and the librarians furnish them with any book they call for.

Among the manuscripts, it is said, the letters of Abelard and Héloïse are to be seen written in Latin. The letters of Henry IV, Fénelon's *Telemachus,* and some writings of Louis XIV, of

Voltaire, and of Anne of Brétagne. The engravings are sufficient to amuse one for an age. Here is all the collection of that inimitable artist Hogarth, and indeed of all the best of ancient and modern artists. Every engraver at this day is obliged to deposit an *épreuve avant la lettre* of his work. By this you may easily imagine what the collection will amount to one day or another.

Among the curiosities to be seen here is a *bouclier* of Hannibal found in Dauphiné in 1714, and another *bouclier* of Scipio's found in the Rhone in 1656. I doubt however if they are properly named. These fragments are much like the cross of our Saviour. If all these pieces were collected together they would make several cords of wood: more than twenty crosses would make. . . .

The *Cabinet des Médailles et Antiques* is the most interesting thing of the kind in the world. They are all arranged in chronological order according to the plan of the celebrated Barthélemy, author of *Anacharsis*. Here is an embalmed ibis, a long-legged bird which the Egyptians worshipped, because it was supposed to have eaten up all the serpents in their country. . . .

I have been to-day with a Mr. Ronaldson to see five thousand troops dine at Place de Vosges. This square is formed of arcades like those of the theatre of Bordeaux, only much wider. At each table was placed nine soldiers, and each one had his bottle of wine. The soups and meats were good, and everything was conducted in good order. On our return from this feast, Ronaldson would go to see the famous lamp-iron on which the infuriated mobs of Paris used to string up and hang without judge or jury such people as did not please them. It is at the Place de Grève. " À la lanterne! à la lanterne! " was the signal of death to every member of the convention, and every leading character who happened to offend the *sovereign people*. The abbé Maury [27] was a distinguished man in the revolution, and is now very near the Emperor. He happened one day to offend one of the factions, and the people were dragging him off to Place de Grève with the cry of, " à la lanterne! à la lanterne!" " À la lanterne! et bien Citoyens, quand je servais à la lanterne," cried the abbé, " y verriez-vous plus claire? " The mob applauded him and let him go.

None but a priest or a Jesuit would have had his wits about him at such a time. Such traits are worth remembering. They are particularly pleasing to the French.

The Prince of Bénévent is very celebrated for these *jeux d'esprit*, though I do not know that he ever made one on so serious an occasion. It is said that not long ago one of the Emperor's favorite generals was invited to dine with him, and came very late. " General," says the Prince, " you have kept me waiting some time." " True," says the general, " a *picard* [28] called on me, and I could not well get rid of him." " What are we to understand," says M. Talleyrand, " by the word *picard?* " " O! " replied the other, " it is a term of derision we military men use when speaking of the civil orders." " Oh! I understand you," says Talleyrand. " It is the same when we speak of any one very unpolished and not very civil. We say he is a *militaire.*"

I send you by this conveyance Gregory's *Legacy to his Daughters*, and Fordyce's *Sermons to Young Women*,[29] two excellent books which I beg you will read carefully. Let me entreat you also to read history. Do not let the first part of it discourage you. The beginning of most studies is dry; but when you once get engaged in them they interest. I love you very much and have a great desire to see you become a superior woman. I wish too you would compose little essays, no matter what they are about. You may take Mary's laziness for a subject, William's *polissonnerie* [mischievous prank], or attempt to draw a picture of your dear mother's serene mind and manners. The first would help to correct Miss Mary; the second would make us laugh; and the third would correct us all. And when forming your style, like the bee, you would be sipping sweets from a stalk where all the virtues have engrafted themselves, and lay up a sufficient store to become, as you advance in life, like her, the loveliest, the most adorable creature on earth. . . .

Embrace the best of mothers for me, and tell her I have received her letter of the fourteenth of December; that I am sorry she is growing so thin, because a little plumpness became her. I shall not love her the less for a wrinkle or two, and as a proof

of it read these lines to her, which came to my remembrance to
answer her fears.

> Though thy beauty must fade, yet thy youth I'll remember;
> That thy *May* was my own, when thou shewest *December;*
> And when Age to my *head* his winter impart
> The summer of love shall reside in my *heart.*[30]

Adieu! I long to embrace you all.
Your affectionate father
Wm. Lee.

My good friend Ronaldson is sitting by and says, "Remember
me to all the family."

To Miss Susan Palfrey Lee at Bordeaux

Paris, December 27, 1809

My dear daughter:

I have just entered from paying my respects at the Minister
of the Interior's, at the President of the Legislative Corps [Cam-
bacérès], and at his Excellency, the Comte de Montesquiou,[31]
Grand Chambellen. Nothing can be more ridiculous than these
visits. Your carriage arrives at the entrance of these hotels in the
file, and you take your turn at descending from it. You pass the
servants' hall, where laced lackeys are crowded together, and
you enter the antechamber, where the *huissiers* [gentlemen-
ushers] (a higher order of domestic, who are dressed in black
with swords and bags) take your name and hand it to another
who bawls it out to another and so you go on from one splendid
apartment to another, and by this time you arrive at the saloon
of reception.

Your name arrives also, but nine times out of ten so distorted
that it has no relation to you. Thus to-night I was announced:
Le Colonel Americain, Le Consul, Le Général Americain; and
as the devils would have it I entered the saloon with *Le Consul
de Malaga.* The company stared and I heard some of them say,
"Il est trop blanc pour un Espagnol." The gentleman who went

with me, a Mr. Von der Leyden of the legislative body, fared worse than I did; but I do not know who was the most out of humor about it, he or those who had to pronounce his name: it was such a task to them. In all the inflexions the Von was carefully preserved, and they actually called him Monsieur Von dit Lanterner, Monsieur Von Lache, and just as he entered Monsieur Von Laid. Did you know the man, you would say, " How unfortunate! "

In these circles you stay fifteen or twenty minutes jammed up, and then you move off to make room for other fools. And as I moved home I found your charming letter, without date. There are some faults of orthography: for instance *in*tertaining instead of entertaining, to for too. The turn of the sentences are pretty good and the quotation delights me. You shall have a master for geography and for *belles-lettres*. It is time also you began to look a little into grammar, which never should be studied before the age of fourteen or fifteen. " On ne peut apprendre la grammaire d'une langue quelconque même celle de son pays, que quand on sait parler, que quand on sait causer." I am glad to hear you have again began Rollin.[32] I hope the second attempt will not be like the first. It is time now you threw by the trifling for the substantial.

You will have something for the New Year, and Mary too, and M. William. What it will be I do not know. Your mother does not say a word of her scarlet and pink dresses. How did she like them? I do not know when I shall get home: as soon as I can, for I long to see and embrace you all. Adieu! I intended to have written you a long letter, but have been interrupted.

Your affectionate father
Wm. Lee

To Miss Mary Elizabeth Lee at Bordeaux

Paris, December 28, 1809

My dear little Mary:

I have this day delivered to a person, who will hand to you Monday Noël's *Leçons de Littérature*,[33] or a collection of the finest morsels of prose and verse in the French language. I intend these two books should be considered as your New Year's gift, and I hope they will be more pleasing (for I am sure they will be more useful) than a doll or a trinket. Mr. Hunt [34] sends you a shawl and Thomas a hat, and William a " three cornered scraper " with a silver button and loop. How fine he will look! particularly if I should send him a hussar's dress, which I may do if he is very *sage* and learns to read.

All the little girls of your age in Paris are straight as arrows, and hold their little shoulders back, their heads up, as if they were really determined to be of some importance in the world. They study drawing, music and embroidery. This last branch the ladies of all ages practice very much, so that they make their own caps, *fichus*, handkerchiefs, and what is more extraordinary, they frequently work the coverings for their chairs. Mde. Haslin has worked all the backs and bottoms of the chairs in her bed room. Mde. Hottinguer, Mde. La Croix and Mde. Vernenac are all employed in the same way, and the young ladies help them. Your mother, Susan and you might soon furnish a room in this way.

I send you the specimen of a young lady's writing, who is under the care of that most amiable and excellent woman, Mde. La Croix. She has done a whole book of four hundred pages in the same way, with a title page and index, which Mde. Vernenac has had bound up in morocco. What would I give to see you and Susan write like that! In one year she arrived at this point of perfection.

How is poor Nipper? I have not heard a word of him. I suppose he lays by the fire roasting his fleas. And Mr. Tom goes quite alone now! You know he began to hobble as I left you. How I long to see you all! You must be kind to your Mamma, and try all you can to make her happy. There are no such good mothers in Paris. Adieu! My paper will scarcely give me room to say how much I love you.

Your affectionate father
Wm. Lee

To Mrs. Susan Palfrey Lee at Bordeaux

Paris, January 2, 1810

I have reason, my dear Girl, to be pleased with my trip to Paris, and when it shall be known to the President what I have done for our country, you will find that no man will stand so high with the administration. I can hardly credit myself with what I have brought about. The thing is finished and you may hourly expect to see a decree in favor of American commerce, notwithstanding the crowd of *mémoires* which interested persons are throwing in to prevent the introduction of certain articles.

The Minister of Exterior Relations [Cadore] has written Gen'l Armstrong requesting him to point out the best mode of preventing the British from partaking in the commerce, which his Majesty is disposed to open between the U[nited] S[tates] of A[merica] and France, assuring him that if this difficulty can be well obviated, that the arrangement will be a liberal one.

I am beginning to think of moving home. If I do not leave this in the course of a week, I will send you the correspondence of my bridge to amuse you. . . . I am interrupted by Barnett [35] Hunt and Ronaldson. So Adieu! dear Girl.

Your Wm.

To Miss Susan Palfrey Lee at Bordeaux

Paris, January 4, 1810

My dear daughter:

I have just returned from the Theatre of the Court, in the Palace of the Tuileries. The Count de Montesquiou, *Grand Chambellan*, sends me a ticket now and then, which even admits me to circulate in the apartments of the Emperor, or in other words, at the Circle of the Court. But, as I have not yet been presented to his Majesty, it would not be altogether proper to make use of this privilege, though many persons do not regard this *etiquette*. I have also another reason for not approaching nearer to Royalty. If the Emperor should happen to notice me, being a *great man*, it might give some offense to General Armstrong, who does not go to court at present, though I have reason to think he will soon make his appearance there.

This *Spectacle de [la] Cour* is one of the most splendid things in Europe. The theatre or more properly *Salle* is richly ornamented, and so highly lighted that you can distinguish all the *trifles* of a woman's dress in any part of it. All the Kings were seated in the box opposite the stage. On the left of them, round to the Emperor's box which is next to the stage, were the first officers of state, their adherents and retinue. Opposite these the Diplomatic Corps, between whom and the box of Kings, were seated all the ladies who had been presented and were to form the Circle of the Court for the evening. Among these I observed Mrs. Gernon. She was dressed in a scarlet velvet trimmed with fur. Her head was elegantly dressed with some display of diamonds.

In the galleries and grill lodges under the boxes, full dressed citizens are admitted, if they show a *blue* card of invitation. In the pit all the gentlemen who have white cards (which permit them to go to Court) are placed, and such a profusion of embroidery I never saw before. All is not gold that glitters! The reflection had scarce passed my brain, when my eyes met an old fellow, who dines sometimes at the restaurateur's, where Sawney and I get our meals occasionally. He had got a new wig on, and no doubt had hired his coat, sword, bag and *chapeau* to enjoy the benefit of a ticket, which the minister of some miserable German prince had given or sold him. O vanity! vanity! Not three hours before, this old fellow was scraping a rind of cheese, and looked so dirty that he almost took my appetite. . . .

The new opera called the *Vestale* [36] was performed by the Italian company. It was tedious enough taken together; though some parts of it were highly gratifying. I think I never heard music before. I was so transported with one piece that I applauded involuntarily, which is very indecorous at this theatre. Vernenac, who sat by me, caught my arm. I understood it; but the whole house observed it, and what is worse observed me. No matter! I had my *harness* on, and my mind, which is generally fertile in difficulties, soon found consolation, by bringing to my recollection an anecdote of Garrick.

This great actor went to hear a celebrated Methodist preacher, who happened to be railing against fashionable follies, and, among others, against the loss of time in acquiring music, which he said would be better employed in endeavoring to conquer our evil propensities. " It is true," said he:

> 'Music hath charms to sooth a savage breast,
>   To soften rocks, or bend a knotted oak,' [37]
>   *But not to conquer sin.*

Garrick, forgetting where he was, clapped violently, and cried out " Bravo! " Thus I found a parallel. And, if I passed for wanting good manners, it must be allowed I had feeling. The account was balanced and I was contented.

Your affectionate father
Wm. Lee

To Mrs. Susan Palfrey Lee at Bordeaux

Paris, January 9, 1810

My much loved S.

My scolding letter had hardly gone when yours of the third came in. If, as you say, I have not written to you (particularly) oftener, you must have seen, best of wives, that you were not out of my mind. That my heart is full of you, loveliest of beings, my letters to my children ought to show. Do not, therefore, suppose that I forget or neglect you, only source of all my delights and comforter in all my love. I will soon press you to my bosom, and convince you of my increasing affection.

Do not despair of riches. We shall have them. And do not let the empty, ridiculous pomp of vain fools distress you. There is only the appearance of riches in the nabob you mentioned, and the very business, which the world supposes is creating so much wealth, is working ruin.

Do not let your drafts on D. distress you. He will be in my debt instead of my being in his; and I shall bring enough home with me to pay off everything we owe; and we will live in a dignified way, seeing a few choice friends, and in a way that our society will be sought instead of our seeking it. You must not be envious. You are beloved, you are adored by all who know you: Mrs. Armstrong and the Gen'l. Mde. Hottinguer was singing your praises to a lady (Miss Hunter that was) a whole hour the other evening. Mrs. Haslin too, and now Mrs. Martini, tells me how much you are esteemed in Bordeaux. Let us, therefore, attend to the education of our children, and set an example of virtue and harmony to our neighbors.

To comfort you about the future, let me tell you that the quarter of the Louisiana purchase, which I am concerned in through and with Barlow, Hunt, Granger [38] and Skipwith, will be in the opinion of Barlow and Hunt a fortune for your children. Thus you see that Providence you have placed so much trust in has already laid the foundation of your future existence.

Mrs. Irwin herself (I do not admire her daughter) is of better origin and of more respectability than W. M.'s family. The story of her not being married is not true. Morton is one of the greatest liars that ever drew breath. The things he has written and said against me to Gen'l. Armstrong and the government, instead of serving his purpose, has rendered him very contemptible in the eyes of both. The Gen'l has let me into some secrets. I wish I had been in Bordeaux. I would soon have put a stop to his airs about Mr. Irwin's going in the *Three Apprentices*. Martini, Ducourneau, Martin and myself own that vessel, a quarter each. The other affair, which troubles you, I will put an end to before long.

The children's *garniture* I shall send to-morrow. The trimming you ask for your velvet, will not do for it by any means. I will find something else. These velvets are high dress, and nothing but fur or an ornamental trimming can be put on them. Feathers and flowers are enormously dear. Shall I bring you a very fashionable silk pelisse, for the evening? Our affairs will be settled with this government. I dined yesterday at the Minister of Foreign Affairs'. The party was very splendid: both ladies and gentlemen, and such a profusion of diamonds! I sat next to the Russian ambassador [Prince Kourakin]. To-morrow I am invited at the Minister of Interior's, and on Thursday at M. Talleyrand's. Ronaldson and Hunt will tell you how much I have been noticed here. As for the bridge, you may tell people I did not come here for that. I gave my *ultimatum* yesterday. I will send it to you to make you laugh.

Adieu! Embrace our children for me, and love him who thinks you the most perfect being on earth, and loves you to a fault.

Yr. W.

To Mrs. Susan Palfrey Lee at Bordeaux

Paris, January 13, 1810

I am very sorry to hear, my dear S., by Meyer's letter that you are indisposed. I hope it is nothing more than a slight cold. I long to see you and the children. It appears to me a twelve-month since I left you.

Our American affairs have taken a darker shade again, and the dispatches which Gen'l. Armstrong has just received from the United States will deepen it. Some of the Emperor's best ministers are highly in favor of an arrangement with us; but his Majesty, influenced by some interested persons about him, does not appear friendly. The question is before him. He is studying it, and he may decide as most of his enlightened men wish, but I doubt it, notwithstanding all that has passed. Gen'l. Armstrong thinks I ought to abandon all mercantile projects and solicit a good place in which I could live handsomely and be respected. I feel almost inclined to it, for the uncertain state of things does not please me.

I have again answered the *Ponts et Chaussées* that I cannot undertake the bridge in any way unless American commerce is opened. You can say to any one, who may ask you questions on the subject, that I did not come to Paris on that project, which is true, and that in the present state of political affairs it is far from being a desirable object.

I hope the bonnets I sent you will please you and that Mrs.

Meyer is satisfied. I expect to receive some money here. If I do I shall lay out six hundred livres of it in linen and hose for you. Mde. Martini told me yesterday that I had the reputation of being an excellent husband even in Bordeaux. I am glad to hear it. But I told her it was impossible to be otherwise, when I had such an angel for a wife. Hunt is coming to see you, and I shall accompany him. We leave this in all next week. My love to the children. Susan ought to have written me. I shall bring the book she asks for. I sent you last post trimmings for the children's gowns.

Yr. Wm.

To Mrs. Susan Palfrey Lee at Bordeaux
Paris, January 16, 1810

My dear Girl:

Your affectionate and kind letter reached me the day before yesterday. I hope this will find you better. I have myself a most intolerable cold which I caught the other day at dinner at M. Champagny's, where I sat with my back to the door. It is now going off.

As this is to go by a private hand, I can say something to you about our American affairs. No dependence can be placed on the Emperor. He acts entirely from the impulse of the moment, and without reflection. All his best ministers and most able men strenuously recommend his coming to terms with the United States. He has gone so far, since I have been in Paris, as to announce to the Legislative Body that he would open again commerce with us. He studied the subject, called for information from all quarters, ordered M. Champagny to communicate his intentions to Gen'l. Armstrong, and to request of him his advice as to the form of a certificate or license, which should be delivered to American vessels bound to France to prevent the English from partaking in this commerce. He ordered a Council of State to decide on the business, and the day he was to meet them, he sat off in a most violent rage to Malmaison to see Josephine. And instead of deciding the American question, to the astonishment of all his ministers, he ordered all the vessels at San Sebastian and Naples seized. After this, the Adams frigate arrives with dispatches &c. &c. &c., and he comes back again to reason, and brings anew the American affairs on the carpet.

In this fluctuating state of things, I asked an interview of the comte de Montalivet, Minister of the Interior, who answered it in a very flattering manner, as you will see by the enclosed. As I have written these memoirs for him on the American affairs, which went a great way towards keeping the Emperor right, and have had several verbal communications, with which he has been highly pleased, I went to him yesterday to tell him what a singular effect the Emperor's conduct had, and that, if his Majesty persists in it, war between France and the United States must be the consequence. He received me most cordially. I passed a whole hour with him. We went over the whole ground, and this is what I have learned. The Minister of the Interior, the Minister of Police,[39] the Minister of State, and some other leading men have come to a determination to use all their endeavors to bring his Majesty to reason on the American question. The Minister [Montalivet] told me the thing looked better yesterday than it had done yet. " France," says he, " must admit your commerce. Our merchants need it. Our manufactures will perish without it, and our national industry be lost." I am now drawing up another *mémoire* of [for?] him, with his own ideas and some of mine, and he recommends my remaining here ten days longer, in the course of which time something decisive will take place.

The bridge is again presented to me. The government offers to build the abutments if I will build the rest. I have answered that I will undertake it, provided the American commerce is opened, and I can get men and timber from the United States, and not without.

I am sure will be in Paris for ten or fifteen days longer, during which time I shall be much occupied, having several very long letters to write by the *Adams* frigate, which has already arrived in Holland from England. I wish much to hear from you, that I may know your indisposition has passed off. Mr. and

Mrs. Hottinguer have been uncommonly attentive to me. Decipher this if you can. My love to the children.

Your devoted Wm.

I have no objection to your expressing to Wm. Johnston, Meyer, Martini or Ducourneau the state of American affairs. Do not make occasion to do it. I believe myself some change will take place.

To Mrs. Susan Palfrey Lee at Bordeaux

Paris, January 22, 1810

Your very affectionate and kind letters of the eleventh and fifteenth have both been received, my dear Susan. The last is one of the prettiest you ever wrote me. You are everything the heart of man can wish: virtuous, amiable, lovely, kind, handsome, endearing, ever studying the happiness of those around you, and not suffering an hour to fly away without an offering to your husband. Your mind is a soil where all the virtues have taken root to bless and delight your family. . . . What a treasure is such a wife! How I long to press her to my bosom, and to embrace her children!

Our American affairs do not look bright. My own opinion is that our government will now arrange with England, provided she will make compensation for the past, and give security for the future, which she appears prepared to do. The system of the Emperor strikes at the sovereignty of all states, and his late unaccountable and unexpected decisions concerning American affairs will do more towards rousing the sensibility and the indignation of the freemen of the United States than anything that has occurred. 120,000,000 fr. of American property has been sequestrated since I have been in the city. If something is not done before the frigate sails, and something very decisive, the American government will take a ground which will change the whole face of things; and, if the Emperor was to live to the age of Methuselah, he never will recover the error he is about to commit. The Spanish affair [40] will be but a grain of sand on the sea shore in comparison to it.

I am much engaged in writing Barlow, and I have also written the President a long letter, which I shall send to Barlow to deliver him, if he thinks proper. I send Barlow also a copy of my *mémoires*, my bridge affair &c &c &c. I have also written him fully on my situation, wishes, views etc. Do not despair! We shall get on with respectability if not with riches; and, as long as my children continue amiable and my wife lives to bless us all, I ask no more. Stuart goes off to-morrow. I do not go with him, but shall reach Bordeaux before him. Prepare a chamber for him.

Kiss the girls and boys for me, and continue to love a husband who prizes your sublime qualities, and who loves you *à la folie*.

Yr. W.

To Mrs. Susan Palfrey Lee at Bordeaux

Paris, January 29, 1810

Your affectionate letter of the 23rd came to me last evening, just as I was going to the *masque* ball of the King of Naples [41] with Gen'l Armstrong. I have undertaken to get this minister of ours out of his cabinet into society. It is a task, I apprise you, but I succeed pretty well. He enjoys this thing, but does not know how to go about it. When he got his mask on last night, he could not see for want of his spectacles. These were put on over mask and all. He found them a difficulty in taking snuff, and by frequently lifting up his mask for this purpose, he pushed his wig off into the back part of his domino. We soon arranged this, but in doing it he was discovered by a lady who lives at Mde. Haslin's, and she sat all the General's acquaintances foul of him, so that at about three o'clock he was glad to retreat. This is the first ball of any description he has been to since his arrival in Paris.

Last week I got him to make two visits to M. Champagny, but to do this, I had to get this minister to give him an opening. The result is they are negotiating again, and our affairs look better. It is a pity that a man, for whom nature and education has done so much, should be so averse to displaying his powers. This is the effect of early habits, or rather of having never mixed much in society. His conversation is instructive and entertaining; his pen is unequalled; and with all this, he has a rudeness of character, a stiff republican frankness about him that is not agreeable to strangers, and is the worst commodity a man can bring to Paris.

Gen'l Clarke,[42] the Minister of War, has taken a great fancy to me. He endeavored to scrape relationship with me. His family was made up of Woodfall or Woodruff and Lees. They took the name of Clarke, he says, by having a large estate left to them, and he concludes that, as some of his ancestors by the name of Lee migrated from Ireland to America, and mine came from Ireland, that we must be related. He says the thing appears so highly probable that he wishes me to examine the business. He is one of the most affable, elegant men I ever met with. As I shall see him frequently before I leave Paris, and have nothing to ask of him, say to Wm. Johnston that I will put a word in for his brother George, just in the way he shall point out. If it does no good, it can do no harm. This I can do in a disinterested way, by stating George's services; William's campaigns; the respectability of Mr. Johnston; the general esteem he is held in &c. &c. &c. I shall take pains to do this, if William approves of it.

I intended, my dear Girl, to have left Paris this week, but the American affairs being again on the carpet, and my bridge project having been again offered to me in another shape, in short in my own way, I intend to remain eight or ten days longer. My desire to embrace you and your children is very great. I shall therefore hasten my return, for I live only with you, best of blessings and of friends. We must not think of Andrews' house. I shall be home in time for all that. Le Comte de Monbadon has offered me his country house, the one we visited last year opposite Mde. Laurent's. He says he has no use for it, and wishes I would inhabit it, in whatever way I please. If things go right, this will be worth attending to.

There is a great deal of political news floating about, such as: negotiations with England; coolness of Russia; the establishment of Ferdinand VII [43] on the throne of Spain; on his marrying the daughter of Lucien Bonaparte, the consent of the Dutch to become a part of the Empire upon condition that they are allowed a free trade with the United States of America; and lastly the marriage of the Emperor with a princess of Saxe. Then we have a few *calembours* [44] such as: I have divorced and am going to marry a wife *de cette rue ci* (Russie); she shall hire fine horses, carriages &c. but not a *beau harnois*. An actor, the famous Brunet, calling for lights, candles were brought to him. "Give me bougies," says he. "Il y a assez de *Sire* à Paris." These, with the Court balls, masquerades &c. &c., fill up the time of the gay, trifling *Parisien*. I am astonished you have not received the trimming for the children's gowns. I gave it to M. Marcotte, whose address M. Martini can give you. Tell Meyer I will bring his books.

Your affectionate
Wm.

To Mrs. Susan Palfrey Lee at Bordeaux

Paris, February 5, 1810

How the time goes! I can scarcely believe we are at the fifth of February. I am so tormented about this bridge that I wish the devil had it. I have succeeded in it thus far beyond my expectations, and I have also completely succeeded in the other object. But, such is the state of things, that God only knows whether they are to be considered benefits or misfortunes. I can do nothing with either until I know what Congress will do, or what restrictions they will lay on our commerce with this country. If I can import the wood for my bridge from the United States, it would be one of the greatest objects a man can undertake.

Congress appears disposed to favor the importation of all French and English manufactures in American bottoms owned solely by American citizens. France will not object to this, and perhaps permit certain articles of the United States in return. Something will therefore grow out of this state of things. I know the ministers are brewing something, and I am waiting to see the issue.

Letters from New York say that Brockholst Livingston [45] is named to succeed Gen'l Armstrong. He will make an excellent minister, being very rich and speaking the French language well. Armstrong is not well with the Court, because he does not dance attendance to them. He would have made an excellent minister to London; but, for want of address, and of those little attentions which please, and above all of a knowledge of the language, he does not succeed here. It has appeared to me, since my residence here, that an American minister, thoroughly acquainted with the interests of the two nations, and with the language, by having access to the Emperor, could do almost anything. Had it not been for the intrigues of a set of men who surround the Emperor, who are concerned in licenses, shares in privateers &c. &c. &c., the enlightened policy of such enlightened men as the Minister of Police, Minister of the Interior, and others, would have been adopted. The Gen'l, by remaining in his cabinet, has no means of combating the machinations of these men, and he sees and depends too much on such unprincipled characters as Parker, whose reputation has become so vile, by being hackneyed in the wiles and mazes of disgraceful intrigues and speculations, that no American minister ought to see him.

The Minister of Foreign Affairs has signified to Gen'l Armstrong that Mr. Patterson [46] of Nantes can no longer be considered as American consul. What he has done to offend his Majesty I cannot learn, but I think it probable he has been concerned in some commerce with England, or has written or said something displeasing to the government.

Do not let any one see the paper I sent you except the persons named, and do not let even them take my three *mémoires* on commercial points out of the house. Let them read them before you.

I long much to see you and your dear children. There are no expressions which can convey to you an idea of my attachment to you, and my adoration for your virtues. I have shed many a tear of affection since I left you, my S., for I love to dwell on your charms &c. &c., to cherish a source of so many delights. Tell Susan I think she ought to have written me. My time is so taken up that I have not been able to continue my long letters to her. Tell William, if he is a good boy, I will bring him home one of the dogs which go about in carts in Paris, and he shall draw him and his brother about all summer. Miss Mary, I suppose, will have no objection to this. Adieu! God bless you! I cannot yet fix the day of my departure.

Yr. W.

To Mrs. Susan Palfrey Lee at Bordeaux

Paris, February 10, 1810

I shall be with you, my dear wife, about the 18th or 20th. If I do not get through my business here so as to bring me home on the twentieth, I will notwithstanding set off and return here again. What Meyer has said to me of your health gives me some inquietude. You fret too much. With a great many blessings, you look grave, and reason yourself into discontent. With good health, a lovely family of children, a husband who loves you passionately, no embarrassments of consequence, you are unhappy because you are not so rich as some of your neighbors, who are not so rich as they appear to be. You lay, Susan, your sorrows in a scale of weightiest lead, and poise your joyful hours in a light ozier basket. Then you say, "Lo! How the scale of grief preponderates! " . . .

The house affair, which has bore as heavy on your mind as the mountain of l'amont on the shore of the Garonne, will be settled without difficulty. And, when I return, all the other monstrous mountains of inquietude shall be removed with great ease. So, my dear wife, do cheer up, and continue to embellish your family and society, and to give a zest to my enjoyments. There is no misery in this world, but what we bring on ourselves. It is therefore in our power to correct them. Trust me, there are no mortals so wretched as those who measure their enjoyments by the length of their purse. But enough of preaching!

It is said the Emperor has dispatched the Prince of Neuchâtel and Wagram to bring the Princess of Austria [47] to Paris, who is destined to be his Queen. She is said to be as beautiful as her great aunt the late Queen of France, and of about nineteen years of age. Thus the scion of the Bourbons will be engrafted to the Napoleons. What a stroke of policy! How worthy of the author! We shall have *calembours* enough now. Adieu!

Yr. W.

On dit que l'Empereur aime sa femme et la chasse.

On dit que le Roi d'Hollande est bien malade depuis qu'il a perdu ses côtes.

Voilà la nouvelle du jour.

IV

A YANKEE AT NAPOLEON'S COURT

1810–1812

After returning from his Paris trip, Lee remained in Bordeaux only three months before business commitments (he was now associated with a Mr. Johnston and his son William at Bordeaux) took him to the United States. He left in July, 1810, and arrived in America in September, traveling via New York to Washington, where he visited Mr. and Mrs. Joel Barlow at their beautiful country seat, Kalorama. Lee returned to Washington in February, 1811, after some business trips to New York, to learn almost immediately that Joel Barlow had been appointed minister to France and that he himself was to accompany Barlow as acting secretary of legation, although he was still in charge of the agency at Bordeaux. Following a long delay, Barlow received instructions from the State Department on July 12, 1811. He and Lee set sail aboard the frigate *Constitution* on August 5, and arrived in Cherbourg a month later.

Because of their difficulties in getting coach transportation, William Lee and the Barlows, with Mr. Barlow's young nephew Thomas, did not reach Paris until the middle of September. Mrs. Barlow wrote to Mrs. Lee that William was distressed at not having gone straight to Bordeaux, " but my husband thinks nothing can go right if Wm. Lee is not at his elbow. And indeed we could not have got along without him." Finally on September 27, William was able to leave Paris.

After a month's joyous reunion with his wife and four children, he returned to the French capital, taking with him six-year-old William Barlow Lee. Staying with the Barlows, William and his son remained in Paris until August 7 — nearly two months after the American Congress declared war on England. Many of the letters in this chapter date from the turbulent period of November, 1811, to March, 1812, and recount for the family in Bordeaux his candid impressions of court life.

To Miss Susan Palfrey Lee at Bordeaux

St. Jean de Luz, April 30, 1810

My much loved daughter:

I have often regretted that your dear mother did not accompany me. The weather has been so fine and the journey so pleasing. Bayonne is beautifully situated on two rivers, the Adour and Nive, which serpentine through numerous vallies. . . .

We have had at Bayonne three fêtes in honor of his Imperial Majesty's marriage. These fêtes were more diversified than those at Bordeaux; and among the exhibitions was a *bull-baiting*, the most incredible, ridiculous, and extraordinary thing I ever heard of. The place of action was on a square, about as large as that where the theatre stands at Bordeaux, every avenue to which was fastened up, and all the women and children were ordered out, though to my utter astonishment some remained. In this square about fifteen hundred or two thousand people of all classes collected together, and the houses were filled with spectators up to the garrets.

At equal distances were let half way into the ground large hogsheads filled with sand. In the middle of the square was a large sign post, on which was hung a man of straw, which was hoisted up and lowered down at pleasure, dressed in a manner to terrify the bull. At equal distances were also driven into the ground large oak stakes, forming a circle, and so close together that a man could creep through between them, but the bull's head and horns could not pass. The circles, four in number, served as a retreat for fifty people to each.

After all this preparation, when the hour was come, I expected to see all the people leave the square *point de tout*. A trumpet was sounded three times to let them know the bull was coming, and those who wished to retire might. At length the stable door opened and a string, which had previously been fastened to the bull's horns, was thrown into the square. Several persons caught hold of this string, pulling and jerking it. The animal made immediately towards them, but with great agility they got out of his way, when he turned on the multitude with such fury that he laid one hundred and fifty of them sprawling in a second. Some ran into the circles; others flew to the hogsheads of sand, the bull pursuing them in every direction. Now and then the people would catch hold of the cord, and throw the animal down. This served to enrage him the more.

The poor soldiers with their red feathers seemed to fare the worst, particularly as they were unacquainted with the game. He made after one, who ran for a door, and the bull butt him on the posterior just as he reached the house, and drove him head over heels into a long entry amongst fifty people. The soldier, who was not hurt, recovered, drew his sabre, and came out into the square to fight the bull and everyone he met with. But the public were so taken up with the animal that they paid no attention to the fury of this son of Mars, who insisted on it he had been insulted and disgraced.

Directly under the window where I was placed, some soldiers and American seamen had placed some planks on a few old brandy pipes, thinking themselves very secure on this staging; but unfortunately a man the bull was in chase of took refuge behind these brandy pipes, and the animal struck them so hard that the whole fabric, people and all came tumbling down. Such screeching, laughing, groaning, noise and confusion would beggar all description. When the poor bull was worried down and panting for breath, he was put up and a fresh one brought out, and so on until the fifth bull made his appearanced, dressed *à feu d'artifice*, when this cruel sport ended, without causing, to my great surprise, any other mischief than bruised bones, bloody noses, torn clothes, etc. This I was told was owing to the bulls being young and their horns growing out straight from the side of the head. You must not suppose I have seen what the Spaniards call a *bull baiting*. This is a very different thing. The bull at such exhibitions is always killed, but not until he has destroyed a horse or two and perhaps their riders. It is a shameful, cruel sport, and ought not to be suffered.

From Bayonne to this place a road runs along the coast in sight of the sea, which afforded me much pleasure, and has determined me to take you all to Royan this summer. The inhabitants of St. Jean de Luz live by fishing and privateering. Fifteen of our countrymen have been brought in here. It made my blood boil to see the cargoes of these vessels going into the stores of these pirates. The town lies at the foot of a mountain, directly on the sea. Upon the top of the mountain is the ruins of an old convent from which I should think, judging from its height, one could see across the Atlantic. I amused myself an hour on the beach, listening to the roaring of the surf and waves, and viewing two British ships in the offing. . . .

This town was once of some importance. Louis XIV was married here, and I have played billiards in the room where the ceremony was performed.[1] Crows would now fly to this house and mistake it for a barn. The people here are very clean in their houses and persons: I mean in comparison with Bordeaux peasants. There is a class of women here called *Bédartines* [Basque women?], whose honesty is proverbial. " He is or she is as honest as a Bédartine," they say. These women go from Bayonne to San Sebastian loaded with smuggled goods. Their whole business is contraband. I have set some of them to work for stockings, muslins &c. for your mother; but they say I am rather out of season, and that there is not much stock on hand. Some of the Spanish women I have met here have very pleasing faces. They wear their hair combed smooth from the forehead over the head, and let it fall in a long braid down the back as low as their hips.

I was preparing to go into Spain, at least as far as San Sebastian, but the brigands are in large bodies between this and that place. They murdered a courier yesterday on the other side [of] the mountains about two leagues from this, and wounded another courier, who made his escape, and is now in the room next to me telling his story to the gaping crowd. Several *gens d'armes* have been hung on trees and the insurgents have dressed themselves in their uniforms. These things are sufficient to deter me from going any farther.

I must leave off to look at the troops, who are all in motion with their horses, going on what the soldiers call " a scouting party." I had rather sleep, and sweat as I did last night over the cook's *fourneau*, like Colman's fat, single gentleman.[2] Such a night I never before passed! I got up and opened the window, but all would not do; and lo! and behold! this morning I discovered my bed was right over the kitchen fires, where supper was preparing for Maréchal Messéna,³ alias Prince d'Essling, alias Duke of Rivoli &c.

Adieu! my dear Susan. I shall be with you about Saturday or Sunday next. My love to all.

Your affectionate father
W. L.

To Mrs. Susan Palfrey Lee at Bordeaux

On board of [the ship of]
Capt. Smith
Socoa, July 8, 1810

My dear Sue:

Your affectionate letter announcing your arrival came to me this instant, and gave me infinite pleasure. As I did not go to bed last evening, I sent an express at three o'clock this morning to Bayonne for it. I could not bear to go away without hearing of your safe arrival.

We have been in a dreadful alarm all day. Orders were yesterday received to stop the ship, or, what is the same thing, to let no passengers go out of France without a special permission from the Minister of Police. The Commissary General of Police of Bayonne came over to stop the ship. Hearing of it, I sent for Prendergast, and made him go to sea last night, and to stand off and on for me. This he has done all day; and I have sent him everything on board, and am now waiting the tide to get off myself with the mate, Boufar, and his wife.

I have come to Socoa, not choosing to go over the bar at St. Jean de Luz. Two boats were upset there last evening and one this morning; but no lives lost, though some luggage. Prendergast was in one, and came near being drowned. The ship is now as far off as you can see her, standing in for me; and I am going off in one of their large tranquedors⁴ with fifteen oars. We have one hundred and ninety-seven seamen on board, besides passengers. I did not intend to take so many, but they crowded on board.

I have been anxious ever since I left you. I love you; I love my children to distraction. Tell them to be good, and push their studies. My poor heart is full. To-night I sleep at sea. If it had not been fête at St. Jean de Luz, we should have been stopped; but now we are safe. Kiss my lovely Susan for me. I hope she will cheer you in my absence. Tell Mary to be good and kind to my poor William and Susan too. Thomas you all love. Get Mr. Griswold to place the credit with Johnston. I have paid all my debts here, and got through all my difficulties *malgré* M. Loures.

Once more adieu! best of wives. I ought to have written Mr. Griswold, but you know how I have been harassed. I approve of your opinion of appearances: of his living in the house with you, and so will he, for he has a great idea of decorum. Adieu!

Yr. W.

Four days later, on July 12, 1810, Mrs. Lee wrote to her husband. This letter is of particular interest because of the account of the famous Paris fire that had occurred on the first of July, 1810:

Twelve days have passed, my dear husband, since your departure; and if all the rest during your absence are to pass as heavily, I do not know what will become of me before your return. I spend all the time in looking at the clouds and watching the winds. But alas I receive but little satisfaction: for the wind has been uncommonly fixed to the westward, with a few variations to the southward; so that I have the pain of thinking that you will have a long passage, which, with such a crowded vessel, will be dreadful.

It has been reported here that the *George Dyer* is carried into England. Mr. Gustier does not believe it. Mr. Griswold is still here, but leaves us to-morrow for the waters. Bordeaux is inexpressibly dull. Mr. Griffon died a few days ago very much regretted. Mr. Forster is getting well. I see Mr. and Mrs. Chalmers oftener than any other persons. They are very kind in coming to see us, and taking us out to walk. Our dear children are in fine health and very amiable. They are a great consolation to me in your absence.

You were extremely luckly in getting off as you did. No one has been permitted to leave the country since your departure. I write this with very little expectation that you will receive it. No one

William Lee 1812

Susan Palfrey Lee 1806–1807

knows here what is the cause of this new order of the police. There are many conjectures. The most probable is that it is to prevent the escape of those persons who robbed jewels to a great amount in the late fire in Paris.[5] As I think it probable that you did not hear the particulars of this accident before your departure, I will endeavor to procure a copy of a letter from Sir John to William Johnston, which is much more particular than the public papers.

Others suppose that this order is issued on account of the misunderstanding among the great in Paris. The report here is that Fouché and Cambacérès are arrested; that Lucien[6] has made his escape to Malta. The King of Holland[7] has certainly abdicated the throne. We have seen the proclamation. I much fear that the intercourse between France and America will be more than ever interrupted.

I sincerely wish that we had all gone with you. Let me again repeat my request that you will not risk a winter passage back, nor even a late fall one. Much as I desire your return, my dear William, I prefer infinitely to suffer a few months more than to endure the misery of knowing that you are on the ocean in that inclement season. When once I hear of your safe arrival, I shall I hope breathe freely, and eat and sleep. Until then the agitation of my mind will make me thinner than ever. Susan wishes to write to you, but I prevent her on account of the uncertainty of the conveyance. I rely, my dearest love, on your sending immediate information of your arrival by all opportunities.

I this moment receive Sir John's letter, which I must copy.

"Paris. July 3, 1810.

"I must begin by relating to you the most horrible event I think I have ever heard of, which took place the night before last. The Austrian ambassador gave a ball to the Empress. Great preparations had been making a long time for it. Two large temporary rooms were erected, the one for dancing room, the other for supper. The company, to the number of about twelve hundred, were in the former one, when all at once a part of an inward room caught fire, which was not observed by those in the ball room. At length they called out 'Fire!' The Emperor, who was talking with some persons not far off, with great *sang froid* said there was no danger. He then went for the Empress, who was at some little distance, and handed her out.

"He had not been gone three minutes, when the fire broke out in every part almost at the same moment, as these buildings were composed of nothing but paper and canvas. The squeeze at the door, as you may suppose, was horrible. Many were thrown down and trampled to death. The fire descended with such rapidity that those persons, who were the last, were obliged to crawl on all fours. The most escaped death, yet the great majority of them were horribly burnt. The ladies were worse off than the men; for their dresses being of a combustible nature, soon caught fire, which communicating one to the other, while they were pressing to get out, made it a most wonderful thing how any of them escaped.

" I happened to be walking by when the conflagration began. In a moment the whole street was full of the company. You saw there ladies with half their dresses burnt; others half naked; some fainting; some wild with despair, not knowing what they were doing or where they were going; happy in meeting the first person they could pick up in the street to assist them; crying out to know what had become of their father, brother, husband, sister etc.; every one supposing it was impossible to escape the fury of the flames. In short never was witness before to such a scene.

" Now the most tragical part of the story is this. The Princess of Schwarzenberg, the Ambassador's sister, a charming young woman of twenty-two years, was in the middle of the room, when the great chandelier falling upon her, cleaved her skull in two, and ripped her body open. Horrible to say, she was four months gone with child. Her body was found next morning in the cellar under the flooring. The Princess Labensky died last night. The Princess de la Leyen has been terribly burnt. She has also since died. The Russian ambassador, whose corpulence and infirmities prevented his being so active as the others, is in a very dangerous way. He was burnt from his legs to the middle of his waist. It is said that he is still alive, but lost both legs. In short no one knows the full extent of the misfortune. None of the musicians are yet heard of. They have undoubtedly fallen a sacrifice. In short the victims must have been innumerable, for every moment they are taking out dead bodies.

" The quantity of jewels lost is prodigious; for, as I mentioned to you above, every woman, glad to put herself under the protection of the first person she happened to meet, found a robber instead of a Samaritan, and most of them lost everything they had. In every part of the town, even as far as the Champs Elysées, ladies were found not knowing where they were going or what doing; but without their diamonds, for, while they fainted, they were at the mercy of these cannibals. The Russian ambassador had diamonds to an enormous amount about him; it is said, all he possessed, amounting to some millions. They were mostly carried off. Also a diamond of some Prince (I forget his name) to the value of 30,000 sterling was stolen.

"In short the whole of this business is the most tragical event in history; when the whole comes to be exactly known, which will not be very soon, for there were a number of persons, who contrived to get tickets, who were not at all known in society. I never saw such a blaze of light. It seemed as if half the city was on fire, which made me see everything distinctly that passed. Though horrible, it was a ridiculous sight to see hundreds of persons decked out in all their paraphernalia of dignity, every coat vying in splendor and magnificence, with all their orders and brilliant stars, some without shoes, some without hats, without swords, running about in search of their families etc. This, my good friend, is only half the history of this event. You shall have more of it when it comes to my knowledge; but this is quite enough for the present."

So much for Sir John. We have since heard other particulars, such as: General Durosne was hurrying out his wife to save her from the flames, when a man in a full suit of black (one of the company no doubt) unclasped her diamond necklace, tore her earrings out of her ears, and marched off with them, leaving the husband too much occupied and astonished to prevent it. A Swedish lieutenant colonel, carrying out a lady, who was much burnt, and who had fainted away, as well as he could, a man full dressed pretending to assist him, took out her diamond earrings and the rings off her fingers, and got off with them.

Adieu! dearest. I am informed I must send this by to-day's post, as Mr. Yates expects to sail on Monday. Mr. Martini is in Paris, and Mr. Ducourneau in Bayonne. We all embrace you cordially. Your affectionate Susan.

To Mrs. Susan Palfrey Lee at Bordeaux

New York, September 14, 1810

After a passage of sixty-three days I arrived, my adored Susan, at New London. We had nothing but calms and head winds all the way, and not a single gale of wind or thunder squall. But one man died on the passage. The rest were all hearty and well able to eat their allowance. I suffered much on your account, from the length of the passage; and therefore made it a point to speak all the vessels we saw, by whom I wrote you several times via London, Lisbon, and Amsterdam; and I hope some of those letters reached you, and eased your anxious mind.

I wrote you also from the beautiful island of Flores, where I stopped to take in some refreshments. Here we found the ship *Margaret*, taken up by our consul at Naples to convey to the United States about one hundred and fifty seamen, had touched for fresh provisions about a month before us. And Mr. Barney found the name of his brother on the book, kept by the collector of the island, on which every passenger writes his name. On the Banks of Newfoundland we spoke the ship *Sheffield*, bound from Norfolk to London, who gave us some papers, by which we learnt the ship *Margaret* had been upset in a squall, and that all perished on board, except a few who had taken to the long boat.[8] But who those few were, and whether Barney's brother was among them, was unknown, and gave him great pain until we arrived here, when he found he was one out of the eight or ten saved.

I too was very unhappy. I feared this story would reach France and make you miserable on my account. I fear too that some of the ridiculous stories, which have been circulated here, will reach you before you hear from me, and make you unhappy. By a vessel arrived at Wiscasset, which we spoke on the banks, it is reported we were short of provisions. By another arrived from Fayal, it is said we had a fever on board, and that a number of passengers died. What could have given rise to such false reports I cannot imagine. I pray they may not have reached you before this letter.

In one of the papers it is announced that my family have accompanied me. They call me, " The Ex-Consul of Bordeaux, who has been driven off by the French government." Among all these reports, however, I have nothing to complain of. One of the papers of this city says, " Mr. Lee passed through this city yesterday for Washington. We congratulate him on his return to his country. The reception his countrymen have met from him abroad, and the ready assistance he has given all those who were in want, will entitle him to the respect of his fellow citizens." A Boston paper puts me off in high style after publishing a note of thanks, signed by about sixty New England men, who[m] I sent to their homes in a small vessel from New London. I have been met everywhere with great kindness and attention by both Federalists and Republicans. Indeed party spirit is nothing like what it was when we left the country. It is kept up in Boston in a degree; but generally speaking foreign principles and foreign attachments are hooted at.

The happiness of the people is very apparent as you ride through the country. The farm houses are generally painted and well furnished. The women are beautiful, particularly in Connecticut. They have fine forms and elegant persons. The roads are incomparable, and the inns better than any I have seen in Europe, not even excepting England. There are more private carriages in this country than in England in proportion to their numbers, and living is much cheaper than we have been taught to expect. My friend Fulton [9] lives in a handsome three story house, keeps an elegant carriage, has four servants, two children, and sees his friends once a fortnight for $4000 per annum. The first people in this city, who dine their friends three or four times a week, and have their town house and country house, do not spend more than $10,000 per annum or 50,000 fr. but then they live in the style of English noblemen and French princes. Their houses are neatly finished and furnished, and there is a comfort and an independence about them that is to be seen in no other country. I stopped one day at New Haven to attend the commencement orations. Such a collection of fine women, such a blaze of beauty and elegant display of dress, together with a native simplicity and innocence of manner, no country on earth can produce. In short, my S., there is nothing like our country in Europe, and we must get back to it as fast as we can.

I met here with Mr. Gallatin,[10] who has persuaded me not to go on to Washington. He says nobody will be there until the first of October. Barlow is at the waters; the President at his seat in Virginia; and the heads of departments at their respective homes. I shall therefore remain here a few days. There is no yellow fever here, nor has there been for four years. This scourge appears to have passed off. If we remain at Bordeaux, I am told, from good authority, that I shall have 10,000 fr., $2000, per annum, and it is probable be appointed Consul for all the ports in Biscay, and agent for seamen. G[eorge] W[illiam] Erving has just returned from Washington, and tells me I stand very high. This is pleasing.

I shall make you a remittance, or rather make Mr. Johnston one for you, by a vessel which is to sail on or about the first of October. Be economical, but do not deprive yourself of necessaries. We are now out of debt, and have promising prospects. Some things have already offered, which will not do to trust to letters. Only let me say that on my return to you I shall have enough to keep us above want, which, when added to what the Consulate will produce, either by fees or a salary, will put us at our ease. If commerce was to come round, I should carry all before me. And as it is I have already made some excellent arrangements for indirect business.

Push our dear children on in their education. Tell my lovely Susan that she must attend to her drawing, music and dancing. Let no expense be spared on their education. I am in great hopes to be able to join you all in November; but, if I cannot get through my business so as to leave this by the twentieth of October, I do not intend to join you until the spring, as I do not like a winter passage.

As I have not time to write anyone, you will tell Meyer so. Tell Ducourneau by note that I have this moment left his friends Caze and Richaud, and shall make arrangements for the payment of the bills on Barlow. I have here also Dr. Romaine, Mr. Griswold's friend, and shall settle with him. I shall make every exertion to join you, for I exist nowhere but in your society. I adore and love you with consuming affection. and were it possible for me to describe the anxious and unhappy moments I have passed since I left you, your affectionate heart would bleed. Teach my children to love a father, whose whole soul is bound up in you all, and whom this cruel separation renders miserable in the midst of all the invitations and attentions of his friends. Adieu! best of wives and of women.

Your W.

To Mrs. Susan Palfrey Lee at Bordeaux

Kalorama, Seat of Joel Barlow,

near Washington, October 20, 1810

I have just heard of a dispatch, which leaves the Department of State by the mail, and have hurried home to scribble off a few lines to my adored wife and her much loved children. My tears begin already to flow faster than my words. How many I have shed since I left you! How many anxious hours have I passed on your account! Could I have imagined that my poor heart would have bled at this rate, I would never have quitted you. Susan, Mary, William and Thomas are forever pulling on my heart strings. If I dine in company, and there are any children introduced, my own crowd upon my mind and occupy my thoughts and render me miserable for the whole day. This is to be the case all winter, for my return is now necessarily deferred until the spring. The great appearance of commerce opening with France will induce me to remain here in order to form connections for the house, and I have no doubt but that I shall succeed greatly to my wishes.

The ship goes out to the address of the house with a cargo. I expect she will sail about the fifteenth or twentieth of November. I have no interest in her, except what is owing me by B ——, say $8000, which I have ordered paid out of the proceeds of his voyage to Mr. Johnston: half of which I intend for you, and the other half I shall draw for, having certain uses for it here. We are now, my dear S., in a better situation than we ever have been since our marriage. My debts are all paid and I have something beforehand. If therefore commerce opens, we shall soon slide ahead. So be patient and be happy. Be prudent too, that if any further restrictions are continued on commerce for two or three years, we may not be in want. Do not let your expenses exceed by any means 10,000 fr. per annum. Have no bills, but pay as you go along. Tell my dear Susan that all the young women here are well educated, and that she must pursue her drawing and other accomplishments with great assiduity. Barlow and his wife have made me promise to send you and her here, when I return, to spend six months with them, and take the tour of the states. I should like the arrangement well, and would take care of the family in your absence.

I am a constant visitor and favorite at the President's. The Government have a wish that I would take the general Consulate at Paris, but I have declined it, on the expectation that the revocation of the decrees will do something for me at Bordeaux. I can have any appointment here that I please, suited to my talents; but the salaries are all low, and I had rather remain in France a few years longer on account of the education of our children.

The Secretary of State, Mr. Smith,[11] is a very gentlemanly man, and his wife a very amiable woman. Mr. and Mrs. Gallatin are charming people to whom I am much attached. Dr. Eustis,[12] the Secretary of War, has married Miss Langdon of Portsmouth. She is about thirty, a fine, handsome, sensible woman. My excellent and estimable friend Barlow is elegantly situated here with an ample fortune and enjoying the respect and esteem of the whole community. His poor wife, in addition to her chronic complaint, has had a fever, from which she is but just recovering, contrary to the expectations of all her friends. She suffers greatly and is much to be pitied. What Barlow will do if he loses her I do not know. He is excessively attached to her.

In a few days I shall leave this for the northward. I shall then turn southward, and go on by degrees to Charleston, S.C., and from thence at New Orleans embark for Bordeaux, very early after the vernal equinox.

I expect to do great things, if the communication is really opened with France after the first of November. If what Meyer suggests to me in his letter, he is not confirmed as Vice-Consul by the French government, I shall send out a Vice-Consul from this appointed by the President, to be under my direction and control. So do not let things of this nature fret you. Everything here is as I could wish. Tell Mary to be industrious and hold up her head. The girls here have the finest forms in the world.

Barlow's house is a little palace.[13] It is situated on a high hill, surrounded with about fifty acres of large forest trees, which he turned into rural walks. He has Georgetown, the President's house, the Capitol, Alexandria, and the majestic Potomac in full view, with a bridge over this river one and a quarter mile wide. The house is new, and much in the style of Barrett's at Charlestown. He keeps four horses, three carriages (one of which is devoted to me) and eight servants.

Will you believe it? J[ohn] B[rown] Cutting is married to a very respectable widow in the neighborhood with five or six children, eighty negroes, and an estate something in debt, but which he is working out with great economy, and will finally finish his days, it is highly probable, very happily. He had no sooner heard I was here than he came to see me fifty miles. . . .

How are my darling boys? How I long to see them! How much I wish winter over that I may join you all! I fear you will suffer much in that house. You must keep a servant man, and a good one, and you must spend money in hack hire. I need not tell you, my S., how circumspect you must be until I join you. I expect now we have much good in store for us, and I expect infinite enjoyment in the society of my girls, whom I trust you will inspire with a love of all your virtues. Barlow says, what is very true, that it is a great misfortune for a man, who has children to be very rich. It creates in them a taste for luxury. If they are girls, they get married to men, who take them for their fortune, and if boys, they turn out very generally vagabonds. Pray, therefore, for a competency and not for riches.

[Written by Mr. Barlow at the end:]

Our dear friend:

You ought to have come along with William and past the winter with us. But he promises to send you to us, when he gets home. We long very much to see you, and show you all our great folks. Your husband has left me no paper to say more.

J. B.

To Mrs. Susan Palfrey Lee at Bordeaux

New York, December 12, 1810

I am afraid, my adored Susan, that many vessels will arrive at Bordeaux from this and other ports of the Union, and you be unhappy on receiving no letters by them from me. The fact is, my dear Girl, that these expeditions are made with such great secrecy, that I know nothing of them until the vessels are gone. This is done to prevent capture by the English, who have so many spies, it is said, in our city. I have however written you pretty fully by several opportunities, and the last letter I received from you came by Gen'l A[rmstrong] who had a charming passage of thirty days; though it like to have ended tragically, for their ship in making the land struck on a reef of rocks in a gale of wind, beat over the shoal and lay at anchor under the lee of it the whole night, with the loss of their rudder, and got into New London miraculously the next morning.

Ever since then we have had nothing but dreadful storms, which lead me to bless my good luck that I did not embark this fall. My life belongs to you and my children, and therefore I shall not sport with it.

Our friend, Mrs. Barlow, is about dying. She has made her will and given the $20,000 left her by her brother, Abraham Baldwin, to Susan and Mary, $10,000 each to be paid to them at the death of Mr. Barlow and he intends to do something handsome for William, so that we shall have to provide for *little Tom* only. Susan and Mary, however, must not plume themselves upon this, for Mr. Barlow may live twenty years yet, but he threatens to give it to them at their marriage, provided they do not, he says, marry foreigners.

By the ship *Ann*, I remitted to Messrs. Johnston, John Barney's [14] bills on his brother Louis Barney, supercargo [agent in charge of the cargo] of the ship *Ann* (which vessel's cargo went to the address of the house) for the sum of thirty-six thousand, one hundred and thirty-nine francs, which I charged them to collect and place to my credit, supplying you with what you might want for your current expenses. I have insured this sum against all risks on board the ship *Ann*, so that if any accident arrives, I shall lose nothing, and I hope, if the ship does not arrive, Messrs Johnston will nevertheless furnish you with [what] you want, as what money I have here I shall make use of to procure other consignments. Under this impression I have taken no arrangements to supply you otherwise than through Mr. Johnston. I have no concern in the *Ann* and have advanced Mr. Barney this sum to induce him to consign to the house. Be prudent and do not spend out of it more than six thousand francs. . . .

I am very uneasy about Susan. She has occupied much of my thoughts and I trust I shall hear in a short time from you. Tell her and Mary how much I love them, and how much I wish to find them improved. They pull upon my heart strings and destroy all the enjoyments I might have here. Thank God December is rolling off. January will soon pass away. February is a short month, and it will take all March to prepare for my voyage. So that by the middle of May I shall be with you, best of beings, and receive new delight in your society from the value this absence has set upon it.

I must repeat to you here how handsomely I have been received in this country by all parties. I am feasted and fêted, and if the communication is fairly open with France, I shall do great things for the house. Indeed I have already secured the best correspondents for them in this country and there are two more vessels loading here to go to their address. Our troubles I trust are now all past. Concerning a house, which I wrote you about in my last, leave all that until my return. We will then adopt a system of economy and regularity for ourselves, and fill all our time up in advancing the children. William and Thomas are always dancing before me. It appears to me the happiness I shall enjoy at the sight of you will be too much to bear.

Attend to Mrs. Madison's memorandum as I have instructed you and complete all the others, if you can, in the manner I have pointed out; but hers above all must not be neglected. Here is one for Mrs. Hopkins. If the *Ann* arrives, Mr. Johnston will advance you for all these things. If she does not arrive, all I wish him to do is to assist you in the order for Mrs. Madison, unless your bill on her can be placed, when the other memorandums can also be fulfilled. Here is a letter to them on the subject.

The children must not expect letters from me. My time is taken up, and the days are so short and so cold that I cannot get through all my correspondence. Adieu! my angel friend. You are the best gift Heaven ever granted to man. Your sublime virtues are a crown of glory to your husband and children. May they long live to offer and you to enjoy the best offerings of their best affections.

[Wm.]

P. S. General Armstrong is feasted everywhere — here, Philadelphia and Baltimore. The military turn out, and public dinners and entertainments are given him where ever he goes. They talk of him for Governor of Pennsylvania, Secretary of State, and even for President. He appears much my friend and has expressed himself so.

To Mrs. Susan Palfrey Lee at Bordeaux

Kalorama, [Washington] March 6, 1811

What I hinted to you, best of wives, has taken place. Our estimable friend, Barlow, has been named Minister Plenipotentiary and Envoy Extraordinary to France. He passed the senate better than Mr. Monroe, Mr. Livingston,[15] or Gen'l Armstrong, when they were nominated! That is to say, they had a bare majority of votes, and Barlow had twenty-one to nine. He stands very high in this country. If he succeeds in arranging our affairs with France, I shall be Consul General at Paris with a salary of $4000 per annum and be chargé d'affaires there during his absence, should he go to Spain, to Russia, Turkey, or Italy to adjust our concerns. At present I keep the Consulate at Bordeaux, and shall in addition assist Mr. Barlow at Paris as Secretary of Legation, with a salary of $2000 per annum.

Mrs. Madison's brother[16] will be attached to the legation, and I believe Mrs. Washington, Mrs. Madison's sister, will accompany Mrs. Barlow, whose health, to the great astonishment of every one, is perfectly established; so much so that she is now better than ever.

We shall leave this, my dear girl, in a frigate in the course of a month or six weeks, as soon as the *Essex* arrives. How my poor heart beats to think of embracing you again! Tell my dear Susan, and tell Mary I have not time now to write them. Indeed I scribbled this off to send to the Department of State, Mr. Smith having promised to put it in his despatch for Mr. Erving, who has not yet sailed from Newport. Mr. Barlow has instructed Erving to pay you 5000 francs. I wrote you a few days ago by the ship *Projector*, which has again sailed to the address of the house. Tell Mr. Johnston of this, as they knew she put back in distress. You [know] my angel friend, that according to the constitution of the United States a man cannot hold two offices; so keep to yourself my being Secretary of Legation. I shall do the business and have the emoluments without the character publicly.

Mrs. Madison wishes her things. I hope Susan will have copied handsomely the miniatures. She has requested me to let Susan spend a couple of years with her, but I expect you will take her with you to Paris. Barlow says he will not live without us. How much I have to tell you which cannot be trusted to letters. I am so well at the President's and did so much with Col. Pickering, Lloyd, and Gilman [17] to secure their influence in the senate for Barlow, that I have been abused in some of the papers. But it does me more good than harm.

I hope Susan is perfectly recovered. What I have suffered on her account! And, notwithstanding your assurances about William, I have been at times very anxious to hear from you, and that his convalescence continues. I will bring him a flying squirrel, and Mary a thimble, and perhaps something for you and Susan; though I think, if I bring myself, you ought to be contented. Adieu! best of beings. Rest assured of my unaltered attachment, and of the influence you will ever continue to have while life continues, and your virtues live ever.

Your devoted
Wm.

A kiss to all my dear children. Be dutiful to your dear mother, and strive to make her happy.

To Mrs. Susan Palfrey Lee at Bordeaux

Washington, March 28, 1811

My dear:

I have just called on M. Sérurier, the French Minister, who informs me of an opportunity to France. I therefore scribble off these few lines, just to say that I am well; that I am anxious to see you and the children, and fretting my soul out to get home.

Mr. Barlow has let his elegant seat to the French Ambassador, who goes into it in fifteen days. The frigate, *The President*, is now at Norfolk waiting for Mr. Barlow; but he does not go until the *Essex* arrives here. In the meantime I am going to New York to spend a few days, and I do not think we shall get away before the first of May. I have been here a month, very busy. I am much abused in the papers with Mr. Barlow and the President. This does me more good than harm.

My friend, Mr. Monroe, is to be Secretary of State. Mr. Smith has retired. That Mr. Monroe is to be is not publicly known. He will probably be the next president, so that my standing will be kept up. I have been mentioned for several places in the papers &c. &c., but I shall stick to my friend Mr. Barlow, and all will go well.

By G. W. Erving I sent you 5000 francs. Do not write me after receiving this. I am very unhappy about William, not having heard of his recovery. Adieu! best of beings. Love a husband who dotes on you. Kiss my little ones for me.

Your devoted
W.

To Mrs. Susan Palfrey Lee at Bordeaux

Kalorama, [Washington]

March 29, 1811

I wrote you yesterday, my adored Susan, a few lines, which the French Minister was kind enough to forward for me. But, lest that channel should fail, I will say a few more words, as it is very probable this may be the last opportunity before my sailing of writing; so few vessels depart for France, and those steal off in such a manner that one does not hear of them until they are gone. . . .

The departure of Barlow and myself will be regulated by the arrival of the *Essex* from France. She is hourly expected; but, allowing her all possible detention in Europe, I think she must be here in ten days. So that there appears to me no doubt but that we shall get off in April. I shall be with Barlow as Secretary of Legation, for two reasons. It will help us live, the salary being $2000 per annum, and then it is an introduction to something better, if commerce does not revive. If I quit the consulate, Mrs. Madison's brother will in all probability be placed there, who is now at Tunis; so that Mr. Morton and all the persons who have been intriguing after the office have no hopes. All this thing is well understood.

I receive from the President and Mrs. Madison daily marks of kindness. In short no one is more intimate there. They are the most amiable people on earth. It would amuse you to see how I am roasted in the papers. One party says I brought over my pockets full of licenses. Another says I have exclusive privileges to trade to France. Then again I have been treated with greater attention in France than even our minister, because I have been so useful to the Emperor &c. &c. &c. Barlow is also getting abuse enough. I shall keep all these scraps to show you. Warden was named Consul to Paris, but Gen'l Armstrong has made such complaints against him that the President has hinted to him that he must return to Washington and clear them up before he can go out. The Secretary of State, Mr. Smith, has been told he may retire, and Mr. Monroe is to take his place. If Mr. Monroe refuses (which is not at all probable), Mr. Livingston, who was Minister to France, is to take it. It is pleasing to see my particular friends named to these important offices; because, if trade does not open, it secures something more to us. Indeed one or two things have already been mentioned.

I hope before I leave this, I shall hear from you and that my anxiety for the health of Susan and William will subside. I have been extremely wretched at times on their account. The change of air from Bordeaux to Paris for a few months, if not more, will be useful for them, and for you. How I long to see you all! It will be, my love, the happiest day of my life. I know of nothing that would tempt me to leave you again. Whole nights have passed without closing my eyes, distracted with the thoughts of home. You will be delighted with Barlow. Such a friend as he is, no man ever before possessed. She is better than she has been for ten years. Her constitution has taken a turn, which appears to have carried off her disorder. She has a great desire to see you. Kiss all our dear little ones for me. In great haste,

Your devoted
Wm.

Have patience, Dear Susan! We shall be along soon. J. B.

To Mrs. Susan Palfrey Lee at Bordeaux

Washington, July 1, 1811

My dear Wife:

You have been uneasy about me, I know, and I have been unhappy about you. Our detention here has been beyond all my expectations, and I have been fretting and worrying my life out. This day I heard of the capture of Capt. Skiddy and the *Osmin*, by both of whom I wrote you. Even the very vessels I wrote by go to England.

Thank God the *Essex* has at last arrived. All our luggage is on board the *Constitution* frigate, laying at Annapolis, about forty miles from this, and Mr. Monroe told me to-day he had begun Mr. Barlow's instructions, and that we should be off very soon. Nothing will ever tempt me to quit you again. It is well, however, that I waited for the frigate. I should have been taken into England in a government vessel. Be patient, dear S.; comfort the children. I shall soon be with you now.

Your ever devoted
W.

To Mrs. Susan Palfrey Lee at Bordeaux

Cherbourg, Monday, September 9, 1811

I wrote you, my adored Susan, a few lines the night of our arrival in the road, which the visiting officer promised to put in the office. We have just landed, bag and baggage; and I have only time, as the post goes off immediately, to say I am well and happy, except that anxiety, which naturally arises from a fear that you or the children may be unwell. I shall leave this to-morrow or next day for Paris, and travel slow, as we must take the diligence, there being no private carriage in this town to be hired; and the minister did not bring his, as it would have taken up too much room in the frigate, in case we had met a brush with the English, which we had reason to expect.

At Paris I must remain several days. Barlow will not let me quit him until he is accredited, and I have all my money arrangements to make. Write me, therefore, fully and particularly about yourself. Make a note of all the money you want, which shall be sent you immediately. I have about 20,000 fr. with me in bills. Did you receive the amount of Mr. Barlow's bill on Parker, sent you by Mr. Erving for 5000 fr? I am afraid you have been in want from the singular letter I received from Mr. Johnston. I am dissatisfied with them. Tell me how they have treated you. I shall break that connection. In short write me fully and correctly, because I shall perhaps read some parts of your letter to Barlow. Mrs. Barlow has some pretty things for you, and Mrs. Madison has sent you a present of a dress or two. What is the state of her memorandum and those of the other ladies? Write me this, as I must get the whole done that remains to be done at Paris to go by the frigate.

Could I only look in upon you one moment, or get a letter, that I might know you were all well! I hope my sufferings are now at an end; for the last three months of detention was insupportable. I never will leave you again. Life is too short to make such sacrifices, and the rest of it must be devoted to the care of my Susan and to her happiness.

We had a fine passage of twenty-eight days from Hampton

Roads to the Lizard Point; [18] but meeting with head winds in the channel, we were seven days from Land's End to this port.

Gen'l Armstrong has conducted so like the devil in the United States as to lose all his standing. He has attacked every one and among the rest me. I gave him as good as he sent, and he sued me for defamation, claiming $100,000 damages. He has retired to his farm in the state of New York, detested by all the friends of the administration, against which he was discovered to be intriguing with Mr. [Robert] Smith. Have you seen Mr. Smith's address and the answer to it? The answer is my work, corrected by Barlow, and has given me a great standing with the President. This to yourself.

Adieu! best of beings. I have some things for all the children I will write to Susan and Mary to-morrow. I will also write Meyer and Johnston.

Yr. W.

To Miss Susan Palfrey Lee at Bordeaux

Paris, November 5, 1811

My dear daughter:

Hand the enclosed to your dear mother, and when the box comes to hand, beg her to open it carefully, as it contains some glass. Tell her, if she will sell all our old casseroles, which serve only for shine in the kitchen, I will lay the proceeds out in such ones as I have sent her in the box. They have this advantage: they are always clean, and there is no danger of getting poisoned by them. They are of Count Rumford's [19] invention, and are getting to be all the vogue in small families. Tell your mother to read Inchiquin's letters.[20] Some of them are well written and will amuse her. I hope my large black trunk has come to hand, and that you have been amused with its contents. You must also have received by this time the box of chocolates. The money the sugar sold for I will send as soon as I can get over to Mr. Hottinguer's to touch the amount, and the tea shall be sent in a day or two.

William is remarkably well. The change of climate has been

of great use to him; though at first he complained for several days, and had a slight fever, which gave me great uneasiness. But by *honey, garlic, beer, beef steaks, côtelettes,* and exercise he is gaining strength daily. He is so reasonable and good-tempered that he makes friends as he goes along. He minds all I say to him, and as a reward, I bought *Robinson Crusoe* for him, which I read through in French, in three evenings, much to his gratification and amusement. I shall bring him home fat and hearty. . . .

I hope the Emperor will arrive soon, that I may join you all, for life is too short to make the sacrifices I am daily making by absenting myself from you. My paper does not give me room to say how much I love you.

W. Lee.

To Mrs. Susan Palfrey Lee at Bordeaux

Paris, November 6, 1811

My dear S.

The ministers begin to arrive from Holland, and I therefore presume the Emperor is not far off. We are all prepared for him when he arrives and I hope and trust he will be led to a different kind of policy from that which he has adopted towards us for four years past. If he does not do something for our commerce, he will greatly strengthen the opposition in the United States and favor the English.

I want him to decide on something that I may join my S., for this is a sorry kind of life I am living. All the pleasure I have ever had is in your society and that I deprive myself of. Shall we remain at Bordeaux or shall we come here? If no commerce is opened to us, we must come here. We can live very well for 10,000 francs per annum. But if we have commerce, we had better stay where we are. Which is your opinion? The consulate at London has become vacant by the death of Gen'l. Lyman.[21] I could have it, but it offers no great emolument, and I had better stick to Barlow, who is a devoted friend. We must have a little patience and take our determination.

William is well. He has been laying on the carpet this evening whistling his tunes to Mr. Barlow. You did wrong to let the Doctors give him so many drugs. I have talked with Haskell and Mde. La Croix's *médecin*, who are of the opinion that his fever was an effort of nature, and was not to be dreaded. He was very unwell for a day or two after his arrival. I suppose it was the change of climate; but he is now better than ever he was in his life. He is very lively and begins to get a color. I can now account for your anxiety for your children by my own feelings. I am unhappy when I am away from him, fearing some accident may happen to him. He loves you and Thos. most dearly, and talks about you with tears in his eyes.

I have been [to] the other side of the river but once since my arrival. I will go to-morrow or next day, and send you the proceeds of the sugar and also send you the tea. I go out in the morning with either B[arlow] or his wife and sister and have purchased all their furniture. They have furnished one room, bedroom, and library. These pretty pieces which they call mine, and the bed is five feet wide which he says is for you. I have taken possession of them to-day and am lodged like a prince. Send me two or three dozen of the new uniform small buttons, which you will find in some of my drawers. I shall hurry home as fast as I can to bring you here or to remain with you, for I will not live thus. Tell Susan to write me. Kiss them all for me. They are dear children and you are everything that a husband can desire.

Yr.

W.

Tell me what you most want from this.

To Mrs. Susan Palfrey Lee at Bordeaux

Paris, November 17, 1811

I received, my precious wife, the things by Bass,[22] accompanied by your four cold lines, which gave me pain, because I had been expecting a letter from you for several days. I will hasten home or I shall lose the affection of you all, and, as I adore my

wife and children, this idea is dreadful. William is getting his
color and really grows finely. He says a great many good things,
and is much beloved by the whole house. To-day we had a large
party at dinner, and William for the first time dined at the side
table. After dinner Mr. Barlow asked him how he fared. " J'ai
diné," says he " comme l'Archi-Chancelier." You know the
Archi-Chancelier [Cambacérès] keeps the best table in France.

Yesterday I accompanied Mr. Barlow to Comte Ségur's,
Grand Maître des Cérémonies, and to Cambacérès', and this
morning we went in high style to St. Cloud, where Mr. Barlow
was presented to his Majesty. It being a particular audience in
the Emperor's cabinet, on the Minister's account only, I could
not be presented to his Majesty. I was introduced to several of
the grand dignitaries as: " Consul for Bordeaux, faisant fonctions
de Secrétaire de Légation," and at the first diplomatic audience
I am to be presented.

The ceremony of this presentation is very stiff. I conducted
Mr. Barlow in my full dress to the *Salon des Ambassadeurs*,
where he was visited by, and I was presented to Comte Ségur
and the Duke of Bassano,[23] who left the minister to learn the
Emperor's pleasure, when two under *Maîtres des Cérémonies* in
their garbs and with their black velvet, ivory headed canes,
threw open the doors and received from my hands the Minister. They conducted him to the head of the stairs, where he was
received by the *Grand Maître des Cérémonies*, who conducted
him to the door of the Emperor's cabinet, where he was received by Prince Cambacérès, who presented him. The Minister
made one bow on entering, another halfway of the room, and a
third when he approached his Majesty. At this moment he addressed him in a very few words, much to the purpose, and the
Emperor answered in a very flattering way, by saying he was
gratified in receiving as Minister Plenipotentiary of the United
States a character so highly distinguished, and whose opinions
and writings were so friendly to France.

This introduction being over, the Minister returned to the
saloon of the *Ambassadeurs*, when I announced him to the
Chambellans of her Majesty the Empress, by whom he was re-

ceived and introduced into the presence of her Majesty. On our way to the city, we called on the Prince of Neuchâtel, and Prince of Bénévent. Our house is now to be open for three days (for so it is printed) to receive visits, and we have, according to the list handed the Minister by Comte Ségur, one hundred and eighty visits to make. Pity me! for I already begin to be tired of it.

All this will be over in three days, and we must then to business to see what can be done. Send me my small and large new buttons. I want them very much. Henit, the courier, will take charge of them. Here is his receipt for the tea and sugar. Do write me how you like the plate &c. Shall I bring William home or leave him here? Mrs. Barlow wants him; and Mde. de la Croix and Vernenac are crazy after him and promise to let him study with Charles, who has good masters.

Tell Susan I expect the Washington head in fine crayons or colors. It will be a very pretty present to Mrs. Madison. I will have *Susan Palfrey Lee* put under it myself. Adieu! my dear S. In your letters press me hard to join you, for when it comes to the moment, I shall have hard work to leave Barlow. I see, and they know they cannot get on well without me. Again Adieu!

To Mrs. Susan Palfrey Lee at Bordeaux

Paris, November 22, 1811

I do not wonder you are dull, my dear S. It is very unpleasant to be separated thus, and we must put an end to it as soon as possible. Mr. Barlow's reception has been excellent, and his standing with the different authorities is such as it ought to be. I think I see some prospect of an accommodation. At any rate we shall know something soon. I am now busy in making up Mrs. Madison's memorandum, and preparing for the frigate; but the chief of my time is taken up in visiting with the Minister.

Yesterday we dined with Cambacérès. This evening we are to be introduced to the Princess Pauline.[24] To-morrow we dine at Bassano's. On Sunday we go to Court. On Monday I do not know what is to become of us, and on Tuesday we are to be introduced to the Queen Hortense.[25] I am obliged to work double tides; and when I leave Barlow, how he will get on I do not know. I have furnished the house elegantly. The clock, candelabras, and *chenets* [andirons] in the saloon cost 6200 francs, the luster two thousand and the carpet 4800 francs. The furniture is crimson and yellow, with a yellow design in the middle and back of every *fauteuil* and chair.

William is hearty and getting red cheeks. I have not yet sent him to school, because he has had, until within these few days, continual sweats every night, which I did not like, and which the doctor could not stop; because he said it was an effort of nature to throw off the fever and humours of the body, and that it was rather a *bien* than a *mal*. He spent yesterday at the Garden of Plants, and is so full of it that he amuses the whole house with the account of the animals.

I hope before this you have received the tea and part of the coffee. The half barrel of coffee and the box of fish you will not have for some time. When the fish arrive, make strong pickle for them, and put them in it. I fear they will grow rusty. Take one out; soak it twenty-four or thirty hours; hang it up in the chimney a day or two, or near the chimney, where it can dry and collect a little smoke, and you will like them. . . .

What can I bring or send you from here? The fashions of the winter are about fixing. Tell me by return post if you wish hats, capes, great coats &c. &c. Barlow and his wife wonder you do not write them. God bless you, my precious wife. I will join you as soon as possible, and try to make you happy. My love to the girls.

To Mrs. Susan Palfrey Lee at Bordeaux

Paris, Monday, November 26, 1811

You cannot suffer more from this separation, my affectionate Susan, than I do, and I will put an end to it as soon as I can. The life I lead is of all others the most disagreeable to me. My wife and children occupy me entirely and in every struggle I make, their happiness is my only object. I need not tell you my S. how much you are admired and beloved. I do not know a woman so universally esteemed. I dined yesterday in a large company where Mrs. Leavenworth spoke of you in the highest terms. How grateful to me! Our children too are spoken of in a pleasing manner. This you see are fortune's distributions to me. She is always equal in her gifts. . . .

William is well and continues to please. In company last evening Barlow quoted his observations and talked of him as I have never dared to, because I always fear the fondness of a parent makes them appear ridiculous. You would have thought it was Barlow's child instead of mine. He did some mischief yesterday to the stove in the dining room. He went immediately to Mrs. B[arlow] and told her of it, begging she would defend him with Mr. B[arlow]. He dined again yesterday at Mde. de la Croix's who tease[s] me to death to let him stay there, which I would do were I not afraid of offending Mrs. B[arlow], for I view Mde. de la Croix and her daughter Mde. V[ernenac] two of the most perfect beings I ever knew.

Since my last, I have been occupied in paying visits with Barlow. We were at a ball on Saturday evening at the Duke of Bassano's. Yesterday we visited Madame Mère's.[26] To-day we go to Malmaison to visit Josephine. It is very tiresome, and having initiated Barlow, who profits well of his lesson, I shall soon quit the job.

Stephen Higginson [27] and Harry Higginson have failed through the extravagance and folly of Stephen. You see how things end and how the wheel goes round. Our friends or rather our enemies at Bordeaux will end in the same way. Even Messrs. J[ohnston]'s credit is very much altered in the commercial world. I sent Mrs. Johnston and Da[niel] Guestier [28] two letters I received from their friends yesterday.

Send me the measure of the glasses in the saloon, or rather the place to put them in; the measure exact of the saloon for a carpet, and of the windows for curtains. If we stay at Bordeaux, I will keep that house, and fit it up handsomely, and as I have bought Martini's *calèche*, and am much pleased with it, I will purchase a horse, so that the distance to your friends shall be shortened. I sent you two kinds of coffee. That in the keg is Mocha, so use that you will receive with the tea first. Lock up your stores and let no one but Susan or yourself go to them. The back room will make an excellent store room, if you nail the windows down. Its proximity to the water closet will do no injury to anything, particularly if you keep the window of the latter open. If this does not suit you, take the closet in Susan's room. God bless you!

On the receipt of this letter send out and buy a box of cologne water, which give to Captain Allen, master of the *Flash*, for Mrs. Baldwin's mother in New Haven. Do not forget this. Just as I got thus far, a servant comes in to announce breakfast. I said to him, " Call the woman to dress William, who sleeps in the next room." All at once the door opens and Mons. W. says, " Je n'ai pas besoin." Behold he has dressed himself from top to toe. But then you must be advised he has elastic garters, elastic suspenders, and his trousers are lined, so he has no trouble. He has contrived to put his suspenders on to the pantaloons first and then put his arms through.

To Mrs. Susan Palfrey Lee at Bordeaux

Paris, November 29, 1811

I received your letter, my dear Susan, last evening. In a few days, something will be decided on, and the frigate dispatched, when I shall be able to join you, and take some decision for the future.

William is well and goes this morning to school for the first time. He breakfasts with us; takes bread and honey for his second at school, and returns to dinner at five o'clock. Barlow insists on my being presented on Sunday. Did I tell you in my last how many pretty things the Empress Josephine said of you? They were kind and very flattering, particularly so as there were many persons present [the rest of this letter has been cut away].

To Mrs. Susan Palfrey Lee at Bordeaux

Paris, Monday, December 3, 1811

Give, my dear S., the enclosed to Martini, and take what money you want of him. I lent him 8000 francs when I left Bordeaux, which he was to return to me on the tenth of November. I have not wanted it. Take six hundred or one thousand francs; the rest he will send me.

You will have seen that I was presented on Sunday. His majesty asked me what uniform I wore. I told him it was the national uniform.[29] " What de Melica? " " No! Sire; the uniform worn by our army and ordered for the Consuls." "Fort bien! très bien! " Whether he meant that I was fort bien, très bien or the uniform I did not ask him. I was also presented to the Empress and to the Queen of Naples. In the evening we went to the theatre and after it to the Circle of the Court, from whence we came out at twelve o'clock at night, to end the chapter, and never was any one so tired of it.

All this ceremony is absolutely necessary. It occupies the whole of the day, and therefore we are obliged to work at night to get through our business. We go to bed regularly at twelve or one, and get up an hour or two before daylight. Sometimes I get but an hour or two sleep. " Savez-vous," says William yesterday to Mr. Barlow, " why you are not as fat as Papa? " " No! " "It's because you get up so early and open the windows, and deprive yourself of sleep. Mama me dit toujours de dormir tant que je peut. That it is the fine way of growing fat." He is delighted with his school, and will soon learn to read both French and English.

I wish you could see me. I am surrounded with your bonnets and the Lord knows what, which I am packing up for the post, the United States and Madame. They are very beautiful. Mde. de la Croix and Mde. Vernenac had them made up for me, and with great taste. These orders completed, and the frigate dispatched, I shall turn towards you. Shall I bring William or leave him? I had better bring him; but then for a school for him! The one he is at is excellent. We had better keep together, and study all in our power to keep our children with us. In this way we shall secure at least happiness.

Mr. Barlow is received everywhere in the most flattering manner. The Emperor told him on Sunday that his answer to his note would be satisfactory, and that he would enable him to dispatch the frigate in a few days. His Majesty said he was happy to have an American minister, with whom he could converse. He conversed with him twice at the diplomatic Audience, and for several minutes at the Circle, which is considered very marked and honorable. It will kill that drill Sergeant Armstrong. Adieu! my S. tell Susan not to forget my last instructions.

Yr. W.

I will send the letter for Martini next post, but I am too late.

To Miss Susan Palfrey Lee at Bordeaux

Paris, [December 1811 or early 1812.]

My dear daughter:

I received yesterday your copy of my portrait, which is a better likeness than the original. I shall send it to S[eth] Hunt, and beg him to send it to your grandmother. You ought to draw from nature now that you are so far advanced.

I dined again yesterday with the Empress Josephine at Malmaison, and had a very pleasant time. The Princess d'Arenberg was there (Miss Tascher [30]) and her maid of honor, who saw you at Mde. Campan's. I forget her name, but never can forget her nose: a most tremendous proboscis, which has been swelled from its natural size by snuff.

That a woman who has any pretentions to cleanliness, to beauty, to wit, to fashion, should be addicted to such a disgusting propensity is astonishing to me. To see a lady at dinner take out her snuffy handkerchief and search for a clean place to put her nose in, is sickening. " Such a handkerchief," says a witty English traveler, " is a flag of abomination." I hope none of my family will ever fall into this vice.

But the horrors of this lady's trunk has driven from my mind what I was going to mention of riddles. In the evening the young ladies and two of the young men of the house played off some riddles, which were really very pretty, and which I will describe to you on my return, as I have not the time now.

William is writing a letter to Mary. He has been ten days about it, and has got to the seventh page. He has nine and a half to do, so that she will have it next week. He is a fine fellow. Everybody loves him. I won't say when I am coming home any more. I want to see you, and I am living a life that is to me distressing. I have no comforts, no enjoyments except my little William. I will write Mamma next post. My love to Mary.

Your affectionate father
Wm. Lee.

To James Madison

Paris, January 1, 1812

Sir:

The answer to Mr. Barlow's note is not what was expected and most certainly is not what was intended to have been given for many days. What can have changed the Emperor's opinion is not known. All the persons about the Court of any influence have been of opinion that complete success would attend Mr. Barlow's mission. No one knows what answer Mr. Barlow has received, but it is feared it is not favorable, from its being kept secret and causing no visible marks of satisfaction.

The hopes of the merchants and manufacturers have been buoyed up for several weeks under the expectation that commerce would revive with the United States. They will soon be disappointed, and if Congress would increase their vexations by laying similar restricting duties on French brandies, wines, and manufactured goods as the Emperor has laid on imports from the United States, it would have an excellent effect here. It would shut up their last resource, and create a general discontent.

To this measure should be added that of preventing our citizens from using Imperial licenses. This cannot be too prompt. The trade between France and the United States has now become the property of a few intriguing individuals to the detriment of the commercial interests generally. It is therefore to be hoped that Congress will not rise until these points shall be established.

The cottons of the Levant pay a much lower duty than those of the United States; the consequence of which is that British cotton and even our own is sent to Turkey, baled over there and brought into France under the name of Levant cotton, and this too in British ships under American colors, who pass the Dardanelles under the English flag and on entering the Russian territory in the Black Sea, hoist our flag.

The people of this country are friendly to the United States. All classes from the post of officers of State down to the merchant and manufacturer regard the policy of the Emperor towards us in a very just point of view, and I am confident, were a total stop to be put to this partial commerce, it would have a wonderful effect. The true cause would be seen, and it would create the same dissatisfaction as the Spanish War.

Rest assured, Sir, that, if *from the answer* Mr. Barlow has received, our vessels should be induced to quit our shores for the harbors of France, that *millions* more of our property will go towards filling the Imperial coffers before this day twelvemonth.

Mr. Barlow's deportment is just what a minister's ought to be. He goes to all the circles of the Court; sees and hears all he can; believes as much as he ought to; and, if he is told anything that he feels is meant to deceive, he favors the deception and profits of it.

> I have the honor to be,
> with great attachment and respect,
> Your obedient Servant
> Wm. Lee.

To Mrs. Susan Palfrey Lee at Bordeaux

Paris, Sunday, February 3, 1812

Dear blessed wife

I am very uneasy not having a letter from you since your last announcing your sufferings with the tooth ache. Meyer says in his of yesterday that you are very unwell. It has rendered me very *triste*. I hope I shall have a letter to-morrow. The present I promised you in my last will not go off until about Wednesday. If your china arrives from Limoges, do not open it until my arrival, as I may send it to the United States, that is if we come here. Be assured, my dear Girl, that I shall make every effort to spend the rest of my life at home. It is cruel to be deprived of such a home as mine. I am likely to succeed in an object or two here of some importance. The success of either will put us at our ease. I long to be with you. You are so superior to all the women I meet with, so kind, so gentle, so much good sense and with all your virtues so few pretentions, that I am daily drawing comparisons to your advantage, and sighing for your society.

The Emperor was very gracious to-day with Mr. Barlow and deigned to say a few words to me. The morning was very fine and the court very brilliant. I go always with reluctance, and only because it pleases Barlow to have me with him, but when I get there, I am very much amused to see them all bowing, " bowing as it were by instinct." There are some of the most *outré* and grotesque figures you can imagine. There is scandal enough moving about too you may be assured, but this I must tell not write to you. I begin to think for the first time that our treaty will go down. They are certainly to work at it. It will do wonders for Barlow, perhaps make him President.

I wish my girls would write me. I will make William write a letter now before them. He gets on very fast and loves his mother dearly. He won't let a dinner pass without your health. He says it is very extraordinary that Mary has not acknowledged the receipt of his present. Do not let Tom forget me.

Adieu! God bless you! It is past midnight.

Your W.

To Miss Susan Palfrey Lee at Bordeaux

Paris, February 10, 1812

My dear daughter:

All Paris are mad, and William has caught the disorder. The ladies have hired him for the day a beautiful harlequin's dress, and have taken him out in the barouche to make the tour of the boulevards, where there are two files of carriages for a league or two, full of beaux and belles, who parade the whole day to see the *masques.*

The Boeuf Gras [31] has been circulating all day through the streets, dressed with flowers and colors, with his horns gilt, and a chair fastened on his back in which a youth sits. He is accompanied by about a hundred butchers in *masques* on horse back, and a troop of soldiers. In this way he is led from one public functionary, Minister, &c. to another, each of whom gives him money. William thinks it delightful, and was out of humor, because I would not let him follow this animal. But he is now more reconciled. For it appears the ox got loose this morning, and before they could secure him, killed one boy and hurt a great many persons.

I had not time to give your dear mother a description of the Emperor's ball and supper. The theatre of the Court was greatly enlarged, and turned into a ball room, the pit being floored over; and the whole was lighted with one hundred superb lustres, containing from fifty to one hundred lamps and wax candles each. In the center and first row of boxes all the persons invited to the ball and supper were placed. In the second and third boxes, all the respectable and fashionable citizens of Paris were admitted as spectators; but they had no communication with the society of the Court. The theatre was newly decorated for the occasion with elegant carpets and velvet seats throughout the part occupied by the Court, except in the center, which was left uncarpeted for the dancers.

The Empress and Queen of Holland opened the ball by a *contre-danse*. When this was finished, a quadrille was danced. Then a Shawl Dance by some of the *élégantes* of the Court, who equaled in grace and agility any of the opera dancers. A species of pantomime was then exhibited, where the Graces, Apollo, Mercury, Zephyrs, and the Hours, were represented with great taste. France and Italy were personified by the Queen of Naples and the Princess Pauline, who are very pretty women. They were dressed in the attributes of Minerva. On the shield of France was the bust of Napoleon; on that of Italy the bust of the King of Rome. The dresses were splendid, and the *tout ensemble* appeared more like magic or the tales of enchantment than anything I ever saw.

From the theatre we passed through the saloon of the Maré-chals to the saloon of Peace, and then to the saloon of the Throne, and from thence into the great supper room. All these apartments are immense, and are decorated and furnished with admirable art and magnificence.

February 12th. I had got thus far in my letter yesterday, when I was called off by Mr. Barlow to take a walk to see the shows, which were indeed very diverting. And last night I again accompanied him to the Emperor's ball, which, to distinguish it from the one given last week, was called a *Masque Ball*. I think it handsomer than the other. The decorations were much the same. The spectators invited were all in full dress; but the Court and its society were all masked. The ladies were all dressed in characters, and continued masked all night. The gentlemen were generally unmasked, but wore colored dominoes. So that the contrast between the masks of the Court and the full dresses was pleasing, and made a fine variety.

To a reflecting mind, the impression that all this luxury leaves is painful. I am so completely tired of such scenes that I do not know what would tempt me to go the same round that I have gone this winter. Those beautiful lines of Goldsmith were present to me all last evening. Speaking of pomp, the midnight masquerade, and all the freaks of wealth, he says:

> In these, ere triflers half their wish obtain,
> The toiling pleasure sickens into pain;
> And, e'en while fashion's brightest arts decoy,
> The heart distrusting asks, if this be joy? [32]

How often have I asked myself this question in Paris! How often have I compared the supreme felicity I enjoy with your dear affectionate mother and her girls (notwithstanding all their little whims and caprices), with that weariness and fretful *ennui*, which this gorgeous grandeur, this barren splendor creates! Trust me, my dear, there is nothing so near to heaven as domestic happiness; and it is the fate of your poor father, who has a greater portion of it at home than any man living, to be deprived of this felicity for months together. He hopes however it is only to make

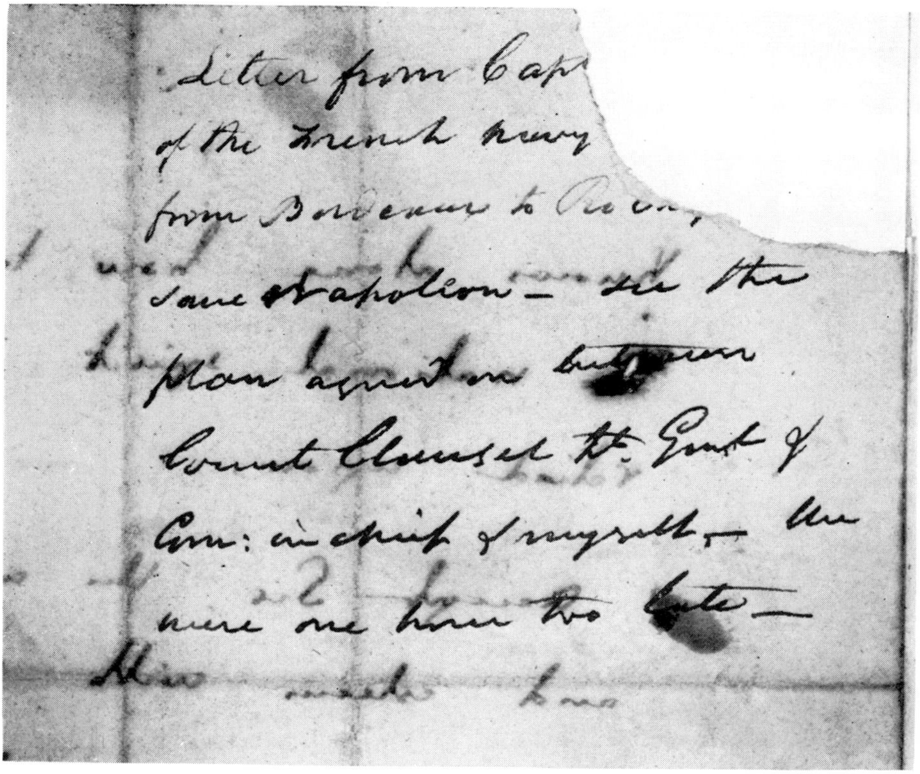

Letter from Capt
of the French Navy
from Bordeaux to Rochef
save Napoleon — see the
plan agreed on between
Count Clausel Lt. Genl &
Com: in chief & myself — we
were one hour too late —

"One hour too late" July 1815

Bordeaux feby 16. 1816

My dear William

I received your letter which, except
one or two words was well written — You must attend
to your hand writing for I find it is not so
fair and legible as formerly —

By this conveyance I send your
brush, and a pair of suspenders, which beg Mr Craig
to arrange for you. — If you want your saddle, and Mr
Craig will tell me how I can send it, you shall
have it. Be a good boy, attend to your studies, and try
to gain the esteem of all your friends. —

Your affectionate father

Wm Lee

Wm B Lee
Jo Jay —

Letter to his son   February 1816

him appreciate it the more. It is with this hope he lives and expects to realize soon by embracing you all.

Adieu! Kiss Mary for me.

Wm. Lee.

Tell Mamma not to worry about her teeth. She can buy very good ones here. I send her a book on the subject, which she must by all means read through. I have desired Martini to pay Mamma money. Let her give receipt, and keep an exact account.

To Mrs. Susan Palfrey Lee at Bordeaux

Paris, March 19, 1812

Parkman has written and said so much about you all, that anybody who has heard his encomiums will be disappointed. He paints you as a most divine woman, great dignity of character and great good sense. He says Mary looks mischievous and Susan — I won't tell you what he says of Susan, for fear it might make an impression, and though the young man has really more sense and discernment than I thought he had, yet I should not altogether like him for a son-in-law. So remember that, sweet wife. I am sorry to hear you have been deluged, and I am uneasy for fear Thomas may get the croup, which is so frequent in damp situations, and so dangerous to children of his age and habit. . . .

I pray, my dear Girl, that Susan may continue to write and cipher for some time, and she ought to continue her drawing. She must copy all my official letters and all my little political scraps together with some trifles I have been doing here, which Barlow flatters me by saying " They ought to be preserved as novels." All these will make a [here the letter is torn] form her style and give her a great many ideas. In addition to which she shall always copy my important letters. There is nothing which feeds and develops the mind like corresponding. Where I get my style from I do not know. It is certainly natural and I must suppose it good, for Barlow, who is so excellent a judge, adopted it in many instances. Some parts of the letter to E. he says is equal to anything in *Junius* [33] and the letter I shall send you to-morrow to read to John Lewis Brown [34] has gained me infinite credit.

William is well and close at work. He reads and writes English from nine until two. I mean to take great pains with his education; he has so fine an intellect. My love to my girls. Tell Mary — beseech Mary — not to be lazy.

Mrs. Barlow was presented to the Emperor with the pretty little Mrs. Sears [35] — a very interesting amiable woman. The Emperor was very gracious to them. Mrs. Sears's dress was a scarlet mantle embroidered all round with gold and the petticoat inlaid with stripes of gold. Her turban was put on with taste. They wore neither of them any diamonds except a rich cross worn by Mrs. Sears — the handsomest thing I ever saw.

> " And on her breast a sparkling cross she wore
> Which saints might kiss and infidels adore." [36]

God bless you, adorable wife. Absence increases my love for you.

W. L.

V

WAR AND INTRIGUE

1 8 1 2 – 1 8 1 6

With the War of 1812 in progress, William Lee was kept very busy at his post in Bordeaux. Although there are, of course, no family letters for the year and one half he spent there, he did write to James Monroe, the Secretary of State, telling of Napoleon's wars and of Joel Barlow's trip to Russia to induce Napoleon to conclude a treaty with the United States. When some time had passed with no news from Barlow, his family in Paris and the Lees in Bordeaux grew exceedingly anxious. Finally, on January 14, 1813, the news reached Paris that Mr. Barlow had died near Cracow without having met Napoleon. Mr. Barlow's secretary immediately wrote to William Lee and begged him — by Mrs. Barlow's wishes as well as his own — to start as soon as possible for Paris in order to assist Mrs. Barlow and to take charge of the late minister's affairs.

Lee accordingly left for Paris on January 23. But in the meantime, David Bailie Warden, United States consul at Paris, had declared himself consul-general and chargé d'affaires. Lee, objecting to this usurpation of power, wrote many letters of protest to the authorities in Washington. This correspondence led finally — but not before Warden had made a great deal of trouble for everyone — to the revocation of his commission as consul. Another American, Daniel Parker, whom Lee neither liked nor trusted, continued to offer advice to Barlow's widow and to his young nephew Thomas. Indeed, Lee wrote on the first of February, " what with Warden's intrigues, D[aniel] P[arker]'s manoeuvres, the distress of this family, and the state of our affairs, I am fairly sick and tired."

Feeling that he could make no progress, Lee left Paris and arrived at Bordeaux on March 12, 1813. His position as consul there had long been fraught with dangers and difficulties, and these were greatly magnified by the War of 1812. Lee spent most of his time during the war years providing for distressed seamen and disposing of the prizes taken by American privateers and brought into Bordeaux and other French ports. When the British occupied Bordeaux on March 12, 1814, Lee, who had gone to La Rochelle to attend to the sale of a prize, wrote to the State Department that he feared for the safety of his family in Bordeaux. The British, he said, hated him for his well-known sympathy with Napoleon and the French. These views were made abundantly clear in his book, *Les États-Unis et L'Angleterre*. The work was published at Bordeaux in December 1814, after Lee had been forced by officers of the French government to add a chapter endorsing the Bourbons.

The political situation in France grew even more turbid with Napoleon's return from Elba, the rallying of his armies, the retirement of Louis to Ghent, Napoleon's "One Hundred Days" in power, and his final defeat by the English at Waterloo. Long an admirer of the Corsican, Lee now entered actively into a plot to take him across the ocean for asylum in the United States, with the cooperation of Captain (later Admiral) Charles Baudin, who held a ship of the French navy in readiness. Baudin's letter, headed Bayadère off Blaye, July 16, 1815, telling Lee of the failure of the plan is of particular interest:

Sir,

All our efforts to save Napoleon from the humiliation of falling into the hands of the English are now to no purpose; for he has on the 15th instant, delivered up himself, with the whole of his attendants and baggage, to the English squadron off Rochefort.

Treachery and deception have opened the mouth of the Gironde to the enemy. Pilots were sent to them from Royan, the white flag was hoisted, they passed uninjured under our batteries and was received as friends, in the name of Louis XVIII; but no sooner were they on shore that they conducted themselves as foes. They broke the guns, burnt the carriages, and destroyed the forts which, *by a previous convention*, had spared them!

Poor France is now in a very miserable situation, torn by savage enemies and divided between two parties, one of which ascribes the whole of our evil to the folly of Bourbon, the other to the ambition of Buonaparte, and are equally both in the right and in the wrong at once. God knows alone how to extricate us! for national spirit is no more to be relied upon.

Accept Sir the assurance of gratitude and esteem with which I remain

Your most obedient, humble servant
Chas. Baudin

On the outside of the letter, Lee himself wrote a note explaining its subject — the plan to save Napoleon agreed on between Baudin, Count Clausel,[1] and himself — and added the rueful comment, "we were one hour too late."

With the conclusion of the War of 1812, following the Treaty of Ghent in December, 1814 (and the battle of New Orleans three months later), international tension abated somewhat. But Lee's own affairs were not going well, for under the second restoration of the Bourbons he was *persona non grata*. He had a disagreeable time in Bordeaux, suffering many indignities at the hands of the Anglo-Royalists. Having requested and received a leave of absence, he set sail on June 13, 1816, with his family and Mariette, their nurse, and arrived in New York on August 2. A month later he wrote to President Madison from Philadelphia resigning his post at Bordeaux.

Once back in his own country, Lee sought to find employment for some of the French artisans who had crossed to the United States with him. Among other projects, he proposed setting up factories for the manufacture of oilcloth and stocking knit and founding a college for the deaf and dumb. His personal career seemed uncertain until President Madison offered him the position of accountant in the War Department to succeed the late Colonel Tobias Lear, formerly military secretary to General Washington. Lee at first refused the post, but, being persuaded by Mrs. Lee of the importance of a certain and regular government salary, he wrote on November 17, 1816, to accept the position. With his appointment by the President on November 28, Lee settled himself and his family in Washington for a residence that was to last for thirteen years.

To President James Madison
Confidential

Paris, May 24, 1812

Sir:

In the letter I took the liberty of writing you in such haste by the *Hornet,* when stating the impression your private letter to Mr. Barlow had made on me, I hope I conveyed no other idea, when I mentioned having heard that letter read, than that Mr. Barlow had communicated confidentially its contents to me. You know, Sir, something of the intimacy that has subsisted between Mr. Barlow and myself for upwards of twenty years, and I therefore hope the careless mention of that letter will not have impressed your mind with any impropriety on his part, if of inconsiderateness on mine.

The satisfactory answer to Mr. Barlow's note on the subject

of the Prince Regent's [2] manifesto has not altered my opinion of the policy of this government towards us. I have lost all confidence in their professions, and suspect their measures. The decree of the 28th April 1811, announced for the first time in the 5th note to the Prince Regent's declaration published in the *Moniteur* of the 8th of this month, was no doubt drawn up for the occasion, and made to conform to the answer prepared to be given to Mr. Barlow. If this decree was really made on the 28th April 1811, why was it not communicated to Mr. [Jonathan] Russell [then chargé d'affaires in London] and promulgated in the usual way?

The very first article in the Napoleon code declares that the laws are not obligatory until the day of their promulgation. A decree of the 6th July 1810 defines the promulgation to consist in the insertion of the act in the *Bulletin des Lois*. All the prohibitory decrees have been inserted in this bulletin, but the decree of the 28th April is not to be found therein to this day. While the promulgation is withheld, captures may occur, unless the Minister of Marine should instruct the privateers to the contrary, which may not always be done, and the decisions of the Court of Prizes must depend in each case by the particular instructions from the Sovereign, which he may neglect to give.

It is thought here that if England rescinds her orders in council [3] and substitutes a blockade, the Emperor will not object to it until our vessels crowd into his ports, when a pretext will be found to repeat the second act of the San Sebastian business. [4] This in my opinion he will not do as long as he can continue the license system, which enables him to calculate with a certainty how to supply the wants of his treasury.

I have stated to Mr. Gallatin that he has issued forty-three licenses for exportation from the United States under American colors, and that eighty more are about to be issued for importations from the United States under French colors! These cargoes by calculation are to produce to the government about 300,000 francs each, so that if we allow only one half of them to come, 18,600,000 francs will be paid into the customs, and if those licenses for importations from England should, notwithstanding the present difficulties attending their execution, be carried into effect, the whole amount produced to the treasury will be about 32,000,000 francs.

If the war with Russia is attended with success, great resources are expected from that country, which if not realized, the commercial system will be, it is said, occasionally relaxed by licenses for a trade with England for financial purposes.

If, by the revocation of the orders in council, our vessels should throng to France, one serious question will arise between Great Britain and the United States. These Imperial licenses are all made out in the names of French houses and appear shipped as their property. Will Great Britain consider these cargoes as American property? In addition to this reason for wishing Congress to do away the use of licenses, they are sold to the American merchant for from $600 to $2000 each, a serious tax on our shipping interests.

The Emperor before his departure signed bills reimbursable at three, six, and nine years to the amount of 20,000,000 francs. He drew out all his funds in the bank and drained the *caisse d'amortissement* [sinking fund]. I mention this, Sir, to show his necessities, and to prove that so far from there being any well grounded hopes of indemnification for past depredations on our commerce, that new ones are to be feared as Europe becomes more exhausted. It is considered that the United States has drawn all their opulence from France. They are therefore to be held in reserve and plundered according to exigencies without remorse.

Copies of a proclamation are now handed about in the high circles said to be addressed to the army, in which the Emperor says he is once more in want of their services and hopes they will prove themselves worthy of him. " You have nothing," says he, " to fear from the Russians. They have good arms but no heads, and I promise to conduct you to St. Petersburg in July." In the same circles it is said that the Emperor Alexander has declared all Russians free who shall take up arms. This may possibly be true as respects his own serfs, but one can hardly think it so as respects others, unless the nobility should have considered their fate annexed to that of their Sovereign and supported the measure.

Be pleased, Sir, to present my respects to Mrs. Madison. I hope the things I sent her by the *Constitution* were approved of.

> With great attachment, I have the honor to be most sincerely Your obedient Servant Wm. Lee

To Secretary of State James Monroe

> *Bordeaux, January 20, 1813*

Sir:

I dispatch a boat to the mouth of the river in hopes of overtaking the schooner *Thebis*, Capt. Bolton, to convey to you the distressing intelligence of the death of Mr. Barlow. He was seized on the road from Wilna to Vienna with an inflammation of the lungs, and died on the 26th of December at Zarnowiec a small town a few leagues from Cracovie [Cracow]. Such was the rapidity of his disorder, that he had no time to make any arrangements for his public or private concerns.

Mr. Thomas Barlow, his [nephew and] secretary of legation, is too young to take charge of our affairs, which must therefore remain in the greatest disorder until the President names a minister or chargé d'affaires. Mr. Erving,[5] the most fit American on this continent to fill either place, is now at Naples.

I shall leave this to-morrow for Paris to assist Mrs. Barlow on this melancholy occasion. As all the commercial and most of the confidential correspondence relating to the negotiation passed through my hands, when acting as secretary of legation, I shall while there do all in my power for the public service.

> I am with great respect Your obedient Servant Wm. Lee.

To James Monroe

> *Bordeaux, March 4, 1814*

Sir:

In the state of confusion and despair which surrounds me, I have only time to say that the enemy is but a few leagues from us; that all the authorities except the Mayor have evacuated the city. I have dispatched all our vessels down the river, some loaded, some partly loaded and others in ballast, with all their crews, to profit of the first occasion to put to sea, having ordered them, should the enemy be off the mouth of the river, as is expected, to put themselves under the fort of Blaye and there remain as long as they can; and should they be obliged to abandon that fort, to run up the river Dordogne above Libourne, where if the enemy pursues them, they can burn their vessels, after landing their goods and sending them into the interior. In such an event, I shall march the crews, about 500 in number into the country and support them there at as little expense as possible. I shall be the last to abandon my post.

I forward you a file of the *Gazettes* by which you can trace the success of the Emperor. The funds continue to rise. Many reports of peace are circulating and of the defection of Austria, which however do not appear to me to merit much confidence, though I think myself the Emperor will succeed in driving his enemies out of France.

With great respect, I am
Sir
Your obedient servant
Wm. Lee.

To James Monroe

La Rochelle, March 20, 1814

Sir:

The departure of the schooner *Commodore Decatur*, from this port for the United States gives me an opportunity of stating to you some of the events which have passed in this vicinity.

The enemy entered Bordeaux on the 12th under the command of Marshal Beresford.[6] They have committed no excesses and the city enjoys a perfect tranquility or rather stupor. The mayor (letters from there say) received them at the gate, threw his decorations of the Legion of Honor, under his feet, and took that of St. Louis with a white sash. The Duke of Angoulême,[7] the representative of Louis XVIII, followed the enemy in, and was received with shouts of *Vive le Roi!* A Te Deum was sung at the Cathedral by order of the Archbishop who was present. At the theatre *Vive Henry IV* was played by the orchestra and *God Save the King* which the populace heard standing with their hats off.

A proclamation has been issued promising commerce, abolition of the conscription, reduction of taxes, and a quiet enjoyment of the purchasers of national estates. But it orders a contribution of four millions of francs and announces that the city is taken possession of by *George III.* A large proportion of the citizens mounted the White Cockade, and the white standard is floating on the public buildings. Thus has this city surrendered to British arms, without firing a gun, and to a force not exceeding five thousand men. If the Emperor succeeds in the north, it is thought they will pay dear for their conduct. If he does not succeed, a civil war will be the consequence. This state of things is distressing and the public mind is greatly agitated between doubts and fears. Paris is in alarm from the slow progress the Emperor is making. The finances are exhausted. Fifty-seven departments are in the power of the Allies, and nothing but a miracle can save the country from destruction.

Marshall Soult [8] has retired to Agen, pursued by Wellington, who it is said has been wounded in the last affair. The French dispute every inch of ground, but are overpowered by numbers. Soult, it was reported yesterday, had received a reinforcement of fifteen thousand men, and General Hullier, who commanded a handful of men at Bordeaux, is organizing an army of ten thousand men on this side [of] the Dordogne at Cavignac. If this is true things in Bordeaux may change. Rochefort is declared in a state of siege, and this place is in a state of defense, being strongly fortified. A brilliant victory on the part of the Emperor, or the reunion of Austria with him (which is still talked of), would change the state of affairs. The fears and apathy of the people are too apparent. The Vendée [9] is in movement and ruin stares all classes in the face.

I have the pleasure to inform you that all our vessels escaped from Bordeaux. Thus by my exertions at Bayonne and Bordeaux not a vessel of ours fell into the hands of the enemy, and a million and a half of dollars at least has been saved to our citizens.

I left my family at Bordeaux, before the enemy entered, for this place, to attend to the sales of the ship *Bachelor*, a prize to the letter of marque, the *Rattlesnake* of Philadelphia, Capt. Moffet. Mr. Crawford [10] will lay before you the difficulty our consuls experience from the agents of prizes, who oppose our administration thereof and plunder the owners, officers, and crews in the most lawless manner. The minister thus far has given me every support, except in the question of commissions or emoluments, which will regularly come before you, and I hope receive that consideration it merits and from the penury of the consuls we are entitled to. By the operation of the law, in prize cases, and the Imperial decree, we are judges, marshals, agents, administrators and liquidators. Surely then we are entitled to more than a marshal's commission, who besides has his fees of office, the clerks of the court their fees and the judge his salary; while we have none of these, nor our traveling expenses, which the marshal's commission of one per cent would not pay.

I am Sir, with great respect
Your devoted humble Servant
Wm. Lee

P. S. The distress I feel on account of my family, who are in Bordeaux, can easily be imagined by you, who are a husband and father. I shall go in quest of them as soon as my public business is closed here. If I am insulted, imprisoned, or my family ill treated, I hope my country will retaliate on the British Consuls and agents in the United States.

To Thomas Jefferson

Bordeaux, December 20, 1814.

Respected and very dear Sir:

I take the liberty to send you a copy of a work [his book, *Les Etats-unis et l'Angleterre*], which I have published here, with a view to enlighten the people of France on the motives of our war, and to help our good cause. I beg you will read it with indulgence, particularly that part relating to the Bourbons, which the authorities here insisted on my inserting before they would permit me to print it.

It is very imperfect for want of documents; but I trust you will pardon its faults, and consider it as a mite in support of an administration, which has contributed so much to the honor and glory of our dear country.

It would give me great pleasure to be useful to you here. I have not forgotten how much I owe to the confidence you honored me with and regret I have never had it in my power to prove to you my sincere gratitude. I have named a darling son after you, who is now seven years old and promises well.

> With highest respect and veneration, I am, my very dear Sir, your obliged and obedient Servant
>
> Wm. Lee

To James Monroe

Bordeaux, March 12, 1815

Sir:

It appears Napoleon has landed in France at Cannes, in the department of the Var at the head of a handful of men, as you will learn by the proclamation I have the honor to enclose.

Private accounts however state that one of his generals is at the head of this band, while he has landed in Italy, and is at the head of thirty thousand men at Milan, directing his march to Switzerland, from whence he is to proceed to Bavaria, Mayence and down the Rhine, where he will be joined by Prince Eugene.[11] Murat and Prince Charles of Austria, it is said, are at the head of powerful armies to second him, and it is reported that a number of generals and several regiments of the line have gone over to him. These are all reports, however, on which no reliance can be placed. The only thing we are certain of is the alarm this news has occasioned throughout the country. Parties are forming, and if the Bourbons do not arrest this evil in the bud, the most serious consequences may follow.

The army, it is feared, are in his favor, while the conduct of the old *Noblesse*, Clergy and Emigrants has disgusted the people, and divided their sentiments. The King is growing very popular, but the rest of the Royal family are not liked, except the Duchess of Angoulême,[12] who inspires a general interest in her favor, from her virtues and sufferings. The English, who are detested on the continent, are suspected of being at the bottom of this affair, with a view to create a civil war in France. Numerous arrestations have taken place at Paris, and some of the first officers of state are, it is said, in the plot. The heads of this department affect to treat this movement of Napoleon's with contempt, and to consider it as the last effort of madness; but I know the President of the Legislative Body has written a most alarming letter on the subject from Paris to his friends in this city.

The Count d'Artois,[13] who commands the National Guards, has left Paris for the south, and the Duke of Angoulême went off of a sudden from Bordeaux for Lyons in the midst of the *fêtes* that were preparing for him. You know France and Frenchmen, and can therefore judge of the effervescence of the public mind on such an occasion.

Italy is up in arms [and] Switzerland is divided in sentiment. The Spaniards are cutting one another's throats. The Netherlands are agitated. The Confederation of the Rhine are all discontended. Austria is suspected of favoring Napoleon. The Saxons are ready to join him. Poland is torn to pieces by faction. In short this continent never presented more discordant materials for ambition and talent to work upon, and what will be the result of this confusion no human mind can foresee. If Russia attempts to mold this heterogeneous mass, it is thought she will not be able to do much, as she is on the eve of a war with the Turks, and has lost much influence by the discovery of her ambitious views on Poland.

In the midst of all this confusion and alarm, the glorious news of the defeat of the British before New Orleans [14] has reached us, and sheds new luster on our Government, which is now admired and respected throughout Europe. Scarcely a political tract appears without holding our institutions and conduct up to view as a model for the rest of the world.

I send you by Mr. Wharton, four numbers of the *Censeur*, a periodical publication much in vogue in France, which I beg you will run over and present to the President. You will, I am persuaded, find it highly interesting.

With great respect and attachment,
I am, Sir, Your humble Servant
Wm Lee

Copy
To The Prefect of Bordeaux

Bordeaux, August 14, 1815

Sir:

I have the honor to enclose you two anonymous letters which I have lately received. I should have paid no attention to these letters, did they not correspond too much with the conduct of certain individuals, who, in passing my house in the evenings, take the liberty of crying, " *À bas les Américains! Vive les Anglais!* " I have been confined during the whole of the interreign to my bed and room by an unfortunate accident. I never when in health mix in society. I go neither to the Exchange, to the theatres or to the Circles. I live entirely in the bosom of my family, nor have I ever manifested opinions hostile to France or to the Bourbons. I have ever been known for my attachment to Frenchmen, and my animosity to the British Government during their inhuman and disgraceful war against my just and upright Government.

If, therefore, some weak, wicked and intriguing individuals of that nation, residing in this city, have taken it into their heads to prejudice certain persons against me and the nation I have the honor to represent, I hope that the authorities will not fail in case of need to accord me that protection I am entitled to, and to do justice to the sentiments which I have, in common with my Government and fellow citizens, entertained for the French nation, and the august family who are now called to reign over them. I have never failed to hoist the colors of the United States and to illuminate my house in honor of the Bourbons, when the authorities have set the example, and why the author of these anonymous letters should insist on my substituting any colors for those of my own nation can only be known to him.

An attempt has been made by a next door neighbor of mine to excite the people to pull down the arms of the United States over my door, and several of my countrymen have been insulted in the streets, and forced to take out of their hats the American cockade, on account of its having the eagle in the center. These things are painful to recite. They do not originate with the true French Royalist, who loves his King and country, but with a certain party of foreigners, who by their machinations do much injury to your righteous cause.

I have thought it my duty to state these things to you who direct the policies of this city, that if any mischief (for I am not without my fears) should arise from any attack on myself or my family, the causes may be known.

I have the honor to be
&c
Wm. Lee

Copy

Bordeaux, August 29, 1815

Monsieur Bergevin
Commissary of Marine
Sir:

A circumstance having taken place on board the American vessel called the *Midas*, which came to anchor in the harbor to-day, I hasten to explain it to you to prevent misrepresentation, and to assure you that there was no intention on the part of the mate of that vessel (the captain not being on board) to insult the people of Bordeaux, as has been wickedly suggested by a certain class of people, who appear to take delight to seize every opportunity to calumniate my fellow citizens, by attributing to them motives and opinions which they are strangers to.

In order to give you a just explanation of this affair, I beg leave to state that on all our forts at the entrance of our harbors in the United States there are two flag staves: the National one, and one for the service of the merchants. Every merchant, engaged in shipping, sends to this fort the private signal which he gives to all his vessels; that when one of his vessels appears in the offing and hoists this signal, it may be repeated by the fort, which is seen from the town, by which means the merchant is informed of the approach of his vessel, and is enabled frequently to save insurance, and to send a boat to his vessel to know if she wants any assistance.

It appears that the private signal of this schooner *Midas*, just arrived, is that of the tricolored French flag reversed. When dropping anchor, the mate as usual fired a gun, hoisted the flag of the United States, and his private signal, which latter the officers of the Custom House took to be an insult, and on their insisting that it should be pulled down, the mate immediately complied with their request. But unfortunately it flew long enough to give a pretext to a certain set of foreigners, who by their violence do great injury to the saint[ed] cause of your beloved Bourbons, and who take particular delight in calumniating my countrymen and government, the best friends of France, attached to your King and country from gratitude and principle, sentiments which the breasts of their violent enemies are strangers to.

If you recollect, a vessel called the *Milo*, belonging to the same owners, commanded by Capt. Johnston, arrived here a few months ago, and on hoisting the same signal, was hissed by the populace, and for which you arrested the Captain, who[m], had it not been for my interference and explanation, you would have thrown into prison, alleging that he had insulted his Majesty the Emperor and the French nation by hoisting the national colors reversed.

I hope, Sir, from the knowledge I have of your character, that you will have the goodness to make use of this explanation whenever you shall find it necessary, in order to prevent my countrymen suffering from having opinions and motives ascribed to them which they are strangers to.

I have the honor to be
&c
Wm. Lee

Note I sent a copy of this letter to the Prefect, the Governor and the Mayor, fearing the mob might attack the *Midas* in the evening. They took measures to prevent any further attack and thus the affair ended.

To James Madison

Bordeaux, September 6, 1815

Sir:

I have of late rec[eive]d a letter from C. Hughes, Junior [15] of Baltimore, who went home from this place in the *Transit* with the Treaty of Ghent, mentioning that a box had been sent to his house from that vessel, containing some French lamps, and the object of his letters is to inquire if I know to whom this box belongs.

As I had before learnt that the wine I sent you by that vessel had been drank on the passage, and been replaced by some purchased here by Mr. Hughes for his own use, I am apprehensive that the box in question may be the one containing the spiral lamp which I took the liberty to send you directed to the care of Mr. Boyd. If this should be the case, I hope, Sir, you will do me the honor to direct its being sent to you. I am fearful that the trifles I have occasionally sent to Mrs. Madison and the wine, cordials &c sent to you may not all have arrived safe.

I must beg leave to apologize for the manner in which this letter is written with my left hand, the right arm being disabled by dislocation & fracture.

I have the honor to be
with the highest veneration your devoted
humble servant
Wm. Lee

171

Copy
To Secretary of Legation Henry Jackson at Paris

Bordeaux, September 20, 1815

My dear Sir:

Your favor of the 15th has this moment reached me. An American vessel [the *Midas*] was boarded in the harbor by the guards and her private signal hauled down and torn to pieces, but no one was hurt on board. We were apprehensive that another attack would have been made in the night, but the affair passed off without further trouble. The enclosed copy of my letter to the authorities of this city will explain to you this affair which I presume has given rise to the reports circulating in Paris.

I have had a very unpleasant time here for several weeks past, but I am happy to find that party spirit is wearing down. An attempt was made to excite the mob to pull down the eagle placed over my door, but the people had more respect for the Government of the United States than their leaders. Another attempt was made to force me [to] haul down the American flag and hoist the white one. Finding I was not disposed to this, it was agreed to force me to hoist the white flag alongside of that of the United States. This I had no objection to; but the demand was made in such an outrageous manner, that I concluded to stand altogether on American ground and see it out. Mobs were then sent before my house to cry, " *à bas les Américains! Ces sont les gueux à pendre. Vive les Anglais!* "

This farce went on for several days, when I thought it necessary to appeal to the authorities, as you will see by the enclosed copy of my letter to the *préfet*. I called also on the Governor and found them both well disposed to protect me. All the Americans here were enraged against the Anglo-Royalists for their criminal conduct, and I am sure had any violence been committed towards me or any of my family, that our countrymen would have revenged us. There were then about six hundred here, and two of our vessels were well armed.

We have two Royal parties here: one composed of Frenchmen

who love their King and country, and who wish to conciliate all parties. The other an Anglo-Royal faction composed of the renegade English, Irish, Russian, Austrian, and Dutch houses, who all hate us, and are for assassinating all who do not go the same lengths as themselves. The enmity of this faction towards me arises chiefly from the publication of my book against their idol, the English Government. All these things will change. " Time obliterates the fiction of opinions and confirms the decisions of nature." [16]

Such has been the conduct of this mad faction towards our American citizens here, that, I am sorry to say, many of them have gone home with the worst impressions, taking the opinion of this domineering party as that of the whole French nation, and no doubt we shall see their opinions with great additions in our gazettes. At a ball given to the Bordelais by the Duchess of Angoulême, my name was erased from the list of foreign consuls, as not worthy to enter the palace; while a few days before during the short reign of Napoleon, I was severely censured for the article in my book in favor of the Bourbons.

Of the opinion and temper of the King I know nothing, but I know from the best authorities that the Duke and Duchess are not friendly towards the United States. Lally Tollendal [17] has, I am told, by his friends, great influence with Louis XVIII, and a more violent enemy our Government cannot have. He is a perfect Englishman. Mr. Lainé [18] is also bitter against us. When *préfet* here, after the famous 12th of March 1814 [when the English entered Bordeaux], I asked him to introduce me to the Duke, as he had introduced all the other consuls, his answer was, "I do not think it proper to present to the Prince the representative of a nation who dared to declare war against the brave English." I turned my back to this *chevalier*, taking leave with as little ceremony as my honest indignation suggested.

Our citizens have deserted the theatres, and we have all been obliged from repeated insults to take out of our hats the American cockades, which we had adopted here last year, with the addition of the eagle to distinguish ourselves from the English, who after the evacuation of the British troops, commanded by Lord

Dalhousie,[19] were daily attacked and ill treated in the streets and at the public places by the citizens.

Having said this much on the little *désagréments* we have experienced here, I beg leave to close by laying before you the affair of Mr. Sasportas, which the enclosed documents will make you thoroughly acquainted with.

Mr. Sasportas is a native of Charleston, South Carolina. His father, a Frenchman by birth, went to the United States an officer in the French army, and [in] 1778 became a citizen of the United States, fixing his residence in Carolina, where he resided for upwards of thirty years. Several years ago he returned to this country with his American wife and family to take possession of some property left him by a relation; and his son has since that period made several voyages to the United States in the trade between this and Carolina. He has always passed here as an American, and has uniformly refused to serve in the National Guards under Napoleon, and under Louis XVIII. His being by birth a Jew and an American is in fact one great cause of the difficulty I have had in obtaining justice for him. Since my letter to the Attorney General of the ——— I have not heard a word of this affair. His assassins promenade the streets exulting in their crime and threatening me with their vengeance for espousing his cause, while he remains in bed with his wounds. He is a young man of talents, of a high sense of honor, of an amiable disposition, and is much esteemed by all who know him. If you should think proper to address a note to the Minister of Justice through the Minister of Foreign Affairs, it will I am persuaded do much good, for if such crimes are to go unpunished, there will be no safety for any American in this deluded and distracted city.

I am &c

Wm. Lee

To James Monroe

Bordeaux, October 20, 1815

Sir:

I beg leave to transmit to you the enclosed copy of my communication to Mr. Jackson of the twentieth of last month. He had heard of the vexations our fellow citizens had experienced in this city after the return of *Louis the Desired*, and as exaggerated reports of the same may reach you through our gazettes, I have thought it correct to make you acquainted with the particulars.

Public opinion is again vibrating towards us, and the English are getting quite into discredit from the imperious conduct of Lord Wellington at Paris. He was lately hissed out of the opera from having favored the Allies in plundering the Museum, and having dared to take possession of the King's box at the opera in the absence of his Majesty. This you may rely on.

The conduct of the Allies at Paris has retrieved in some measure the character of Napoleon. His generosity and magnanimity towards them as a conqueror is openly spoken of, while their disgraceful conduct towards their ally, Louis XVIII, is reprobated.

The Museum, Garden of Plants, and Public Library have been stripped of all their most valuable articles.[20] The monuments of Paris have been degraded. The Champs Élysées has been much injured by the English cavalry quartered there, and in the Bois de Boulogne they have not left wood enough to make a toothpick of.

I enclose to amuse you a spirited caricature, the original of which was put into my hands just long enough to take a sketch of it. I also transmit you by this vessel the answer of both houses to the King's speech which I sent you some days ago.

> I have the honor to be
> with great respect
> Your humble Servant
> Wm Lee

To James Monroe

Bordeaux, October 20, 1815

Sir:

Some of the most valuable manufacturers of this country, Switzerland, and Germany are daily making applications at this office for passages to the United States. Through the generosity of our shipmasters I have been able to pass many, and had I the means, I could send over crowds of these people. This week I have sent out a valuable dyer, who has discovered the means of printing woolens and cottons with various indelible colors, by one and the same operation. Next week I shall embark a whole family, who carry with them ten or a dozen looms for manufacturing of cotton and woolen hose, pantaloons, undervests, and petticoats. This family will prove a valuable acquisition, particularly for the article of cotton hose, as their loom for this purpose is so simple that a child of twelve years of age may work it, whereas those German looms at present in use in the United States require a long apprenticeship to learn the use of them.

Viewing the present distracted state of Europe, and the growing taste for manufacturing in the United States, it is to be desired that our Government could devise some means of authorizing our consuls (without alarming the Governments of Europe) to defray the expenses of the passages of some of these manufacturers to America. I can always find ship room enough for them; it is only the expenses of their provisions which is wanting, as our Captains do not feel justified in subjecting their owners to the charge of from two to three hundred francs for their sustenance during the voyage.

There is another point which I think merits the attention of our legislature: I mean the patent laws. It would prove highly useful were we to introduce into our patent law, as the French have done in theirs, a clause allowing the same privileges and advantages to the *importers* of useful machines and discoveries, as if they were the inventors thereof. By this means many useful arts would be carried to the United States, from the importer being thus secured for at least the expenses he might be at for such introduction, with a probability of some benefit. There are but few men of sufficient patriotism to pay several hundred dollars for a machine, which, on its arrival in the United States, anyone may copy and use to the same advantage as himself.

I beg, Sir, that you will not imagine that I am a great partisan for the introduction of all sorts of manufactures into our country. A few useful ones which would in time of war lessen our dependence on foreign nations is all that we ought to wish for. A hardy, manly race of yeomanry are preferable to a puny population of manufacturers. Our great and leading branch of industry should be confined to the raising of the raw material and transporting it to the work shops of Europe, to be returned to us in a manufactured state. Thus the Royal subjects of this quarter of the globe would naturally become " hewers of wood and drawers of water " [21] for the *Freeds* of the United States.

Besides the advantages of vigor of mind and strength of body which our citizens would enjoy from directing their industry in these channels, our raw materials would in a short space of time become so abundant and cheap when compared to those of the colonies of the European nations, that when we found it necessary to prohibit any intercourse with them, their manufactures would suffer greatly by being either entirely deprived of our produce, and shut out of our markets, or forced to communicate with the one and receive the other through a third power. Thus it is evident that in the course of time *restrictive measures* would prove our best and greatest means of annoyance to an enemy. But I have forgotten that this subject is already so familiar to you that were I to reason a week on all its points and bearings I should produce nothing new to your mind.

> I have the honor to be
> with great respect
> Your very humble Servant
> Wm. Lee

To James Madison

Bordeaux, February 16, 1816

Sir:

I have been honored within these few days by your letter of the 21st December, to which I shall pay due attention.

The confidence you have reposed in me, by continuing me for so many years in this office, has been highly flattering, and has proved my greatest consolation in all the painful occurrences I have of late experienced in this city, which has now become peculiarly disagreeable, from the alarming state of party spirit, and the great influence of a predominant foreign faction, who, not content with heaping on me personally every species of insult, have of late extended them to many of my countrymen and to my family.

Although these attacks have united all my countrymen in support of my public and private character, as you will see by this handsome address to me, a copy of which I have sent to the Secretary of State, still I feel my position so very irksome that I have a great desire to return home.

As I am not richer than when I took this office, my surest means of existence in the United States will be the continuance of my commercial house here, and in seeking when there to increase its connections. The office of consul, the fees of which can never support a family, would contribute greatly to the success of that establishment. Shall I therefore venture to recommend my friend Mr. Strobel, lately named Consul for Nantes, for this appointment? Should he be thought eligible, the arrangements we have made together will contribute to the support of his numerous family and mine, through our joint commercial exertions; while the influence the office naturally gives would supply the want of a greater capital than we possess.

If this arrangement should not meet your approbation, will you permit me, Sir, to make a visit of a few months to the United States for the purpose of adjusting my accounts public and private, during which time the rancor of parties may subside? In such case, may I be permitted to name Mr. Strobel my agent here? He is a native American, well known and respected in this city, from a former residence in it of ten years. His having already been named to Antwerp and Nantes, from numerous recommendations lodged in the Department of State, sufficiently prove that he is in every way qualified to discharge the duties of this troublesome office.

I will not, however, hide from you, Sir, how agreeable it would be to me to be restored to my country. My family, at least the female part, have now become of an age to think of establishments, which never can be had to our minds in this ruined, distracted country. If I have hazarded too much in this respect, I beg leave to ask forgiveness.

> With the highest veneration
> and most sincere respect and attachment
> I have, Sir, the honor to remain
> Your obliged humble Servant
> Wm. Lee

To Thomas Jefferson

Bordeaux, May 11, 1816

Sir:

I beg leave to enclose you a letter from Mr. Garde, professor at the Deaf and Dumb College in this city. He is considered in this country as a phenomenon; for, though deaf and dumb, he is familiar with every branch of science and literature. He wrote the enclosed himself, and brought it to me to correct, but I thought it best to make no alteration in it.

There is no one, Sir, who can appreciate his merits better than you, or who can determine how far those rare talents he possesses can be made useful in our country. I can assure you he is considered far superior to the abbé Sicard,[22] who has acquired so much celebrity in Europe in instructing the deaf and dumb. Being but twenty-eight years of age, and of an excellent constitution, he has a large margin for improvement; and, if fixed in the United States, would in all probability live to see his proposed institution carried to the highest perfection it is susceptible of.

He will be highly flattered in receiving a line from you. I have led him to believe that, if our Government, to whom I have written on the subject, should not think proper to favor his project, he would find no difficulty in procuring individual patronage.

> I have the honor to be with high esteem
> and respect, Your very humble Servant,
> Wm. Lee

To Thomas Jefferson

New York, Oct. 25, 1816

Revered Sir:

The letter you did me the favor to write me,[23] under the date of the 24th of August, after having traveled from Boston to Philadelphia, and then back to Boston, found me here a few days since, which will account for my not having acknowledged the receipt of it before this. I have not forgotten, Sir, the great obligations I am under to you; and that I have lived so much in your memory as to have merited this amiable mark of your regard is particularly gratifying. Your opinion of my book is very flattering. It did some good, while it drew upon me all the venom of the party at which it was aimed, and has been the great cause of my abandoning a situation which was in every point of view agreeable to me.

I shall succeed here for Mr. Garde. We have had two meetings, composed of enlightened, patriotic men, who are digesting a plan for his establishment in this vicinity. I will not fail to make known to him your friendly sentiments.

Your observations on the state of things in Euorpe are very just. The best informed of all nations in that section of the globe are looking towards us with wishful eyes, particularly those of the French kingdom. The languishing state of our infant fabrics, and the prevalent opinion on our seaboard that we cannot become a manufacturing people for ages, may check in a degree, for a moment, their immigration; but, as that opinion will prove erroneous, we shall not fail to reap great advantages from the Gothic strides of legitimacy. That we cannot for many years become a manufacturing nation is certain; that we may not become so for a lapse of time is desirable; but that the germs of useful fabrics, producing from our raw materials articles of the first necessity, ought to be protected and encouraged will not be denied.

The seeds of the dissolution of European governments, which the commercial despotism of England has sown to her own and their inevitable destruction, have taken such a deep root of late, that the most superficial observer must see the consequences. The crimes of the legitimates [retributive measures of the legitimate monarchs] begin to operate in this country by the throngs of useful artisans who are daily arriving in our cities, in the same manner as the [revoking of the] Edict of Nantes operated in favor of England, who at that period was considered the bulwark of freedom.

The French people, at the commencement of their revolution, threw off a part of the scum of their population. Napoleon, when he became the champion of privileged orders, called them back; and the consequence has been that they, in revenge, have warred against the people, who in their turn are forced by a vindictive policy to seek an asylum in other countries. The result of this struggle is favorable to America.

The first immigration from France to this country was of the worst kind; so much so as to prejudice our people against that nation. The men who then came over brought from France and her colonies only their idleness, ignorance, debauchery, and decorations: " the engines of the woes of men," while those who now come among us bring the arts and sciences and manufactures. Even the Dukes, Counts, and Generals, who were created by Napoleon, are very different men from most of those of the ancient French school. They rose by their merit, not by hereditary right. Having received their education in the walks of private life, we find them here returning with ease to the source from which they came, and to the dignity of useful citizens.

Look, Sir, at the crowds of civilians: chemists, mineralogists, naturalists, engineers, geographers, mechanicians, engravers, sculptors, dyers, opticians, weavers of cloth and stocking knit, gold beaters, hatters, tanners, gun and locksmiths, cutlers, distillers, gilders in wood and metal, founders, glove makers, fringe makers, glass makers, gardeners, vignerons cultivators, lampists, surgeons and dentists, which have passed through Bordeaux only, and have been patronized by my small means, and I am sure you will find your wise predictions fully confirmed. I brought over with me in the same ship sixty-nine of this list, for all of whom I have found employment and happiness.

The received New England opinion, that European immigrants bring only their vices with them, cannot certainly be applied to the French. They are undoubtedly the *most virtuous* nation in Europe. The middling and lower classes are sober, amiable, and industrious. The vulgar vices of swearing, drinking, fighting, and petty larceny [are] unknown among them. There is a degree of civilization and good manners in their social intercourse, which is very pleasing, and, when contrasted with their neighbors, highly honorable to them. You must have observed an essential difference between them and all other immigrants. They never interfere improperly in affairs that do not concern them. If you will examine the conduct of the respectable French merchants, artists, and manufacturers settled in Baltimore, Philadelphia and New York, you will scarcely find an instance of their meddling in our party disputes, or making a bustle at an election. If they have acquired rights, they exercise them with a moderation and decency, which seems to say: " This people have received us among them. We must not abuse their indulgence." We ought to cherish such men, and I am happy to find public opinion is growing up in their favor.

I hope this winter to have it in my power to present my respects to you in person, and at the same time to present to you my friend and intimate, Marshal Grouchy.[24] I have taken the liberty to give to the celebrated *ex-législateur*, M. Pénières,[25] a letter of introduction to you. He is one of the best informed men of the age, and will let you more into the secrets of the late affairs in France than any other man can do. He is at the head of the company now forming, for an establishment on the Ohio, to be composed of Frenchmen altogether. My paper scarcely gives me room enough to say with how much veneration and respect I have, Sir, the honor to be

Your obliged humble Servant
Wm. Lee

To James Madison

New York, November 8, 1816

Sir:

By a confidential letter received yesterday from an obliging friend at Washington I learnt you had done me the honor to appoint me accountant to the War Department, and that the commission had been directed to me at Philadelphia, where I presume it still lies in the post office, as it has never come to hand, which I am a little surprised at, as several letters directed to me in that city have been sent to me since my return to this place.

This new mark of your favor has caused, Sir, at the same moment both pleasure and pain — pleasure from the proof it affords of the continuance of your confidence in me, which I know not how to thank you for, in a manner agreeable to you, and at the same time do justice to the sentiments of gratitude your kindness inspires me with — pain from my finding it impossible to accept the appointment owing to the nature and extent of my concerns in this city.

I had rather settle at Washington than any other town in the Union, but, such was my situation on arriving here, that it became necessary in order to save expense I should immediately determine on the spot for my residence, as the sixty manufacturers I brought out with me, fifteen of whom were at my charge, would, if unemployed, soon destroy my resources. After visiting Philadelphia, I concluded to form my establishment here. I have expended considerable sums in building up an oil cloth manufactory, a specimen of which I take the liberty to enclose, and I have erected another fabric at Manhattanville near this city composed of thirty stocking knit looms. Both branches are new in the United States, and if they meet with proper encouragement, will give employment to several hundreds of poor people, and create for me an influence in society here which will be agreeable.

Such is the present state of these fabrics that, were I to leave them under the direction of others, I should not only suffer myself, but my failure in the enterprise would really be a public loss. In addition to these objects, I am engaged in establishing a

Deaf and Dumb School, and I have formed a company composed of French immigrants for the purpose of making a settlement in the western country, and, as this project is in some forwardness, my residence in a sea port is necessary in order to assist the persons we expect from France on their way to Proscripolis.[26] Large subscriptions and a hundred subscribers have already been procured, and M. Pénières, the celebrated ex-legislator, experimental agriculturalist and naturalist, has been dispatched to the Ohio and Mississippi in search of a tract of land in a climate which will produce, among other things, the vine and olive. I am confident this interesting settlement will soon surpass that of Vevay and Harmony.

We shall draw over from France in the course of a year or two six or eight hundred Protestants. I am doing all this, Sir, by the dint of hard work. I never expect to be rich; I must therefore content myself with being useful. Were I to fix myself at Washington in the office in question I should do but little for myself and family and less for my country. From my long habits of business, I have acquired a facility and turn for almost all occupations except that of exclusively pouring over accounts. There I find no variety, nothing that can occupy the mind agreeably. It is of all others the most irksome task. It was once my *fort* and my experience therein carried me through great embarrassments, but at the same time gave me such a surfeit that I dread to encounter the like.

I never can forget, Sir, the great obligations I am under to you, and that you should have thought me worthy this new mark of your esteem, is to be one of the most flattering and agreeable circumstances that has ever occurred to me. That you should have named me, Sir, to the first vacancy because you thought I stood in need of it is so extremely kind that I know not how to give vent to my feelings on the subject. It is more than I had a right to expect, if not more than I deserve for my feeble services.

With the highest veneration,
I have the honor to be
Your obliged and devoted humble Servant
Wm. Lee

To James Madison

New York, November 17, 1816

Sir:

Some circumstances having occurred since I had the honor to write you on the subject of the appointment you had the goodness to offer me, I have thought it best after mature reflection to accept the same, if you have not, Sir, before this gets to hand, selected another person. It will take me from ten to fifteen days to close all my concerns here, and at the farthest, I can be in Washington in the first week in December. If it is not incompatible with the public service that the place should remain vacant for that time, and no choice should have been made, will you do me the honor to confirm me therein?

I will not occupy your important time in stating my reasons for this sudden change of mind. I will reserve my explanations thereon until I reach the seat of government. Mrs. Lee, a confidential friend, and the great difficulties I daily encounter here in maturing my establishments have brought about this determination and induced me to abandon my plans here to those who have more ample means of executing them.

I have the honor to be
with the highest veneration
Your obliged and humble Servant
Wm. Lee

VI

THE TREASURY DEPARTMENT, WASHINGTON

1817–1822

Some four months after his appointment to the War Department, William Lee was made second auditor of the Treasury on March 6, 1817, and this responsible post he filled with distinction for the next twelve years. During most of this time in the capital Lee lived in one of the so-called "Seven Buildings," a row of houses on Pennsylvania Avenue erected about 1794 (six of the row — numbers 1901 through 1911 Pennsylvania Avenue — are still in use). At one time or another a great many prominent people lived in these buildings, among them the James Madisons and Commodore and Mrs. Stephen Decatur. Lee himself mentions as his neighbors in the row of houses the Reverend William Hawley, rector of St. John's Church; James Kirke Paulding, secretary of the Board of Navy Commissioners; Postmaster Munroe and his family; Mrs. Constant Freeman, and several other leading citizens of Washington.

The first letters in this chapter form part of the correspondence between William Lee and Thomas Jefferson on Lee's proposal to establish in Washington a factory for a group of immigrant Swiss stocking weavers. Despite the interest and help extended by Jefferson, the venture failed, and Lee evidently lost money on it.

The other letters, limited to the years 1820–1822, deal primarily with the life of the family. Since the Lees (except for William Barlow, who was studying at West Point) were all together during the winter time, most of these letters were written in the summer, particularly the summer of 1822. During that time Susan and Mary Lee went with their mother, whose health had been seriously failing, to Schooley's Mountain, New Jersey. Lee's letters were obviously written to cheer his anxious family. Mrs. Lee died (probably of a bowel complaint) on July 22, 1822, before her devoted husband, who had endured so many enforced separations from her during her lifetime, could reach her side. She was buried in the cemetery at Schooley's Mountain.

To Thomas Jefferson at Monticello

Washington, June 16, 1817

Respected Sir:

The little Swiss colony of stocking weavers to which the letter you honored me with refers [1] is composed of three heads of families, their children, and four workmen with twenty four choice looms, many of which are after the English model, with the newest French improvements. I am half concerned in this factory, the whole of which has cost me, in the purchase of the looms and the passage & sustenance of the workmen, a considerable sum.

It would give me great pleasure to meet your wishes, but having but four good workmen and the looms being assorted for the weaving of hose, pantaloons, petticoats, drawers etc., I cannot separate them at present without injuring the establishment; the four workmen I have being necessary to instruct the apprentices I am about taking. An intelligent lad of twelve or fourteen years of age becomes a good weaver in the course of a few months, and as I have with me mechanics to make as many looms as I want, my plan is to take twenty apprentices, and while they are learning the art of weaving, to make a number of looms for sale, and on selling them, allow my apprentices to engage with the purchasers. By this means I shall distribute them about the country and do much good. A loom or two in a country town would employ the yarn spun by the women and supply the neighborhood with stockings and coarse pantaloons, drawers, under vests etc.

Charlottesville shall be the first town I shall supply, and if you know of a smart boy or two in that place that would like to learn the trade, I will thank you to send them to me, and next year they shall return to their own village good workmen.

One loom can turn off a pair of pantaloons in a day without the help of a tailor, except for the button holes and running up the seams halfway up the legs, which can be done by a woman.

We can board our apprentices here at $2 per week, and our head workman finds all sorts of yarn here better than in Europe

— the woolen in particular he says is far superior. I have been very anxious about this factory, but I now think our success will be complete; our work is so much superior to that imported. One pair of our cotton, silk, or worsted stockings will wear as long as four pairs of those imported from England.

> I am Sir with great respect &
> attachment your obliged & obedient
> Wm Lee

To Thomas Jefferson at Monticello.

Washington, January 12, 1818

Respected Sir: . . .

This is an unlucky experiment for me in every way. The persons who induced me to bring these weavers here, by engaging to form a company to set them at work, have failed to fulfill their promises. and a second company in Georgetown have also declined doing anything. I have therefore discharged all the workmen except Keller, and his three countrymen, who bring me in debt a trifle every quarter.

The word *fabric* is sufficient to destroy the monied credit of anyone. I preach patience, but these poor devils think the land of promise I held up to their view is the land of starvation for all manufacturers.

> I have the honor to be
> with the highest veneration
> Your humble Servant
> Wm. Lee

To William Barlow Lee, St. John's College, Annapolis, Maryland

Washington, March 25, 1820

My dear William:

You have not mentioned the receipt of my last letter enclosing you two dollars, though I requested you to do it. If your mother does not hear from you every week, she begins to be uneasy.

Poor Commodore Decatur is no more.[2] He fell in a duel with Commodore Barron, a very worthy amiable man. Yesterday the Commodore was buried in Mr. Barlow's tomb. The concourse of people was immense. He is much regretted, and the other is much pitied, being a very excellent officer; but a most unfortunate one, with a wife and eleven children. The city is quite gloomy. All parties are suspended. Mrs. Decatur is, as you may suppose, very wretched.

We are all well, and hope soon to have a letter from you.

Your affectionate father
Wm. Lee

To William Barlow Lee at West Point

Washington, June 12, 1821

My dear William:

I have just received your second letter and two from Dr. Cutbush,[3] whose kindness I hope you will remember. He is a very worthy man and an excellent scholar. I spent Sunday with your mother and sisters. They are well and delightfully situated at the house where you joined Col. Thomas at breakfast, three miles beyond Bladensburg.

My library was sold for only $400, and bought in by Gen'l Parker [4] for me. Everything goes on now as I could wish. Tom is well. He and Mariette went with me to see your mother. About the time you depart for Boston I shall send you some letters for your relatives and friends, all of whom you must continue to see.

The Goldsborough family have been distressed beyond all measure from a report, which proved not true, that Louis [5] had been shot in a duel. His poor mother was in the deepest distress, and, had they not found out it was a wicked report, she would have died. Remember that it is a received opinion of old military men that the greatest cowards are the greatest duelists; and that a man never gains honor nor credit, successful or not, in a private contest. Men of cultivated minds, and elegant manners avoid quarrels. They never offend, and avoid those who are given to disputes from ignorance and clownish manners.

Dueling is a mark of the want of civilization. The French, who are the most polished nation in Europe, and whose manners and literature have done more towards civilizing Europe than any other nation, fight but few duels, and those like gentlemen with the small sword. The rude English and Irish introduced the *brutal* practice of pistols, and our *Cossacks* of the south and west have imitated them.

I hope you will get in the same house with your friend Robert Wirt,[6] who you know is a great favorite of ours.

Tout à vous
Wm. Lee

To William Barlow Lee at West Point

Washington, September 14, 1821

My dear William:

Your mother was much pleased with your letter, and I was full as well so, by finding you had determined to attend to your French grammar. And, should you be so fortunate as to get the situation of assistant professor of the French language, I shall be content; for it will necessarily follow that you will finally get a taste for French literature, which, as Mr. [John Quincy] Adams observes (who is unquestionably the first scholar in our country), is superior to that of any other nation. This you will also find to be their reputation in the exact sciences. There are no such mathematicians in the world.

I hope you will find time to attend to drawing. You will not repent of it. It is [so] useful (I mean as relates to maps, plans, architecture, views of the country, mathematical instruments, and hydraulics) that, old as I am, I have sometimes thought of attending to it; which I do believe I should have done had I been in easy circumstances. To be a distinguished painter requires a peculiar talent, and years of study; but more necessary drawing, as relates to civil engineering, is easily acquired, and through life will afford you rational enjoyment.

Upon the score of handwriting I shall never cease tormenting you, until I find you sound in that particular. Your style is excellent, and will probably always be so, because it is natural; but it is almost unintelligible from the cramped formation of your letters. Make it a standing rule to form every letter perfectly, and in a very short time you will succeed in writing a good hand.

It has been an uncommon sickly season here. All parts of the city, except ours, has suffered. One of the Miss Thompsons has been at death's door. Her father [7] is also sick, owing to having water in their cellar. Mr. [William Harris] Crawford is dangerously ill. Justice Varnum is dead. In short about eight hundred persons are down with bilious fever. If people will eat, while the thermometer ranges from 80 to 96, smoked hams and fish and rancid bacon boiled with fat cabbage, they must expect to become bilious; particularly if they drink whiskey or any ardent spirits. We stick to soups, fresh meat, and claret wine, and water.

I hope you have thrown aside cigars and tobacco, the use of which is not only injurious but dirty and vulgar. They destroy the breath and debilitate the stomach. I had as lief have a man go to stool in my parlor as to smoke in it. We often hear people seriously deny the destructive influence of tobacco, because they can produce a few rare instances of persons who have lived to an old age under the regular use of it; but a similar argument might be advanced to prove that the plague is innocent, because a few individuals have escaped its contagion.

Colonel Tayloe,[8] *our great spendthrift,* is it is thought on his last legs at the springs.

Your affectionate father
Wm. Lee

To Mary Elizabeth Lee at Schooley's Mountain, N. J.

Washington, Sunday, June 9, 1822

My dear Mary:

No letter from you yesterday. Of course I am to conclude you were on your way to Trenton, from whence I expect a letter to-day,[9] which I am impatiently waiting for, being very anxious about Susan only. For, from what I have read yesterday at the French book store in a work called, "L'Ami des Femmes," I find such complaints as your mother has been afflicted with, when they fall on the bowels, terminate favorably.

Shall I send you the papers? There is one (and I may send more) which puffs Miss Onis. *À propos,* Tom Munroe [10] has seen her, and has been dancing attendance on her and on the Russian Ambassador's lady in London. He has been to the Italian opera with them. Only think! the opera! And has sent his father the piece in Italian with an English translation, with which the old gentleman is delighted, and was so engaged last evening in spelling it out that he bored me excessively with it, and Tom's description of London, which he does not appear to be much pleased with. I hope, when my Tom goes, he will give me an account of some manufacture, new invention, or discovery in the sciences.

The city is full of parsons, "a regiment of black coats," as Red Jacket [11] calls them. St. John's has been open every day and every evening; and such feasting and carousing among the faithful was never before seen here. Hawley's house is the rendezvous, and mother Calhoun the *major domo.* . . . She first comes with her carriage full of reverends, and then returns with it stuffed with eatables. She was over at Mr. Martin's yesterday cheapening brandy and scolding him for selling such deleterious stuff as whiskey.

In the midst of their dinner yesterday, the Captain's chimney caught fire, and the roof followed suit to really an alarming degree, when such a scene took place as Hogarth only could do justice to. There were fat priests and lean priests; scrub headed and bald headed, all running and bawling to and fro, with meager Mrs. Lear, oily Mrs. Ramsay, fidgety Mrs. Calhoun, and sweet Mrs. Hawley piping and swarming like blackbirds in a swamp.[12] The fire out and the danger over, they returned to their repast with additional vigor; for fear, you know, affects the bowels, and when past leaves an appetite.

To-day the Unitarian Church [13] is to be consecrated, and no doubt at St. John's these infidels will be lashed by the only true believers. It seems the establishment of the Unitarian seat here has given great alarm to the Episcopalians; and that the assemblage of this convention, synod, or whatever it is called, has for its object the building and endowing of a Theological College in or near this city for the purpose of preparing Episcopalian youth for the work of the true calling. . . .

To-morrow, James Baker told me, they are all to dine with Mr. Canning,[14] when I am sure the corkscrew will be in greater demand than the prayer book. But I must stop, lest your mother should call me a pupil of Barlow's. And now for a most extraordinary thing which happened yesterday to myself. After Hawley's farce was over, I returned to my mutton cutlet, in the little back room, which I sat quietly picking with the window open, when casting my eyes on the pavement, I beheld a *huge black snake* staring me in the face. My blood ran cold to my toes. I flew hollering for Ann and Mark, and seized the scrubbing brush which stood in the passage, and broke its back the first stroke. Mark threw one of the boxes of flowers on its head, and thus we subdued it. When dead I measured it, and found it four feet, ten inches long, and as large around as your wrist. Where the devil the creature came from we cannot imagine. The stable door had been shut the whole day, and we think he must have been brought to Smith's or Johnson's stable in a load of hay, the morning before, and had found his way into the yard through the hole in the wall leading into Mrs. Coolidge's. All the neighborhood came to see him. If you had all been at table, what a scene I should have had. I must make a good story of it, and send it to G. at Berlin and to Tucker at Brussels.

I left off here to go to dinner, and, before I finished my solitary meal, I got your letter of the seventh from Trenton, in which there is not a word of my dear Susan, and nothing pleasing of your mother, who I beg and pray will stick to those rhubarb pills, notwithstanding they may fatigue her. When you get at your journey's end, or before if you are detained on the road, write me, for you have no idea with what impatience I look for the post.

William will be within one day's ride of you, if I can judge by the map. But for God's sake do not entice him from his studies. I fear from his letter to Emily that he expects to retrograde another year. Upon the whole I will send you the papers. They will serve to amuse you. I am sorry you were not fitted out well (supposing you would do that in Boston) before you left Philadelphia, as you may see much company. Is there no getting anything to you from Philadelphia?

Mr. Erving has arrived at New York from Paris. Baldwin is still sick at Bomford's. Our neighbor Brengle is dead, and Col. Towson is to take his house. The good Vice-President has gained his suit against the United States — $136,000! [15] James Lloyd is coming, it is said, Senator from Boston in the room of Otis, resigned. All were well at Valparaiso on board the Franklin. De Neuville is still here. It is said he is troubled for money. What a fool, if this is the case, to live so expensively! hence no doubt the sale of furniture. . . .

I think in conscience this is enough for one mail. I have heard no scandal, or you should have had it. I hope Tom will pick up some books. This is a serious loss of time to him at a moment when he begins to be lazy.

W. Lee

To Mrs. Lee, Susan, and Mary at Schooley's Mountain

Washington, June 14, 1822

My dear wife and children:

I have just got a letter from the amiable Mr. Wilson announcing the return of the carriage, after your safe arrival, and stating that you had changed your lodgings for the better. I shall now look anxiously for a letter, and for some cheering things of Mamma and Susan's health.

Goody Freeman,[16] it seems saw you into the steam boat: at least so she said to me. I have seen nothing of them and will not. Mark and John are off. I keep Ann to take care of the house, not choosing to lose so good a creature. She washes and irons for me. I breakfast at home, and dine at Mrs. Coolidge's, to save trouble and expense. Ann brushes my coat, and cleans my boots very well.

I am pestered to death with inquiries about you, though I visit nowhere except the President's, who are all still here. Mrs. Decatur has come out quite charming, handsome (they say), and brilliant. Therefore some ill-natured things are said by the gossips. Poor Baldwin is very ill with an abscess in his side, and very much reduced. He is really sick both in mind and body; which I regret, as he is the best of the whole Barlow connection: a man of the true worth and talents, though somewhat of a raw material.

What a crash! A long, slab-sided Kentuckian, in passing through our office passage, has hit the large lamp, which made a tremendous noise in its fall on the brick floor, after covering him with fish oil. The clerks have all deserted their desks, except the Duke of Vinegar,[17] who[m] nothing stirs when once his breast touches it.

I expect Susan, when she gets well, will let me see her talent in a description of mountain scenery; but those hills are pigmies when compared with the Pyrenees, which she was too young to enjoy or remember. How is Mariette? The sight of a Bonaparte[18] is enough of itself to cure your mother, and make her amiable chambermaid dance in ecstasy. You have a friend now to draw upon to amuse me, and I expect Mister Tom will tell me all about the manufacturing of iron. Gen'l Dickerson[19] must be near you, if I recollect right. At least you are in his district, if not in his county. I have nothing new, except that I am exceptionally annoyed by the honeymoon of Mr. and Mrs. Beall, and as much amused with the never-ending toilette of Mrs. Hill.[20]

God bless you.
W. Lee.

To Mary E. Lee, at Schooley's Mountain

Washington, Sunday, June 16, 1822

I find, my dear Mary, that the post leaves Schooley's Mount but once a week. But then I trust you can at times find persons going to Philadelphia and Trenton, who will take a letter for you, and throw it into the post office at either place, for to be a whole week without hearing from you will be insupportable. Look out, therefore I pray you, for such occasions, that I may be kept constantly, if not daily, informed of Mamma's and Susan's health. Neither must expect to get well all at once. The effect of change of air is not so rapid as that of a dose of physic. It is slow and sure; and the very circumstance of its influence on the system being unfavorable at first is among the proofs that it will eventually be beneficial. Persevere, therefore, in giving the mountain atmosphere a fair trial, and insist on your mother's taking freely and regularly of the waters. And let Susan take Epsom salts and working things. If Dr. Mongez is with the Count [Joseph Bonaparte], your mother must consult him. He has very justly a high reputation in medicine, and, as he sometimes travels with Joseph, I hope he is now in his suite. Tell me all about the Countess and her father.

We have nothing new here, not even any fruit fit for hogs to eat; and the people are all much distressed, for an additional scarcity of money which pervades all classes. In Boston too it is the same. Tell your mother that these such times were never known. The papers are full of it, and the numerous failures it has occasioned in that town, among which I expect to hear of our friend Rice.

We have had disgraceful work here about Mayor.[21] Weightman did not succeed, which enraged him and his friends so much that they disputed the legality of the votes. This war raged for a whole week, when Capt. Carbery of our ward, a poor devil (though one [of] the people), succeeded in getting installed. In consequence of his success, the mob who supported him paraded the streets all night with music as abominable as their vulgar propensities. Before Weightman's house they played "The Rogues March," and broke his, John Law's, and Seaton's, windows. The fact is that both candidates are poor, ignorant men.

> "Strange all this difference should be
> 'Twixt Tweedledum and Tweedledee." [22]

Our swarm of parsons have all disappeared, like a flock of swallows at the approach of autumn, and left poor Mrs. Hawley in the quiet enjoyment of her house. Mrs. Munroe is getting uneasy about Emily for what cause I do not know. Her house is filled every evening with Hay, Bibby, the Randalls,[23] and other clerks: a very edifying society for young ladies, where, so far from genius and good sense or any germ of intellect, not even good manners is to be found.

We have had the most severe thunder gust I ever knew; and the rain fell in such torrents that it tore up everything by the roots. It was ankle deep in our yard, and back and front area. Old Salomon[24] sat with me through the whole of it, exclaiming " Dat is very fine; c'est magnifique." I was thinking of my wife and children, and once his wife crossed my brain, which is more than she does his. How different we are composed! Some men can bury all in a whiff of tobacco, " content to vegetate and rot," while others, alive to everything, are probed to the quick by every adverse wind.

I expect in your next a bulletin of your mother's and Susan's health: how they rest, how and what they eat, their symptoms, favorable or unfavorable, the exercise they take, and how they pass every hour of the twenty-four. I can then judge for myself of their progress, and be fixed as to the time I am to join them. . . .

I was going into [the] Munroe's last evening, when I discovered the pastry cook auditor and his wife, and turned back happy in the escape. Mons. and Mde. de Neuville saw me on the pavement yesterday, and stopped their barouche to inquire after all of you. C'est bien aimable. Vive les Français! for good manners, soit imperialists, royalists, ou republicans. Two Englishmen have opened beer shops between this and the President's house, and have erected, on gallows as wide as the front path, swinging signs high in air. These people are so accustomed in their own country to see the gallows, that they think it is a mark of civilization to have it always in view, that their children may have the fear of the law, if not the fear of God, continually present to them.

I hope you will be able to decipher this. For, having left my knife at the office, my pen is so bad, that I can hardly use it. Besides which, I have written it *à la hâte* to create for myself a few happy moments. Not that I would have you think it is when writing to you only that I think of you all. You are ever present to me, and hope cheers me that I shall see you all restored to health.

I am fully convinced now that I can beat Helen Davis[25] at thinning out a letter; and, not like the lady who bet she could write a letter without a postscript (and, who actually wrote one, and then opened it to say, " N. B. You see I have won the bet."), add anything by way of annotation. To fill up my time, I am writing a little biographical sketch of poor Desnouettes,[26] which I shall publish in the *Intelligencer* and send to you.

Here are my letters and papers arrived and none from you. I did not much expect one, and yet I feel disappointed. I fear I shall not get one until next Saturday, if Wednesday is your post day at the Mount. Well I must put up with it. I shall send you some money through Mr. Wilson in a day or two, having made an arrangement therefor in anticipation of my salary.

God bless you all.
W. Lee

To Mary E. Lee at Schooley's Mountain

Washington, Sunday, June 23, 1822

Your two last letters, my dear Mary, were dated the 17th, five days ago. So that you must be in error, when you say the post leaves Schooley's Mount three times a week. Here are some newspapers to curl your hair with.

We have nothing new. I had a hint from the sweet little Miss McKnight [Commodore Decatur's niece] that Mrs. Decatur wondered I had not been to see her. Wonders never cease! Miss de Wolf picked up a husband in New York the other day, who chose her no doubt as you

> " Would old plate
> Not for the fashion but the weight."

The weather is getting excessively warm, but the city continues uncommonly healthy: at least so the doctors say; and I suppose it is true, for the two apothecaries I am acquainted with complain of the dullness of the times.

Mr. de Neuville is at last preparing to go, having concluded a commercial treaty. Bon voyage! The Consul General Baker lies dangerously ill. The Baron sputters more than ever. Gen'l Van Ness [27] has fallen from his horse in a fit, but luckily fell upon his head, which brought him to. Thus a new cure has been found for epilepsy: viz. a severe stroke on the head. No doubt it will be reported in the *Medical Journal* among the new discoveries of extraordinary cases.

I am sorry Thomas is losing so much time. Is there no parson or no school near you, where he could go and study his Latin and Greek? He will get into such habits of idleness, that it will be impossible to correct them. His is a dangerous age. I hope your next will relieve me in my anxiety for Susan. As your mother improves, she must be careful of her diet, be abstemious, and avoid all heating and high seasoned things. She must stick to the water.

God bless you all.
W. L.

To Mary E. Lee at Schooley's Mountain

Washington, Friday, June 28, 1822

On examining the back of your letter of the 24th, I find it is marked "Post Office, Schooley's Mount." Therefore it came through the regular mail via Trenton, which leads me to suppose that the mail leaves Schooley's Mount every Monday and perhaps every Thursday — say twice a week. Look into this fact, and if so do not miss a post.

Dr. Huntt [28] has just returned from a visit to his Dulcinea, whose father, it seems, objects to the match, giving [as] a reason that he has no idea of his daughter marrying a man as old as himself. The Dr. you know has been 33 years old ever since we have lived in this delightful place, this seat of science, the Muses, and of pleasure.

199

Report says that Mr. Canning is agoing to marry Mrs. Decatur. It is all stuff, though he visits there frequently. She is ten years older than he is, though she has had *address* enough to get him there, her riches however artfully won, will not entrap or hold him. He knows too well that family influence in England is everything, and that, were he to desert that sure way to honors in Britain by marrying an American, that his fate would be like his predecessor, Erskine,[29] who in doing so fell into disgrace with his Government, and his father, the Lord High Chancellor.

All de Neuville's family go off on Monday next. Mr. H. and Miss C. T. are shedding salt tears the whole day to the great amusement of the gossips of the first ward, and it is said that the tall attaché, Monsieur Count what d'ye call him, is to be married immediately to the other Miss T. She, it is said, is very sick, which is more than probable, as they are no longer seen at eve sauntering over the green fields of Washington sipping the sweets of white clover. What silly, romantic, consummate fools, American women are, and how much these foreigners must laugh at them. Your mother, I am sure, will think with me.

That estimable worthy man, Mr. Wirt,[30] is in the deepest affliction. His vicious son has attempted to commit suicide by taking two ounces of laudanum. His poor mother has gone to him to New York. What a wretch! Is there any punishment too severe for him? He knows the ill state of his excellent father's health, of the helpless state [in which] his family would be, was that indulgent father to die, and leave ten children, and, instead of studying with his father, taking up his profession under his auspices that he might be a stay to his family, he launches out into every species of wickedness, and then attempts to put an end to his existence. Hanging is too good for such a villain. He ought to be quartered in the public market place, as an example to all parricides, for he is no better, instead he is worse. For a parricide murders his parent at once, while he kills him by inches by the wounds he is every day inflicting through the sorrows he is heaping on his venerable head. In escaping from his society what a happy circumstance for William. Mrs. Munroe said last evening, " What a prudent boy Wm. Lee is! He knew well Robert's character, but we never could draw anything out of him respecting him. The most he ever said was, ' I fear he will not fulfill the expectations of his father.' "

Captain Hook has just returned from West Point. He says William is in fine health and is much beloved in the Academy; that his examination was thought very favorable to him, considering he had been absent six months. We would all be happy now, Mary, were it not for Susan. Can it be possible she will continue to harbor such dire ideas and thus retard your mother's recovery and throw us all into the depths of misery? Will she have no consideration, no commiseration for any of us? Can you not convince her that the happiness of the whole family now depends on her, and paint to her in gloomy tones the inevitable heart-rending scenes we are to go through, if she persists in indulging her gloomy caste of mind. I will not, cannot, dwell on this dreadful subject. The idea is so painful that it ought to be chased from the mind the moment it enters. For, when once it takes hold, adieu to all hopes of peace and comfort in this world.

God bless you all
W. L.

To Mary E. Lee at Schooley's Mountain

Washington, Saturday, June 29, 1822

No letters yesterday or to-day. This is very painful, my dear Mary, but I suppose I must put up with it. . . .

Enclosed is another newspaper — dull enough you will say. The whole city are occupied about R. W[irt]. The friends of the family now say he took laudanum to relieve him from violent pains, but took accidentally too much. Happy will it be for his future reputation if they can make it appear so, but happier still for his family if the fellow dies.

Mr. and Mrs. Middleton [31] have returned to Mosquito Hall in Bog Mire. The father-in-law has recovered but he looks like death and rates. Colonel Tayloe it is said cannot live over to-morrow. I went to see them a few days ago, and was not a little surprised to find them so tranquil. They all want feeling and as to the mother she is a sordid creature, a penurious hag. I asked her if the Colonel did not intend to go to the north. She said, " No." They have traveled so much and *found it so expensive* that he had concluded to remain at home.

Mr. Mark has left me. He had too many visitors in my absence, though I believe him honest. Ann remains yet, but I intend to engage her master to take her home; she will get spoiled having nothing to do. Little John has run away from his mother and she cannot find him anywhere. I like that poor little fellow.

The house is very dull. There is nothing to amuse me. Last evening Mr. Wood was fiddling to Capt. Hook and singing " All's well," over and over again. Then Hook would begin with his flageolet. Mrs. Hill was screaming, " Lullaby, lullaby," to her piano. Then at Mrs. Handy's someone was murdering " The Soldier's Bride," and Emily and Bibby were playing and singing God knows what, as the noise only vibrates on my ears, while at the same time I was assailed by a negro's jew's-harp and the noise occasioned by a group shuffling to the time, the howling of dogs and squalling of cats. Yelling of savages in the wilderness would be as much if not more entertaining. I went to bed doubtless comparing myself to Hogarth's enraged musician, and this morning at break of day, I was rambling over my favorite hills " looking through nature up to nature's God." [32] This is true felicity.

[No ending.]

To Mary E. Lee at Schooley's Mountain

Washington, July 1822

My dear Mary:

I have nothing to say, and only write to state I am well, and that the weather is delightful. Madame Campan died in May. I dine at Mr. Munroe's to-day by special invitation. Mr. Adams has given Jonathan Russell [33] another tremendous dressing. The President left town yesterday for three weeks. All the rest of the family remain here on account of Mrs. Gouverneur.[34] The doctors have forbid Emily [Munroe] riding out. She is condemned to sit perfectly still. She is very low in spirits.

Mr. [John Caldwell] Calhoun is losing ground as the presidential candidate. Mr. Crawford remains stationary, and Mr. Adams is rising greatly. I spent last evening in close confab with Madame la Présidente, who intends *entre nous* to give no more dinner parties; to give drawing rooms once a week and two balls. I agreed with her that it would be by far the best mode of conciliating all the beaux, belles, gentlemen, and Cossacks.

Your last was dated Friday. I hope to-morrow to get another. I wrote Ronaldson yesterday about the fifty dollars. Our cats found they must starve or go to war. Of course they commenced hostilities against the rats, killing hundreds, and forcing the remainder to retreat to our neighbors. As Tom's dog was in a starving condition, I gave him to Mr. Mitchell. Peters continues ill. The Duke of Vinegar has got over Gen'l [Winfield] Scott's sortie against him without a bilious fever.

Mrs. Bomford has arrived safe with her carriage [and] horses and bantlings at New Haven. The Colonel called at my office to announce the news — as if I cared a fig about it. " Only think " said he, " it cost her but $100 — all the expenses on the road." He will lie gratuitously farther than a horse can trot. Poor Mr. Baldwin, the worth of the whole family, is very ill at Bedford Springs. I fear it is his last illness.

God bless you all
W. L.

To Mary E. Lee at Schooley's Mountain

Washington, Sunday, July 7, 1822

My dear Mary: . . .

I every day rejoice that your mother and Susan are not here in this excessive heat. I do not know how they would get through these melting nights; and, as to that bed of your mother's, it would sweat an elephant down to the size of a grasshopper. I shall alter it immediately by lowering the front and back part several inches, narrowing the steps on which it rests one half, and mounting it on good rollers. And I will finish it so that in summer the head can be turned to the wall, and the side in winter.

I am rejoiced to hear that Susan is getting more composed. Your mother brought on in a great degree her [own] sickness by her inquietude. For two years back her physical and moral properties have been in conflict, until the first gave way. She ought to have studied LaSalle's *Balance Naturelle*, which maintains that you may cure a moral evil by opposing to it a physical remedy; and a physical disease by a moral one. He says that two drams of *Bois-Robert* [35] cured the atrocious Cardinal de Richelieu of that deep melancholy, the result of so many crimes meditated by his genius. We know a calming potion will cure a project of vengeance; a cordial expel fear (take it, I pray you, in a thunder storm); bleeding will moderate anger, pride, vain hopes, and all such chimerical ideas as possess Mrs. Tudor, which begin by amusing, and finish by tormenting us. What a pity her family had not known this! A little vivisection now and then would have made her a discreet, prudent, valuable woman. I have a notion of writing her a chapter on the subject of hallucinations (errors of the imagination). Is it too late? "Yes," you will say. Well! we will not then touch on it.

I am rejoiced to hear Mamma has determined to renew and continue the waters, and not to neglect her rhubarb jelly. This is right. She ought not only to change the air, but her diet, remedies and regimen. Should she have occasion to take castor oil, enclosed is a preparation of it, which renders it an agreeable medicine to take. Annexed to it another prescription for an indigestion. I found them at the end of an old journal of mine, and showed them to Dr. Craven, who called to see me this morning, and was so pleased with them that he copied them off.

I have nothing new to tell you, and the weather is too hot to go among the gossips to hear tales of imagination or reality. The greatest comfort I have had has been in the use of a little instrument called a back scratcher. I take so much pleasure in it, in getting up or going to bed, as ever any lady did with hunting fleas . . . [William Lee included a drawing of the back-scratcher with the following labels: " a. A small brush an inch in diameter; b. A whale bone handle two feet long."] It is indeed a great luxury. Thanks to the Chinese for their invention of it. William was well a few days ago. It is time I had another letter from him, and I hope you have had one before this. I expect he will make an effort to get to see you all.

Adieu

W. L.

To Mary E. Lee at Schooley's Mountain

Washington, Monday, July 8, 1822

Your letter of Friday last, my dear Mary, reached me this day. . . . You need not be concerned about my being dull. Keep yourselves lively. I have enough to occupy me the best half [of] the day. As to my coming to you before August, it is out of the question. So be quiet about it. I am happy to hear my dear wife is so contented that she begins to get a relish for society, and that Susan follows suit. *Tout ça est fort bien; mais n'êtes-vous pas une petite menteuse?* and fabricate all this to keep me easy? *Je voudrai bien savoir la verité. Envoye moi donc des bulletins.*

The fourth of July I spent at home, and sent into Mrs. Coolidge's for a vegetable dinner. We had no oration; the toasts I sent you. But here enclosed are some of Dr. Cutting's, drank at Mr. Harrison Smith's [36] in the country, where there was a large party of literary people such as Dr. Thornton &c. &c. And here are also some lines on Miss Smith's birthday: all very pretty.

As you suppose the gossips have not yet killed Tayloe. They swear that, like their own cats, he has nine lives. " Well Mistress! Have you heard the news? " " No! What is it? " " Tayloe is dead." " And I told you so, Colonel. He would not live the day out." " Well damme! if I did not see him this day in his carriage." " It is not possible! " " Well! well! it is no matter (snuffing); die he will, and so will you, Mistress; and I suppose there will be just as much sniffling over the one as the other." This is exactly what I heard the two say the other day at Mitchell's, and I unfortu-

nately met them, and they were uncommonly civil: too civil by
half.

All the accounts I get from Cadets Lewis, Washington, and
others, who are here, of William are flattering. But the truth is
he is so amiable, such an offhand gentlemanly fellow that all his
comrades like him. I fear he is a clever fellow in the American
not the English acceptation of the word.

Tom had better hunt up the philosopher's stone. Now is the
time to impress upon him that:

> " The mind untaught
> Is a dark waste, where fiends and tempests howl.
> As Phoebus to the world is science to the soul." [37]

Loadstone is found everywhere among iron ore. It is in fact a
rich iron ore, found in masses, of a deep iron grey when fresh
broken, and often tinged with a brownish or reddish color. No
doubt there are great quantities of it about you, and I hope it
will communicate to you some of its attractive qualities, should
any Adonis move near your orbit, and be found worthy of such
a jewel.

We have nothing new. The President and Mrs. Monroe have
returned to the city, having gone, it is said by the ill-natured, for
the mere purpose of getting rid of the fourth of July. I wish upon
the whole they had remained away ten or fifteen days. I do not
know what is the matter, but I suspect the President feels the
pressure of the times. In speaking to Mrs. Monroe the other evening of the troubles and vexations I have encountered the last
three years, she fetched a deep sigh, and said " We all have our
share," and then went into some particulars, which convinced me
all is not right. These Virginia estates are getting to be great bur-
dens to their proprietors.

Mr. Adams and Mr. Russell occupy the public mind. The latter
has replied to the former in a sort of whining, labored perform-
ance. I am not sorry to see the diplomatic gas, with which this
gentleman has been inflated, end in a combustion that will reduce
him to his proper state. In comparison to Mr. Adams he is a mere

butterfly, fluttering round this sun of science, exhibiting his gaudy colors to amuse children.

The theatre [38] is to be opened to-morrow night. I do not think I shall trouble it. One must love the drama much to consent to pass three hours amidst tobacco smoke, whiskey breaths, and other stenches, mixed up with the effluvia of stables, and miasmas of the canal, which the theatre is exactly placed and constructed to receive. It provokes me to think that a beautiful spot or site as this for a city should be cut up into such small lots, and that people begin to huddle together on that stinking avenue in preference to stretching out into ample spaces with small gardens around their houses. But our people have no taste in this vicinity. Hog and hominy; whiskey and cigars, are superlative enjoyments with them.

Tom will see by the paper that poor John Cronier is no more. Mrs. Decatur has gone to the *Manor*, a high-sounding name. How much there is in sounds and in showing off! " All the world is indeed a stage and the men and women merely players."

God bless you all
W. L.

To Mary E. Lee at Schooley's Mountain

Washington, Saturday evening,
July 12, 1822

Dear Mary:

I sent you in the midst of office business this morning a letter from Mrs. Stewart, and two newspapers, and shortly after received your letter of the last Wednesday via New York. I have not complained of want of letters of late. You have been so good in writing. But methinks you might tell me something about the various characters which surround you at present, and among whom, as at all watering places, there must be some oddities; some queer fish in religion, politics, eccentricities, or fopperies. I am sure you could make a perfect magic lantern for me if you chose.

I do not know how it is my children have always had an antipathy to exhibiting in any way. They are not idle. They are always gathering information for what? To hide it under a bushel: and that too in this country of pretensions, where everything is made to pass for a *great deal more than it is worth*. Now I think there is a just medium in these things, and I desire you will try to arrive at it. For a stupid sensible woman is just as insufferable as a silly trifling one. If you cannot do better, collect yourselves around a table, and give me the result of all your observations: a family piece. Color it, if the originals are not sufficiently striking. I am sure Tom and Mariette could add some shades, and Susan, if in the humor, could give some dry rubs. As to mother, she is a perfect oyster; all goodness. Having nothing about her to ridicule, she is averse to, and never would, ridicule any one. If she happens to hate anyone, you may now and then find it out so *distinctly* as not to be mistaken.

Mrs. Munroe fell in love with my back scratcher; and, as I could do no less than give it to her, I observed on presenting it that she had a store of bosom friends, who all loved her, but that I sent her a *back biter*, which by irritating, assuaged all those little humors which heat gave rise to. She was pleased, and I was happy in administering to her comforts. We fat people labor under many inconveniences which Pharaoh's lean kind [kine] know nothing of. I like Mrs. Munroe much. She is a very friendly woman.

You object to sending me a bulletin of Mamma's and Susan's health. My reasons for asking it were to find out the state of Susan's mind from her observations, and to learn the state of your mother's stomach and bowels. I am sensible her recovery will be slow, but I want to watch it, to see if something cannot be thrown in to aid nature in her work. Does she continue the waters and the rhubarb pills, those friends to the bowels? Has she a sick stomach? . . . What does she eat and particularly drink? No heating things I hope. American beer I have found out is very bad for her. . . . And yet beer and porter is good if you are sure no aloes have been used in making it. . . .

I believe I told you in my last that some fears were entertained of the yellow fever at Philadelphia. And Mr. Stiles of Baltimore told me to-day there had been several cases of it there. This alternate hot and wet season will make our city unhealthy. How much better you are off where you are than you would have been in Boston, where the thermometer has been as high as it has been here! Your mother never could have supported the heat in this place the last fortnight. It has been very oppressive. Thunder gusts have been very frequent and severe. To-day it has been literally pouring down all day, with occasionally moderate thunder and lightning. What effect so much moisture and heat will have I do not know. Thus far the city never was healthier at this season. But as green apples, pears, etc. with cucumbers, squashes, salt and smoked fish, and ruined bacon is now the food of all, I expect disease will crop in among those who love these delicacies, moistened with grog and toddy.

Accompanying this is the evening's paper with some rattle-snake stories for Tom, which I hope will make him cautious how he frequents their haunts. There is also more of that ridiculous, atrocious duel of McDuffie's,[39] with a vile federal attack on the Vice-President. You know he was sued by the government for $11,000, while he claimed of them $150,000. The jury gave him $136,000. He plead his own cause to admiration. I have seen some extracts from it, which pleased me much. The whole trial is now in the press. When I get it I will send it to you. His farm, furniture, horses, carriages etc. have been sold by his creditors. A general sympathy exists in his favor. And, had he not taken to the sordid, solitary bottle to drown his cares, his poverty and misfortunes, so far from injuring him, would have been of infinite use to him.

How such amiable men, with such friends, and so elevated by a free people, can fall into such a low degrading vice is inconceivable. How many instances do we see of it in England and America; with this difference: that in England it is a sort of convivial crime. Gentlemen get intoxicated there, while discussing various subjects, and enjoying the charms of conversation over wine. But here they get drunk with ardent spirits for the pure *pleasure of drunk* as the Indian said. Let it, I pray you, be an article in your marriage contract that your husband is never to touch spirits of any kind, and keep him from smoking and chewing, which create thirst, and tend to all the low vices. . . .

Adieu! I must go to bed, without a soul to say " Good-night " to me, and rise as usual to pursue my monotonous course without a charm to beguile the heavy, tedious hours. How can it be otherwise? The same sorrow rises as the day returns. My Susan suffers, and my daughter succors.

God bless you all.
W. L.

To Mary E. Lee at Schooley's Mountain

Washington, Sunday afternoon,
July 21, 1822

I have just come in, and opened your letter of the 18th.[40] The effect it has produced it would be vain to attempt to describe. I shall leave everything and join you as soon as possible. I shall be with you before the week is out. We will go to the seaside: perhaps to Long Island, Newport, or Boston. We must now try a damp moist atmosphere, such as the sea coast and fogs will give.

It happens that my affairs (private ones) can be easily left; and as to my public ones, they must get on as they can. I regard no sacrifice, if I can only restore your mother's health. For on that depends all our happiness. Not a word have you said of Susan.

Judge, my dear Mary, of my feelings and sufferings until I reach you, and until then God bless you.

W. L.

VII

WASHINGTON SOCIETY

1823 – 1829

After Mrs. Lee's death, Susan and Mary returned to their father's house in Washington, and after a suitable period of mourning, they began to go out in society. As for the sons, William left West Point before being graduated and seems not to have settled down to a serious job until middle life, when, in 1851, he obtained a clerkship in the War Department that drew upon his knowledge of French; [1] Thomas was graduated seventh in his class at West Point in July, 1826, and thereupon entered the Engineer Corps.

In December, 1823, Louisa Kalisky, a young German girl of seventeen, became a guest in the Lees' house through rather unusual circumstances. She had come to Washington by stage coach from Philadelphia to stay with the German minister, Friedrich Greuhm; but he died just before she started on her trip. It was decided, however, that she should continue her journey. Greuhm's widow had taken refuge with the Lees, and when Louisa arrived, she also became a guest in their house. During her stay with them she wrote a delightful diary [2] in which she says:

I naturally receive many marked attentions as the guest of the Ambassadress and of the eminent Lees. . . . Susan and Mary Lee are the acknowledged leaders of society here and their word is law in regard to social customs. They were educated in Bordeaux and are very handsome and very charming. Mary is very musical.

It was about this time that Mary Lee was being courted by a young Russian diplomat, and on June 6, 1825, she was married in her father's house by the Reverend William Hawley, rector of St. John's Church, to Jean-François-George-Frédéric, baron de Maltitz. Mrs. Adams, Lady of the President, was one of the witnesses. The Baron was secretary of the Russian legation in Washington, and acted as chargé d'affaires *ad interim* from March 14, 1826, to December 20, 1827. He was then stationed at Berlin and afterwards at London; and finally served as Envoy Extraordinary and Minister Plenipotentiary to Holland during the reigns of William I, William II, and William III. Susan Lee never married, and remained with her father in Washington until 1829, when she crossed the ocean to be with her sister.

When Andrew Jackson became president in 1829, the end came for William Lee's career. The spoils system, wherein everyone who differed politically from the victor was summarily dismissed from office and replaced by a member of the winning party, fell hard on Lee, who had served the government of the United States faithfully for almost thirty years. A commentary in the Washington press (written as an historical sketch of the second auditor's office and quoted in *John Leigh of Agawam*) summed up his character and his service as auditor:

Mr. Lee was a gentleman of the old school, though without that primness so often associated with the character; he was fine looking, large of frame, free and jovial in his manner, and indifferent to the minor cares of life; but no one who examines the records of the office for the twelve years during which he had charge of it, can fail to be convinced that he was a gentleman of culture and business method. The successful organization of his bureau on a systematic plan which has not been found to need essential modification under all the vicissitudes of the sixty years since passed, shows that he possessed ability of no common order.

To William Barlow Lee at West Point

Washington, March 24, 1823

My dear William:

I am anxious to know how you get on. I mean in respect to money. I wish you would let me know whether you meet your expenses by your pay. I know you are not extravagant, and it is my wish to help you all I can; though my great expenses of last summer have kept me much behind this winter, from which I am just recovering.

Have you received your shirts &c? Having heard that the Mansion House in Philadelphia had been destroyed by fire, your sisters are apprehensive your friend might have been there on his way to the Point, and lost your box in the conflagration, at which I laugh. But you know how whimsical they are.

Miss Ann, our cook,[3] was brought to bed last night without any one in the house suspecting she was with child. *She says she did not suspect it herself.* And the first thing we heard was the squalling of the black brat, without doctor, midwife, or anything else. Mariette is as busy as a bee in a tar barrel. I shrewdly suspect that Mr. Mark is the father.

When am I to see you at the head of your class in mathematics on the weekly report? Do you chew tobacco? If you do, I shall give you up; for I never knew a man possess talents or genius, who chewed the cud. And as to a man's being a gentleman and chewing, it is out of the question; unless you call a *Cossack* or a *forecastle* buck a gentleman.

We are all well and shall make you a visit this summer.

Your affectionate father
W. Lee

To Baron de Maltitz

Washington, June 20, 1824

My dear Baron: [4]

It was with infinite pain that I learnt of your attachment to my daughter. And I am much surprised that a man of your superior acquirements and excellent understanding should have indulged in a passion which does not promise the faintest glimmerings of happiness. Such is my esteem for your excellent qualities that, were I a man of fortune, and my daughter was pleased with your attentions, I would willingly share it with you to make you both happy. But, as that you know is not the case, and as you have not yourself the means of making a suitable establishment for yourself and her, it would be the height of imprudence in me to countenance your addresses.

Riches are not necessary to happiness. This is exemplified by the perfect union which has ever existed in my own family without them. But a competency is necessary, and neither of us, *malheureusement*, my dear Baron, have it to bestow.

Under the most advantageous circumstances, a father who marries his daughter to a stranger to be expatriated by following his fortunes, makes a sacrifice, which, such is my attachment to my dear children, and so much is my happiness interwoven with theirs, that I never will bring my mind to consent to it.

I hope, my worthy friend, this fever of the brain will pass off, and that, with your sober, discreet, enlightened mind, you will see the picture and propriety of my determination.

With the highest esteem for
your many excellent qualities,
I am, my dear Baron,
Your sincere friend
W. Lee.

To Mary E. Lee at Boston

Washington, Saturday, July 24, 1824

" I will write you from *Broomley Vale*." [5]

There is a charm in that name, my dear Mary, not to be described. The instant it met my eye in your delightful letter of the 19th my tears flowed copiously. There passed the scenes of my early life with that perfect object of affection, which my heart will never cease to wear. I followed you into the hall, to the library, parlor, dining room, along the canal, round the garden, to the opposite hill of granite, the little river between, its bridge, and the tanyard on its banks. I coursed all the neighborhood, then " back-glancing memory, acting her busy part " brought all the members of the revered domestic groups to view. Even Dinah, the faithful servant of Master John (for so she always called the patriarch), was not forgotten. . . .

That those of the much loved family, who still live, have not forgotten one the virtuous departed were so kind to, is consoling to my widowed heart. The attentions you will receive from all the friends of your adored mother I shall feel grateful for; but there are none can reach the recesses of affection like those bestowed on you by the Lowell family. As I do not expect this letter will reach you while under their venerated roof, I beg you will take the earliest occasion to say how much their kindness has touched me. Tell Sally there will be softness in my regard when we meet, for she has not a relative on earth that loves her better than I do. I am much pleased with the kindness of Mrs. Bethune. She was always very amiable.

I am gratified with your contemplated visit to our dear and good friend Mrs. Tudor, who owes me several letters, and who I am sure will smile at my epitaph to her old beau, Dr. [John Brown] Cutting, who has obtained at last through my exertions a comfortable living, and has bought himself a new wig. You have both laughed at my attachment to this extraordinary amusing man. Recollect it is of about *forty years* standing, and learn, I pray you, to bear with the foibles of eccentric old age towards which I am traveling fast. You do not know how much I regret Father Law.⁶ He is very different, you will say, from the Dr., though in caste of character as rare. One may be compared to an instructive interesting book; the other to an index or chronological table. " Il y a entre un homme de lettres et un érudit la même différence qu'entre un ouvrage et un table de matières." Now in this golgotha of numbskulls, where for six months in the year now is seen but worms of the desk creeping out on the commons, at stated hours, from those hospitals of incurables, the public offices, to their hog, hominy, and hemlock from the still, if one did not cherish such intellectual beings as Law and Cutting, one should have no amusement, and shortly have as little wit as we have of the *savoir vivre*.

I have not yet heard of William's arrival at Northampton. If that boy was as studious as he is virtuous, what a rare man he would make. I feel anxious to hear how he gets on in his chosen profession. I fear he never will succeed. It is ——

[The rest is missing.]

To Mary E. Lee at Boston

Washington, Sunday, July 25, 1824

In the letter I wrote you yesterday, my dear Mary, I said nothing about the Baron, as it was meant for you to show to the Lowells and Mrs. Bethune; as you requested me to say something about them for their kindness. Immediately on the receipt of your letter of the nineteenth, I wrote the Baron to this purport:

That the consent of his parents and the approbation of his government must be had. As I knew in some nations of Europe the marriages of such men . . . were null and void without this formality. That, when these were obtained, I would consent to his paying his addresses to you, provided he obtained your consent, and that nothing should swerve me from that decision.

This is as it should be, and you must not be in a hurry to give that consent. I must not permit him to visit Boston. If he does, all my prudent arrangements will be of no avail, and we shall all be made unhappy. " Absence, like the wind, extinguishes small flames and increases large ones." [7] The affair is now at rest as respects me, unless I see cause to change my opinion; and you are left perfectly free to act as you please.

You will see all the Munroes by the tenth of August.

In haste

W.L.

To Mary and Susan Lee at Boston

Washington, July 28, 1824

My dear children:

Mr. Salomon called to tell me that by dispatches received within a few days by the Russian Minister, it appears Baron [de] Maltitz is named Counsellor of the Legation in the place of Ellisen who has resigned.[8] If this is true (for Salomon cannot vouch for it as he has it not from the Minister, but from one of his household), his next step will be, when this minister leaves here, chargé d'affaires, and the next step, when a new minister comes, he must go home; because a chargé d'affaires cannot go back to a counsellor of legation. What he will become, when he gets home, is in the womb of time.

The Munroes left here yesterday for Boston. I am sorry for it; because *he* [the postmaster] is an ignorant, vain, purse-proud, jealous, censorious fellow, and, if he finds you are much noticed, *à la mode de Madame la dowager* [Mrs. Constant Freeman], he will not be sparing of his ill-natured observations. He is as bad as they all are good. I hate vulgarity in a coach. Bank bills are too often in our country the *tapestry* of fools.

I shall not write you a long letter, as I have been without any from you for several mails, which proves you only write your father when you have nothing better to do.

W. L.

To Mary and Susan Lee at Boston

Washington, August 13, 1824

I have nothing to say, only that I have been three days without any letters from either of you. When you see the good Lowells, you must say that, when you return home, you will send Nancy's letters to them, for I cannot find them anywhere.

I took a walk last evening with *mon garçon* to Commodore Porter's,[9] and there took tea *en famille*. Miss Jane Watson being present with all her airs and graces, which she directed with all her accustomed force against the Baron, who made some shrewd observations thereon on our way home *en faisant des jolies comparaisons* all in your favor. So you see he is a man of merit and discernment. I do not say that I see, but that you see it. Since our walk, I have not seen him, as his minister gives a great dinner to-day to the French *nouveau*.

I saw Mrs. Graham at Mrs. Munroe's yesterday, at full length on the sofa, trying very hard to look interesting as usual. She has fallen away very much and looks very pale. Her articulation, however, is much clearer, and no longer gives the idea that she had swallowed her nail brush. The Vails[10] may certainly be considered as belonging to the South American Legation, for they are eternally there, and the harp and the *gosier* [throat — voice] are always on the strain. They practice in the morning to display in the evening. Who makes the puddings and darns the stockings I cannot say, knowing nothing of their interior economy. Mrs. Stone, Mrs. Wilson's daughter, looks very kind at me, so much so that Anderson [Joseph Anderson, first comptroller] and myself have had many good laughs about it.

What a vulgar set I am surrounded with! I know not which

217

way to turn, nor where to go, to see a pleasing male or female. This had never struck me so forcibly as this summer. Ruff scruff: fit only for the cellar or smoke house! O yes! I must except Mrs. Adams, for she is charming: like a rose among cabbages. I have dined at Paymaster Kuhn's [11] new house, the envy of all the vain. She is a pretty woman, but rather vacant in the attic story. She speaks five languages, and none well, if no better than her French and English. She talks like Mrs. Pleasanton, a good deal about style, and has all the display and ostentation of her slave-holding neighbors. They have set up their carriage.

This passion for carriages here always puts me in mind of the Italian proverb: that " he who rides in his carriage and has a bad dinner at home, draws his coach with his teeth." I know I have quoted it before, but no matter; it is so applicable to all around me. Besides I am an old man, and begin to *radote* [talk drivel]. I might have said the same thing in fewer words. Liveries and smoked herrings. If I was at Athens, as you are in the center of wit, beauty, taste, and fashion, I could answer you. How is that charming, lady-like woman, Mrs. Sullivan? If she has not been kind to you, I will never admire her Austrian lip again.

Old Cutting has enamoured a lady from Virginia, *owning to fifty-five*, who has $30,000 and ten negroes. His poetry is flying about her like *gulls* after *bait*. I expect to be bridesgroom [bridesman — best man]. Mr. Crawford has left the city, very sick indeed. He told a friend of mine, who asked to see him, that his physicians have " *killed him up*": a favorite expression with all our public men, who come like him from the verge of civilization, and means, I suppose, sending a man to Heaven before his time. Of course, " killing him down " must mean sending him among evil spirits, or to Georgia, which is the same thing. I have not seen the dowager since your departure. Her *homme d'affaires* told me this morning that she was shortly to make a visit to Philadelphia and will, no doubt, torment Cousin Zeke [12] on her way. She is determined to hold on and see it out. . . .

This is nonsense enough for one evening. Spell it out if you can. I have written it with a steel pen, which I bought to do away [with] the necessity of nibbing and mending. It is so sharp,

Mary Elizabeth Lee Baroness de Maltitz

Susan Palfrey Lee's miniature of Mariette

and I have such a heavy hand, that it does not turn a corner quick, but sticks to angles. I shall wear it smooth in a day or two, and write plainer.

God bless you, my dear children.
W. Lee.

To Mary and Susan Lee at Boston

Washington, August 27, 1824

My dear children:

I suppose what with the arrival of Lafayette, and commencement, this will prove a busy, fatiguing week to you. I expect to hear all about it by Sunday next.

Mrs. Greuhm's mother has reached here at last. The Vails gave her a party last evening, at which, not being invited to assist, I did not make my appearance. So I cannot say what sort of a woman she appears to be. Our neighborhood is noisy and lively. Mrs. Wilson is full of long, lean, ghastly looking people from the south, driven from the springs by the *cold* weather, and who praise our delightful air: the thermometer being at 84 the last three days, and not a drop of rain for five weeks. You know what Washington is under such circumstances. I observe that all who come south and west from the verge of civilization think it a most delectable place.

At Kervand's we have all the youth attached to the French legation: about as noisy, impudent, indecent [a] set as I ever met with. And at Gadsby's [13] that vulgar Englishman, Jackson, has taken up his abode, and feeds all the foreigners, among whom is a young flaxen-haired, blue-eyed Russian, Count Medem,[14] the bearer of the treaty, one of the most delightful fellows you ever saw, about the size, but much handsomer than Capt. Randall.[15] I should pity the lady's father he should make a bow to, for he certainly would disturb the lady's tranquility. He goes off in a day or two to Niagara, and from thence to Boston to return here. You will therefore see this Adonis, who looks very much like Susan, but *malheureusement* is too young for her. Otherwise I should stand a good chance of having another feudal sprig

219

engrafted on a democratic stock. The Baron loves me to death. He sits whole hours in the library admiring your poor mother's ivory likeness, which he says resembles Mary so much that he cannot keep his eyes off of it. "Pauvre homme! Il est bien malade." I hope it will last.

Mrs. Adams left here yesterday for Bordentown. Mr. Adams is to join her in a few days. She took your shawl, and said, if she did not go on to Boston, with him, she would put it in his trunk. She is indeed a very charming woman. But of all the women I have met with since my return home, Mrs. Towson is by far the most agreeable. I am astonished we have not discovered this before. She has not a spark of vanity; is beautiful as an angel, graceful as Psyche, tasteful in her dress as Mde. Récamier, with a mind stored by choice reading. In short she is natural, beautiful, sensible, witty, elegant, and enchanting: a diamond among the pebbles of Washington.

It is said the stupid Daniel Brent [16] is agoing to be married to the vulgar widow Graham. These are the sort of beings who pass for something here: your *good* old-fashioned hog and hominy people, who have not been dressed clean but once a week in their lives, who never took a bath except in the puddles of a corn field, having as great an aversion to water as if they possessed the hydrophobia, and whose taste is so exquisite that they prefer a bed of cabbages before their parlor windows to a *parterre*.

Colonel Tayloe lays very ill. This old fellow and his hyena have fretted themselves to death because their negroes have fallen fifty per cent in value, and wheat and corn are a drug.

My Duke of Vinegar set off yesterday on his annual tour to Mount Holly in New Jersey. Of course I shall be closely confined to the office until his return. The President is to be here to-day to make, I presume, arrangements with the Corporation [17] for the reception of Lafayette. Mr. Crawford is very ill at the waters. Mr. Adams will most assuredly be our next President. The opposition to him by certain *Ultras* in New England has been of infinite service to him with the moderate men of all parties. It is " the homage that vice pays to virtue." [18] Tell Davis [19] this, and beg him not to oppose the Essex scouts in their doings against

Mr. Adams, but to encourage them therein as the surest means of increasing his popularity with the great body of the people.

Miss Mary came very near losing her lover the other day. He attempted to cross the Potomac below the Great Falls; was swept away by the current, and saved by catching hold of the cane of another fool who was following, but did not venture so far. And yesterday he set out to go to the falls with Count Medem (How pretty these Counts and Barons sound!) in a hired gig. The horse took fright and went over the bank into the river; but the gentlemen leapt from the vehicle, and saved themselves. What wonderful things to write home about! It is a pity these people were not born or educated with a little common sense.

The ladies of Baltimore are gathering all the roses far and near. They have even sent here to know if they can have some to brighten the way for " Amicus humani generis ": the friend of the human race [Lafayette]. This will be very pretty. I am sorry it was not thought of in Boston.

God bless you, my dear children.
Wm. Lee

To Susan and Mary Lee at Boston

Washington, August 29, 1824

My dear children:

Susan's letter of the 25th has this moment reached me. I expected, from what you said in one from Nahant, that you would have been spending a week at Mrs. Lloyd's when Lafayette arrived there, and was a little mortified to find you had not yet been introduced to him. I want him to see you. Under the supposition that he will take the road from Boston to Springfield, and Northampton to Albany, and down the Hudson to West Point, I have written William, and sent him a letter to him [Lafayette] that he may notice him, as these things animate and encourage young men.

I see but little of the Baron. He is taken up with Count Medem, who appears determined to see all he can, and be pleased with everything. But he calls daily for a few minutes. I like him. He certainly is very much attached to Mary, and that is the main point. But the idea of her living in Europe mars all my enjoyment. This is a dreadful country for old people, when they have not their children settled around them, on whom they can lean for comfort.

I am sorry to find you consider the reception of Lafayette "exactly what you have seen" of the artificial pageantry of royalty; got up, paid for, and directed by the creatures of Kings. This is the overflowing of honest grateful hearts for a simple citizen without titles and place: homage to virtue. Its moral effects will be felt from the Bosphorus to the Baltic; from Terra del Fuego to the Texas. I hope you will be introduced to him at Mrs. Sears' as the children of his old friend.

I am glad you have seen Jamaica Pond. Dubullet did not build that house. He bought it, and sold it to Mr. Ritchie's former father-in-law. You must see Fresh Pond or Lake. I recollect that vain fool Monsieur Bussey,[20] who being bred a tailor in the town of Dedham, would (it was said at the time) always ride cross-legged on the seat in his carriage. I well recollect the day he first drove in his carriage to Dedham to show himself. I do not care what a man's origin is if he has mind. Asses I hate.

I am pleased with what you say of William, who has not written me but once since his departure from this, and it mortifies me, when asked when I heard from him, to say, "Not lately," for I dare not say, "Never." Seeing nothing of Mary's handwriting of late, I wrought myself up into a belief that she was sick, and Susan was hiding it from me, and did not in consequence sleep all last night, which on the whole I believe was chiefly owing to a strong cup of tea Mariette gave me.

Poor Miss Hopkinson that was has lost her husband very suddenly. How unlucky for Mrs. Adams, who is there! We are beginning our preparations for Lafayette. The Corporation have hired the east house of Gadsby's, and are going to fit it up. It will make our neighborhood very lively. Mrs. Monroe is very ill. I fear she will die. If she does, the President will not survive her long.

Your devoted father
W. Lee.

To Mary E. Lee at Boston

Washington, August 30, 1824

Here is a letter, my dear Mary, from your sprig of nobility, the Baron. Now, if his friend, Count Medem, had a few more years over his head, I should advise Susan to set her plumes for him, and if she succeeded in captivating this *heart smasher* (to use the elegant phrase of the Kentucky belles, who rise up now and then from the verge of civilization), your democratic father *de bon gré ou malgré* would have to embrace the *tenets* of these phantoms of feudal tenures in order to live in peace and quiet with his aristocratic children. As things have gone so far, it appears to me you ought to write the Baron. You have a thousand objects about you to fill a letter with; and even letter after letter. And, if you find nothing else, I would tell him how a pumpkin pie is made; or get Pickering's *Dictionary of Americanisms*,[21] and select a few quaint sayings for him, which would amuse him, as he is so much of a linguist. Or, as he is like yourself very fond of fresh butter, I would tell him how it is produced, and describe the ventures of a New England churn. As you value your future happiness, say not a word about Lafayette to him; for the very name has made the whole diplomatic corps so sick that Dr. Huntt has as much as he can do to preserve them from the dire effects of this fever of liberty, whose contagion is spreading far and near.

Indifferent subjects treated by your fair hand would electrify the poor Baron, *qui se meurt d'ennui.* It is not necessary to dwell on the *tender passion*, for a lady should never acknowledge more than *friendship* even for her husband. The northwest corner of the heart is all she ever ought to admit as possessed. The remainder of the palpitating, panting little thing should be carefully guarded, and reserved for *hope* to dwell on and feed the imagination, which in a German, and a German Baron too of the Duchy of Courland, is always extremely vivid. . . .

As to keeping this thing a secret, as you desire in one of your last letters, that is out of the question. All I can do is to affect to know nothing about it; and *par force* to say, when the subject is mentioned to me, that I never intend to control my children in affairs in which their happiness so essentially depends. It is proper you should know, however, that you are considered as mortgaged, and that, among the weddings to take place this fall, yours is the first on the list. And, will you believe it, your old father's about the middle of it. Poor gossips! If they get no wedding cake until they get mine, they will lose the taste and art of making it. On this subject as related to myself I get necessarily out of humor, and say some very impudent things, which the Baron says is " váry rhûde ".

I expected sheets of paper filled with the reception of the Marquis, and commencement; but you are both such provoking, matter-of-fact girls, that I must content myself with newspaper accounts, which display as much fancy as a merchant's bill of parcels. If that angelic mind of Nancy Lowell still embellished life, what a treat I should have from her divine *plume*.

Adieu. Your affectionate father,
W. Lee.

To Mary and Susan Lee at Boston

Washington, September 5, 1824

My dear Girls:

In writing to William, you had better tell him how much his manners please, and encourage him by telling him also of the good accounts you hear of his progress and studies, and how much all his friends are delighted therewith.

As to the Baron, I can only say that he is *excessively hurt* that Mary does not write him. If he was an American I should be delighted with the match. I have found him to be such a high minded, honorable man. His being a foreigner is all that can possibly be brought against him. But native or foreigner, I see plainly that the thing will take place and under those circumstances Mary ought to write him pleasant agreeable letters about her parties &c. But you have no address, no tact, either of you, nor never will have. Luckily there was a friendly expression in one of your last letters about him which I showed him and it lighted him up and made him happy. Every day he calls to get a letter, but finding none, goes away despairing and melancholy.

You will suspect that I was opposed to this affair, and had I not discovered how much he loved Mary, and that she was also attached to him, I should never have consented to put it on the footing I have. Being a foreigner from an *iron climate* and of a noble family, who have great merit, were great objections in my mind, but, since the affair has gone so far, I am for treating him with all possible kindness and attention, while you appear to be indifferent to his feelings. There is a *bienséance* in all things.

Tout à vous
W Lee

To Mary and Susan Lee at Boston

Washington, September 8, 1824

My dear children: . . .

The Munroes have arrived and do not seem over and above pleased with their visit to Boston. They tell me Susan has grown fat, handsome, and saucy, and of course very gay, while poor Mary is moping. That you should wish to return to these dreary commons so soon appears to me very extraordinary. I believe you both want to see the Baron as much as he does you. He has been with some of the French legation on a shooting party, the last two days, to the Great Falls. Of course I have not seen him, and therefore cannot tell whether his pulse beats high or low. . . .

Poor Stewart, it is true enough, has not made over $20,000. He has, or will call for, a court of inquiry to pronounce on his conduct.[22] He has been shamefully calumniated, but he will come off with flying colors. I hear not a word of her. As to avarice, he has not a particle of it. No one who knows him can call him an interested man. He is generous, noble, and brave. How they will get over her secreting the Royal officer, if true, I know not. It was a humane act of hers, if she did it, but an excessive imp[r]udent one, as it was calculated to injure her husband's hard earned fame. Let there be no change in your conduct towards her when you meet. The more the world censures her, the more kind do you be to her. Never abandon your friends for the howling of the multitude. I wish one of you would write [to] her. It would be pleasing to her; and I beg you will do it, and do it at once.

If this finds you with my dear friends, Dr. and Mrs. Freeman,[23] give my best love to them. I have not another idea.

Your devoted father
W. Lee.

To Susan Lee at Boston

Washington, October 12, 1824

My dear Susan:

Mr. Fitzgerald, the purser of Stewart's ship and friend of his, told me on Sunday (in such a way that I am sure the Commodore gave him the hint) that Stewart's house and farm were in such disorder that he could not prepare it this fall to go into it, and that he contemplated taking a house at Philadelphia for the winter, the expense of which fretted him much. On this information, I immediately wrote Stewart to bring his wife and children here and spend the winter with us. To put him perfectly at his ease, I told him we would divide the expenses of housekeeping, as this would be economy both for him and me. . . .

Our city is full and overrunning. I expect Mrs. Adams, Calhoun, Wirt, Towson, Kuhn, Ramsay and families [24] (as I invited them all to keep out the rabble) to grace my windows. . . .

I was at the President's all day yesterday. He sent for me to consult about receiving Lafayette, as he did not like the arrangement of the Corporation, who proposed that the President and all members of the government should join in the procession. This is what we concluded on: [25] We have the Gen'l to the Corporation. They will meet him at the city bounds, conduct him to the Capitol, address him there, and then proceed with him to the President's gates. Here *he only*, with his suite, and a few revolutionary officers, are to enter; and the President, surrounded by the Heads of Department, officers of the government, navy commissioners, Generals Brown and Macomb, will receive him in the saloon. None of the city authorities or populace will be admitted. After the ceremony is ended, we shall deliver him over to the Corporation at the gate, who will conduct him to Gadsby's, where eighty people are to dine with him. On Thursday, he dines with the President with a select party composed of all the members of the government.

We shall get on pretty well, notwithstanding all the blunders of the Corporation, who are all common people, and do not know how to arrange such things. Goldsborough is the best of them. He has tormented me for advice and assistance, so that with him and the President I have had my hands full: to say nothing of the Miss Wrights, who look to me as their protector.

Mrs. Greuhm [26] has got out, and is ducking about on horseback with Laborie. The Baron is gaining strength fast. The more I see of him, the more I like him. The avenue is full of Virginia and Maryland equipages. It is a perfect carrouse[l], Mardi Gras: but caricatures. Where they all came from God only knows. The attempt at style and splendor is marred by some *outré* appendage, such as ill-dressed negroes dancing around the carriages like pages round royalty: while the ancient forms and dirty appearance of some of the vehicles would beggar all description. But of all the fools, the most errant fool, is our neighbor. His pomposity and ignorance is insupportable. The man will become a laughing stock.

[W. Lee.]

To Susan and Mary Lee at Boston

Washington, October 29, 1824

My dear girls:

I have been several days without any letters from you, and to-day our very kind friend Mr. Colden's [27] letter tells me that the steam boat has arrived and you are not on board. This will make me very unhappy until I hear from you. My dear Mary, I fear, is sick. I hope the next mail will relieve my mind. The bank has bought the house, and are to begin next week to fit it up. I shall begin with your rooms first that you may be comfortable. The Baron's fever has left him for ten days, and he now goes out daily. He is however very thin, but his cough has left him altogether.

I do not believe the Munroes will call upon you when you come back. He and myself have had a dreadful quarrel about the house. He insulted me in such a gross manner at the bank that I sent Major Kuhn to him to demand satisfaction. *The triumph was complete*. Nothing else is talked of, and everybody is rejoiced at it. He will now take special care how he makes use of my name again as he does everyone's. It was full time he received a lesson, and he has got it.

I hope and pray I may have a letter from you next post. How good and kind it is in Mrs. Colden to ask you to her house! How many obligations I am under to this excellent, worthy couple! If Stewart does not come to us (and I have no reply from him on the subject), I should like to have David and his wife spend a month with us this winter.

God bless you, my dear children.
W. Lee.

Mary Elizabeth Lee was married to the Baron the following year, in 1825. She and her husband continued to live in Washington until 1827, when he was sent back to Europe in the Russian diplomatic service. She wrote the following letter to her brother, William Barlow Lee, at Michigan, on August 31, 1827, the day before she was to sail to Europe: " If Papa has not written to you lately, you will be surprised by this: to learn that we are in New York, and intend sailing to-morrow for Liverpool in the packet of the first of September. It was very hard parting from Susan. But from every account we receive directly or indirectly, it appears she now bears our temporary separation very well. She is cheerful as usual, and visits every evening, and from her letters appears in very good spirits. We shall be back in a year's time: perhaps less. My health is good, and I depend much on a sea voyage to confirm it. Our accommodations are the best. There are few passengers, and a very good captain. I did not at first much like the season; but every one says it is excellent, and that the equinoctial gales are nothing on the coast of Europe.

" We sold the furniture and got ready in a week's time, which was very fatiguing, but I am glad it is over. When we come out, we can get handsome French furniture for what ours sold for. Krudener [28] who is here, tells the Baron he must be sure and come back within a year; as he cannot stand the heat and must and will go home. He tells him, ' Revenez bien vite, pour vos intérêts et pour les miens.' (This is *en confidence*.)

" Thomas spent five days with us, but got tired of New York, and returned to his quarters. Ochando we left in Washington, bemoaning your absence. ' Oh! Si William était ici. Quand revient'il donc, William? ' When he came to take leave of us, your dogs jumped round him as though it was you. I hope you still continue to be pleased with your situation. I little thought this voyage was so near when we parted.

" Adieu! dear brother. The Baron desires to be affectionately remembered. Think of us sometimes, and, as Tom says, not with anxiety. This voyage will do us both good."

The only letter of William Lee during this period is one written to the Secretary of the Treasury, Richard Rush, on the 28th of February, 1828: " In reply to your letter of the 15th inst., accompanied by a copy of the communication addressed by you to the Chairman of the Committee on Retrenchment, requesting information whether in your opinion there be any ' officers in your department whose services may be dispensed with without detriment to the public interest, or if the salaries of any of them can be reduced consistently with justice and propriety; and in general whether any of the expenses incident to the department can be reduced without impairing the efficiency of its operation,' I beg leave to state that as far as relates to this office I must truly say, considering the mass of business transacted therein, that I do not see how the number of clerks employed can be dispensed with, without detriment to the public service; nor do I see how with propriety, the salaries of any of them or of the messenger can be reduced, as the stipend each receives furnishes him with only a bare subsistence (and hardly that to those who have large families) without the hope of laying up anything for old age.

" The clerks in the accounting offices earn their salaries. They are the dray horses of the government. To them is confided all the details of the public expenditure, and during my public service for the last thirty years, I have observed that the faithful, laborious clerk, however firm his constitution, has generally been worn out by disease from close confinement, before he reached the common age of man, finishing his useful career by dying penniless.

" To give you an idea of the labor performed in this office, I beg leave to lay before you the statement herewith enclosed, exhibiting an expenditure accounted for therein under about sixty heads of appropriation, of nearly four millions of dollars annually, which exceeds by far, not only in its amount but in its detail, that of any other office under the government, and by which it will also be seen that besides the pay and clothing of the army &c. &c. &c. and the perplexing and endless details of the Indian Department, the military property of the United States, or what may be more properly called the 'material [matériel] of the army' is also accounted for in this office, amounting in value, on an accurate calculation, without including the arsenals, to about eleven millions of dollars.

"In relation to the question 'whether any of the expenses incident to the office can be reduced,' I beg leave to observe that the contingent fund is managed with economy, and if the extent of its correspondence with several hundred officers, most of whom make quarterly returns, is taken into view, the expenses of stationery and other items will not be found extravagant."

Ironically enough, Lee himself was removed from office with the change in administration in 1829, a piece of party politics that caused Mary de Maltitz to write: " Poor Papa! After serving his government faithfully for thirty years, that it should come to this." Mary's concern for her father is shown in the letter she wrote from Berlin on May 30, 1829, to her sister Susan in Washington: " I need not tell you what grief and distress I have experienced since I heard Papa had lost his place, and your silence increases my unhappiness. Lovl. feels it very deeply and sensibly. *Son bon coeur ne s'est pas démenti*. Rothschild will send you immediately by his order about six hundred dollars, through the hands of Phillips and Company, Philadelphia, who were also ordered by him to remit you nearly the same sum, which we calculate must have reached you near the middle of May. I hope you have received their letter announcing it, and pray it may have got in time. The rest will reach you the beginning of August.

" What a misfortune we are not in Washington at this time! Take courage, my beloved Susan. How I wish I was with you! Poor Papa! After serving his government faithfully for thirty years, that it should come to this. If you do not feel the courage to leave him and William, perhaps you had better take a house by the year, and keep the little furniture, piano and silver we left, for which L. has sent Papa an order to dispose of at his pleasure, and we can make out to spare you a thousand or twelve hundred dollars a year. Lovl's appointments are the same as at Washington; but the expenses of living are not so great. The least he can expect from his farm is a thousand pounds a year. So you see we can comfortably spare it, and perhaps more as things may turn out.

" I fear the season will be too advanced for you to sail, and that under these circumstances it will be painful to you. Therefore act as you think best. That I have missed you, since we parted, more than I can express, is but too true, and to have you with us is the greatest comfort our hearts can desire. Mrs. Sands, whose husband had this place, enjoyed the happiness to have her sister with her. Attachés and counsellors of legations with families are more common at this legation than single ones. If you do not like to come this year, on account of leaving Papa and William, you can come the next. Take the most prudent step, and especially do not sail in a bad season. Bring Mariette with you if you can. Do, my dear Susan, be calm and patient, and think you have enough to live upon, as long as we possess anything. I wish my poor William could get a situation. Thomas, I hope and trust, is provided for. My dear Papa. How I feel for him! Lovl wrote him three days ago and sent the order mentioned.

" Adieu! Dearest, and best love and sympathies to all. Your Mary." On this letter William Lee wrote: " This letter with the generous offer of assistance from the Baron made me weep with affection."

One more letter from his children is included here, this one from his daughter Susan, who had left Washington in order to join her sister in Berlin. She wrote to her father from Berlin on November 15, 1829: " My dear Papa, It would be very cheering to us to hear often from you, but we have not that pleasure. I have only had one letter from you since my arrival, and am much distressed to learn that you had been indisposed on your return to New York and I begin to fear that you have had a relapse. When I left New York, I felt quite sanguine in the hope of seeing you here in the spring, and that you would bring Mariette also. Now I begin to think that I flattered myself much in thinking so, and that I shall be quite disappointed.

" I scarcely know where to address this letter to you. In Washington post office it may lay a long time and do not know where to find you in the other cities. What a painful state of things! I am very impatient to know something positive concerning you, dear Papa, and should like also to know what William is about. I think he might write. And poor Mariette! Do tell her to write often to us. I feel quite lost without her, and I would give a great deal to have her now with us. I hope that if you can spare her, she will find courage to come in the spring, when the season is fine, for the navigation to Hamburg is very dangerous and tedious whilst the northerly winds prevail.

"Mary's health is still delicate. She has a very celebrated physician, Dr. Hüfelande. He gives her strengthening things, among the rest baths of strengthening herbs. But the season is much against a person's recovering entirely. You know it is in Europe the worst season in the year, so very dull. In fact I am horribly homesick, as you may see by my letter, although I am quite delighted at being again with Mary; yet I am constantly thinking of Washington and so very desirous to know what you are all about. Although I must own this is a splendid city, and is conducted in the greatest vigor and justice under the King's [Friedrich-Wilhelm III] paternal government, and it is quite a pleasing sight to see him riding about in an open carriage without any guards, the people bowing as he passes along. They are very contented and enjoy a steady happiness.

"The Baron's trunk (I suppose the trunk of papers) was shipwrecked at Cuxhaven (the entrance to the Elbe), supposed lost, but he has just received a letter from Hamburg telling him that it is found again but it has not yet reached here. Dear Papa. I have written you from Dover, Hamburg, by Shepperd and through London, two of which letters I addressed to Mrs. Street's. I hope they have all reached you. I am daily expecting to hear from you and hope and trust that it will be good news. Yours very affectionately, Susan."

VIII

LAST YEARS

1830–1840

After his daughter Susan had left to join her sister in Berlin, William Lee went to Boston to live in 1830. Lonely for his daughters to whom he wrote often, and discouraged at the loss of his government post, he little dreamed that his fortunes would soon rise again. At fifty-eight, Lee was still handsome, vigorous, entertaining, and attractive to women. During his residence in Boston he renewed an old friendship with Ann Amory McLean, widow of the wealthy merchant, John McLean. The two were married on November 4, 1830, in a wedding attended by many distinguished guests, including Daniel Webster and John Quincy Adams. In his *Memoirs* for that date (VIII, 244–245), Adams movingly described the wedding:

At six o'clock to Mrs. McLean's, No. 44 Beacon Street, where I was present at the ceremony of her marriage with Mr. William Lee, which was performed by the Rev. Mr. Green. There was a peculiarity in this solemnization which excited feelings and reflections different from those of any other wedding at which I had ever been present. The parties are each about threescore years of age. I knew them both in the heyday of youth, before either of them was first married. I then also knew their former partners, now in the grave. The numerous family of the Amorys in both branches were social companions of my youth. Of six brothers of the present bride, the three survivors, John, Rufus, and Francis, were now present, as was the youngest sister, Mrs. Bethune, with her husband. But Mrs. Codman and Mrs. Lowell, with her husband, were not there. Mrs. McLean has no children, but about half the company present were of a subsequent generation — children of my old acquaintance. There were of the former generation also Daniel Davis, George Blake, John Gray, Joseph Russell, Jonathan Davis, and his wife; H. G. Otis, who did not speak to me, and some others. Mr. Lee's son Thomas was there, and Mr. Green prayed for him and his sisters, as part of the marriage service. This was one of the singularities of the occasion. The couple thus united cannot have many years to live together. Their contemporaries, blooming in youth as I had seen them all, are now, some bending under the weight of years, and faces where I had seen roses in bloom were now furrowed, wrinkled, and haggard. I, too, have gone through a corresponding change, and was an object of meditation to them, as they were to me. Cupid and Hymen! what worshippers of yours are these! There was a numerous evening party invited at eight o'clock, from which I made, however, my escape.

The second Mrs. Lee had inherited considerable wealth from Mr. McLean, and she and William Lee, except for the winter of 1831–1832, which they spent in Washington, lived comfortably in Boston. Although retired from business and government service, Lee kept busy with literary interests and with the activities of the Massachusetts Historical Society, of which he had been elected a corresponding member back in 1822. Lee's second marriage lasted only four years, for in 1834 Ann McLean Lee died of " bilious fever," and was buried beside her first husband in Boston's Granary burial ground.

Although he had been left a substantial inheritance, Lee was again forced to live in loneliness. He thought and wrote repeatedly of joining his two daughters in Europe, but the decline of American prosperity — culminating in the Panic of 1837 — and the general political unrest of those years kept him from making this decisive move. He was fated never to see his daughters again. Of all his four children only the elder son, William Barlow Lee, was in Boston at the death of his father. William Lee died, possibly from a heart attack, on February 29, 1840, and was buried in a vault under King's Chapel, Boston.

Dr. William Lee quotes in *John Leigh of Agawam* the following passage from William Lee's Excerpt Book:

The question was asked, where this fellow (meaning my Excellency) got his knowledge. He does not know the life I have led among distinguished men and great events, amid revolutions and convulsions, hovering around Napoleon, and the enlightened men of all Nations who surrounded him, amid the glare of conflagrations, and the ruins of falling Kingdoms. Wonderful times they were. The mere souvenir of them is enough to chase dull care away for the remainder of life. The very last winter I passed in Paris, I went regularly to Court, and every Thursday I dined with the inimitable Josephine at Malmaison. But more of such things when I shall set myself down to write my Memoirs. . . .

This, unfortunately, he never did. But his diary and letters, spanning the full scope of his rich and varied life, perhaps give a more vivid insight into his period than an autobiographical account would have done.

To James Madison

Boston, November 9, 1830

Very dear Sir:

In all the events of my chequered life I have ever considered you and Mrs. Madison my best and dearest friends, to whom I owed more than to all the world. Through good and through evil report you were always the same, and I therefore experience much delight in announcing to you both my marriage with Mrs. Ann McLean, the widow of the late munificent John McLean, which took place on the 4th inst. Mr. Adams, Otis, Webster and many other distinguished friends did me the honor to assist at the ceremony, and in the evening all the respectability, fashion and beauty of the city filled our apartments to offer their congratulations.

As this event places me in opulence, I am persuaded it will give you pleasure. I beg you will say to Mrs. Madison that I bear her in sweet remembrance.

With the highest veneration I am
affectionately and devotedly yours
W. Lee

The following two letters were written by Lee's children on the occasion of his marriage to Mrs. McLean: the first from William Barlow Lee to his father on November 12, 1830, the second from Mary Elizabeth, Baroness de Maltitz, to Mrs. Ann Amory McLean on January 10, 1831.

William Barlow Lee wrote: "I returned yesterday from a shooting excursion into the country, where I have been for about a week, and found your letter announcing your marriage. I congratulate you and my good mother with all my heart, and wish you both all the happiness that you both so well deserve. Mariette joins with me. She says, if she can only see you both, she will be perfectly happy. I hope this will be shortly. Your bad season is no doubt setting in, whereas here we are enjoying by far the pleasantest part of the year. By what Tom says in his last letter, I shall expect you about the last of the month. I should like to hear from you what to do about lodgings.

"There is nothing new here. The Washington world is very much taken up with your marriage, which has not as yet, however, appeared in the papers. I hope Tom has made his arrangements with Mr. Stevens. I have said nothing more about it here than was absolutely necessary. I am getting so fat that I am afraid in a few years I shall become a sight. And what is the worst part of it, nothing that I can do will stop it.

"I am very anxious to know whether you have heard from the girls by the late arrivals, and to hear from you myself about everything. I have thousands of congratulations for you, which would be too tedious to particularize. You must take them all in a heap. Give my love to mother. Tell her I long of all things to see and embrace her. Tell Tom to write me soon. Believe me your affectionate son, W. B. Lee."

Mary de Maltitz wrote to Mrs. Ann Amory McLean Lee: " When my sister and myself had the pleasure of becoming acquainted with you during our visit to Boston, and when we received from you so many marks of friendship and such kind attentions, we felt all the gratefulness due to so amiable and cordial a reception; but we were not then aware that we should one day be indebted to you for the happiness of a beloved father, who owes you the recovery of all those endearing ties of which fate had deprived him.

" Allow me to mingle the expression of my love and my congratulations to those of my sister, on this occasion. The wishes I form for the welfare of my father, are blended with those I utter for yours, and the feelings I have ever cherished for so beloved a parent inspire [in] me the most tender [feelings] for one who has been the means of securing his happiness by uniting her fate with his.

" Although the separation from him will never cease to be painful to us, yet it is now softened by the comfort we derive from the knowledge of his having a companion such as you. The loneliness of his situation was ever a source of anxiety and unhappiness to us. This separation is also softened by the fondly cherished hope that a favorable and by no means impossible change of circumstances, will occasion our return to America. I shall then be most happy in introducing to you my excellent husband, who is very anxious to become personally acquainted with you and who unites his wishes and sentiments to mine. Believe me, Your affectionate and devoted daughter, Mary E. de Maltitz."

To Susan Lee and Mary, Baroness de Maltitz at Berlin

Boston, January 12, 1834

I write, my dear much-loved children, just to say we are all well. William and Dash are with us. The latter, like myself, begins to show marks of age. Thomas is at Washington; but in the course of this month will return to his post at Annapolis. Our Arab [1] President has scattered all the topographical engineers by ordering them off from the city to their different regiments. Tom says he is not sorry for it. His toil was so great and his health endangered by exposure to all weather and climates during most of the year. He has a healthful post, and will have full time to read and study. Mariette continues in fine health. I was fearful, when she came here, that the climate would not agree with her; but the contrary has proved to be the case. She is now entirely free from those coughs and bilious febrile attacks she used to have, and is as gay as a lark.

Except a violent cold, which confined me at home some time, I have enjoyed the last year my usual good health. On the first of January I passed into my sixty-third year: the year of the Grand Climacteric. According to the ancients and some moderns this number sixty-three is the critical year. It is generally thought by those who have studied the human constitution, that it undergoes a sensible change every seven years. If you pass, they say, nine of those points, your chance of living until eighty-four is double that of your living from forty-five to sixty-three. Having lost, since marriage, forty pounds of flesh and most of my *bas ventre* [abdomen], I feel light, can move easier, and stoop as well as I did at eighteen. I am in hopes, therefore, I shall weather the cape and coast along to the 84th degree, when it will be time to look out for the promised Haven. . . .

You will recollect that I have had but two letters from you since last spring. The last was from my dear Susan, dated August 15th. On the arrival of every packet, I flatter myself I shall hear from you, but I am continually disappointed. I console myself with the persuasion that you are all well and enjoying yourselves. It is painful to be separated from my children. For, after all, no one cares a fig about you, particularly in this *trading* country, where, when old age advances and activity closes, you are laid on a shelf like a yellow admiral.[2]

I am happy, however, having resources in myself. My greatest annoyance is that of being surrounded by a set of religious maniacs: a vile clique of Calvinistical fanatics, who have been courting my wife, and plundering her of from $1200 to 1500 a year ever since the death of her former husband. I have curtailed their robberies a little, and put an end to evening lectures and prayer meetings at *home* and *abroad*. I like some of the traits of character of old Luther; but that vile murderer Calvin,[3] and his doctrines, I ever did and shall detest. The descendants of the Roundheads and Puritans in this country are full as bad as the Jesuits were formerly.

Tell the Baron the great tariff storm has passed over, but a more serious one is arriving: a *Mungomania*,[4] the emancipation of the blacks. I have long seen this storm a brewing. The Calvinists are beginning to preach and to pray about it, with the Bible in one hand and a dagger in the other. I fear I shall live to see rivers of blood flow from that source. That slavery is the great curse of our country no good man can doubt. But they are the property of the planters, guaranteed to them by the Constitution; and we have no more right to deprive the southern man of them than he has to deprive us of our oxen, ploughs and ships. If you free them, *pay their masters for them*. Freeing them by stirring them up to rebellion and setting them to work to slit their masters' throats is criminal in the highest degree. I tremble for the results. This is the leading bone of contention among these states and the great rock on which the Ship of State is to be wrecked. . . . I can see no difference between the people of America and the people of Europe. They are governed or led, according as they are deserted, by bad or good men. So much for the good Baron to reflect on.

Mrs. Randall, Laura Wirt, died lately leaving five children. Mr. and Mrs. [Henry] Clay have been here. We saw much of them. He is growing very popular, and may be our next President. I hope so on William's account. Old Jackson is popular as ever with the rabble; but is hated and despised by the good and high-minded.

God bless you, my dear children.
W. L.

To Mary, Baroness de Maltitz at Berlin

Lancaster, Massachusetts
September 11, 1834

My dear children:

William, Thomas, and Mariette are well, but my precious wife is no more. She died of a bilious intermitting fever at one o'clock this day, after severe suffering of fourteen days. I am in the depths of affliction. Be not anxious about me. My health is good, and a competency is secured to me. She loved me dearly and I had a sincere regard for her, and I shall forever cherish her memory. I made her happy, which no other could have done in all probability. Our habits, tastes and inclinations were totally different, and from gratitude I made it a duty to conform to hers as much as possible.

Adieu! much-loved children. William and Mariette, who are sitting by me, send their love.

Wm. Lee.

To Mary at Berlin

Boston, September 20, 1834

My dear Children:

This is the second letter I write to announce to you the death of my wife, who departed this life on the 11th inst. at Lancaster. I am exceedingly cast down by this event as you may suppose.

By her will she has left, not as I supposed $10,000 to Susan, but that sum to my children, the interest of which after a certain time is to be paid to that one of them which I must say stands most in need of it, and the survivor of the four children is to possess the whole sum.

She has left me the house, horses, carriages, plate, furniture, and an income which will vary from 4 to 5000 dollars a year during life. Have I not reason to bless her memory and be grateful to the Giver of all Good for His bountiful protection of me in my old age? Being up to my eyes in business; proving and recording will; taking inventories; and distributing innumerable little gifts to her friends as memorials of her affection, I have not time to say more; only that Tom you will now most certainly see before many months and William probably.

By my wife's death $25,000 goes to the University of Cambridge [Harvard] to establish a professorship of history and $25,000 to the McLean Hospital, to whom her husband [5] gave at his death $120,000. A small portion of her estate goes to her family (who are all rich); at my death the bulk goes to public institutions. The family are very much dissatisfied with the will, but as it was made ten years ago, I could have no hand in it. Of course they do not blame me. When it was read before the whole family, who were totally ignorant of its provisions, the sensation was painful. Mr. [John] Lowell rose up and said: " Mr. Lee, since none of us are much benefited by this will, I hope you will live 100 years to enjoy the property left to you, and that these priests and deacons may not come into the possession of it until that time." Now you see how wonderfully well this turns out to me. Had the property gone to my wife's relations after my death, they would all have wished me dead and would all have looked upon me through life with an evil eye. But as it is they are disposed to be *very kind — excessively kind*. Homo homini lupus [Man is a wolf to his fellow-man].

Rufus Amory [6] and Mr. Lowell were both very distinguished lawyers. They and all the family were opposed to the marriage under the fear I should have influence with my wife to divert some of her property to my children, and know[ing] she had in 1824 made a will, though they did not know its contents, which she carefully kept from them, by getting Mr. Shaw [7] (now justice of the state) to make it for her, they in drawing up the contract of marriage made that begin at 1st page, will irrevocable, supposing its dispositions were in favor of her family. She always told me that if her family knew her will, they would not oppose the marriage. I think myself it is a most extraordinary will. It shows how much influence these religious sects and these priests have over the minds of their associates. My wife was deluded by them. They courted and flattered her by placing [her] at the head of their institutions and robbed her and her family.

She was enthusiastic, sincere, and immovable in her religious opinions, and believed in all the doctrines of that murderer Calvin. I have scolded her, read to her, coaxed her, persuaded her, but it was all in vain. You might as well attempt to throw a ray of light into a block of granite as into her mind. Finding I could not succeed and that I was doomed to suffer torments, I came to a determination, as she had generously given herself and fortune to me to yield to her. She is as a spoilt [child], accustomed to govern with despotic sway all about her, and as since one must yield, I took upon myself to yield in everything and she was happy, but I was not; on the contrary as miserable as a man could be; for in addition to her religious frenzy she was the most penurious being on earth: eternally hoarding for what she thought the cause of God. Next to Him she loved me most ardently, and seeing it I bent to all her wishes, to the astonishment of all her family and friends. Had I not done it we should have both been very miserable. Had she married a rude headstrong man, she would have been a most wretched being.

Her gifts of plate, jewels, linen, pictures, books, statuary, and some valuable articles of furniture to her sisters, brothers, nephews, and nieces as memorials of affection are numerous. By her will, as I said before, nothing was to be yielded up until my death, but I thought it was due to her memory and to the friends she loved to order them distributed immediately, which is thought among these close-fisted people of trading habits to be a mighty generous act. " How nobly he acts," they all say, and the relatives are all pleased, *and so am I*. Enclosed is the copy of the 77 circular letters I have written to all the legatees of these objects. Do not you think I have done right? William is outrageous about it. He was for not giving up one cent.

The parson of her church is agoing to give us a funeral sermon next Sunday. I will send you a copy. I shall have from custom to be present, and a barbarous custom it is. I have put all the servants, her physician, pastor, and deacons in mourning, and done everything in a style far above their commercial habits here. I can say no more at present.

God bless you,
Affectionately
Wm. Lee.

I have not used black wax nor mourning paper fearing to alarm you when the letter gets into your hands before you open it.

To Mrs. Henry Codman [8]

Boston, September 20, 1834

Madame:

By the will of your much lamented aunt, dated in 1824, she bequeathed to her relations and friends, as memorials of her affection, all her plate, linen, pictures, furniture and clothing. And, notwithstanding she did by her marriage contracted with me in 1830 so far revoke her former will, as to leave me in possession and full enjoyment of all these objects during my life time, I have thought it due to her memory and to the friends she loved, to order these tokens of affection to be distributed without delay.

Will you do me the favor to send for her best silver bowl and cream pot bequeathed to you, and to request Mr. Codman will have the goodness to call and sign a receipt therefor.

I have the honor to be, Madam,
with the highest respect
Your obedient servant
Wm. Lee

[This letter has a wide black border.]

To Susan Lee at London

Roxbury, near Boston, December 26, 1836.
Direct to me always at Boston.

I have been anxiously waiting for the last six weeks to hear from you, my own dear children. From all that has been said in the papers about your coming to America (I presume you have seen the paragraphs), I have at times brought myself into the belief that you were on your passage. Are we to be forever separated? Is my old age to be a life of suffering with no one being near me to soothe and comfort me? Alas! I fear it is so. Even your letters are few and far between. The last from Mary was by Mrs. Bethune, and Susan's was dated in I think September, though I cannot tell exactly, for I sent it to Thomas. But I will not complain. Since the death of your ever regretted mother, and my expulsion from France by the French Bourbons, my life has been a life of suffering — at times of intense suffering, and though inured to it, I begin, as old age approaches, to wince under it. If I am never to taste domestic enjoyments again and my eyes are to be closed by menials only, be it so. . . . But enough of this. It cannot be agreeable to you, and to dwell on it is certainly painful to me.

From what I learn from Mrs. Bethune and your own letters it appears to me the Baron does not wish to come to America. In this I must say I think he is right. To a man of ambition and his standing in the diplomatic corps, it would be a sort of exile, and its consequences would be to throw him back for years in his career of European policy and relations. Therefore, however much I should be gratified to see him at Washington, and to embrace you, my dear children, I do not think that either of us ought to wish him to make the sacrifice. A residence at an European Court would be more congenial to him and more consonant to his feelings and interests. I state upon mature reflection this, as my firm belief and conviction. On this point I hope your next letters will fix me. If you remain in Europe, I will join you, for I cannot live in this forlorn, forsaken way any longer. At least I will try what running backwards and forwards will do to relieve me and spin out a hale old age. I should like, if you remain in Europe, to visit Switzerland, parts of Germany, and Sweden, Denmark and Norway. I should prefer a northern to a southern tour. England I dislike. France I have seen enough of, and Italy I never had any desire to see.

William is well and now in great hopes, as Van Buren is to be

President, that he shall be able to get some employment. Tom, as I have written you, resigned his commission in the army and is now employed in engineering in Maryland. He stands high in his profession and will realize from $3000 to $5000 a year. He is now attending as a witness the Court of Enquiry on Gen'l Scott [9] at Fredericktown in Maryland. He was Scott's aide in the Creek war. While he was engaged in that inglorious Indian warfare, I had no rest. So many lives were lost by the scalping knife and tomahawk, that I had no peace night or day. Among them were two of his friends: Izard and Lane,[10] who were continually at my house, the finest West Pointers I ever knew and young men of great promise.

Mariette is well. She had her trunk stolen and rifled of all its contents on her way from Lancaster. She cried like a child about it. All was lost except her pins of gold and watch. I in vain endeavored to console her by promising her another trunk of clothes better than those lost; but she said that was impossible as the best of them came from you. Luckily for her, the two robbers were arrested, all her clothes found, except two or three pairs of stockings, and the fellows sent to the penitentiary or state's prison to hard labor for seven years. This severe sentence was owing to their having been in prison three years before. The most painful part of the business to Mariette was her being obliged to attend the court several times, to swear, hold up her *best* hand, as she called it, and go through an examination. She now pities the creatures and would have prevented their punishment if she could.

I have purchased a large brick house at Roxbury, where I now am with Mariette, my cook, Mary, and a servant man. It is 50 feet square three stories high, has twenty-two rooms and stands on an eminence which commands the view of Boston, its islands, harbor, Nahant and all the country round. It is a beautiful spot. I bought it of the widow and heirs dog cheap and was offered $4000 for my bargain; but as there is 1 acre of ground to it, which may sell well for house lots, I thought I had better keep [it] and have let it at $800 a year for a boarding house. The necessary repairs occupy me much. I shall put it in Susan's name, so that when I am gone, she will be independent, as the rent will always support her.

Mrs. Bethune says everything about you, and I am tormented for letters of introduction to you, *which I do not give*. I fear you would be overrun. Should you hear of Mr. and Mrs. Thorndike, who are very rich and she a fine woman; and of Mrs. Cobb,[11] who is also a charming woman, I wish you would pay them some attention, as they are friends of mine.

I wish when Susan writes she would tell me all she sees and who[m] she sees. If you go to Cheltenham, make yourselves known to Dr. Newell,[12] a first cousin of mine, who I am told is rich and much respected.

I will continue to write you and oftener under the full impression that you are not coming here, and when the spring opens, you may look out for me.

God bless you all
Your affectionate father
W. L.

To Susan Lee at London

Roxbury, near Boston, yet you
had better to direct to me [at] *Boston,*
February 19, 1837

I have just received, my dear Susan, your letter from Hastings. I began to think you cared little about me. Children soon get weaned from their parents, but the parents never from the children. Of the removal of you all to London I never heard, until I got it through the Lowell family, who had it *from the Bethunes at Paris!* At length comes a letter dated in August from Mary, by the Bethunes, who did not arrive here until November. Then one or two short letters from you in the fall, and after the arrival of (as the newspapers say) forty-seven vessels from England in the course of a few days, your Hastings epistle reaches me. When I shall be again favored time will show. No news is good news, and to know that you are happy is perhaps all I ought to desire.

My life is a dreary one. Old men in this country no one cares anything about. Like admirals of the yellow, they are laid on the shelf. The news from Liverpool that the Baron was to be named and then again was named to Washington, which ran through all our papers, has died away, and I am left without any idea of your movements as well as of your hopes and wishes. I must wait with patience and, as I do not know what would be best for the interest of the Baron — to remain in Europe or to come to Washington — I have come to the determination to wait patiently events and yield to circumstances.

Washington I have not seen for three years. Everybody complains of the change for the worse there, as far as society goes. Perhaps now that rich old Arab [Jackson] is about leaving it and Van Buren, who is much of a gentleman, takes his place on the 4th [of] March, he may give a different tone to things. But the whole country is changed. We have now every sort of excitement and as much superstition as any country in Europe. The great bone of contention now is emancipation of the slaves, 3,000,000 in number. Rivers of blood will flow before it can be brought about. If the northern states insist on it, I presume we shall separate into two or three governments. Next to this mungomania is the Great Temperance Societies. We are all to become water drinkers, stupid Boeotians; [13] for I never knew a water drinker yet who had any talents or genius. Then comes your antimasons, the most ridiculous of all societies, except masonry itself; and then your bible society, the great gem of all; your missionary societies, *mite* societies and the devil knows what all — all of which I have taken upon myself to ridicule without measure.

Tell the Baron I have concluded that wherever we find excitement we find error, and wherever we find fanaticism we find crime, and that I am opposed to all this nonsense and stuff now floating about in the world. Tell him further that go where he will, he must expect me to follow, if it be to the uttermost parts of the earth. I will not live any longer from you the moment I hear you are permanently fixed.

Tom, since he resigned, has always had employment, and what is singular is now at work in the Bureau of the Topographical Engineers in Washington! He will always do well. William will now get something, I have no doubt. He is a favorite in the Van

Buren family. He and the young Vans have always been intimate and last fall at New York were inseparable. Mariette is as gay as a lark. She pleases herself that Mary is coming out, and that our French cook, and a very respectable woman, is to go with her to Washington to help Mary keep house.

I wish you would write one long letter, and tell me all you see, hear, and know. I do not envy your living in London in winter. To me at that season (and I tried it twice) it was the most detestable place I ever knew. But then you have more comforts as to house and fire than I had at the London Coffee House, Ludgate Hill. Do you see any Americans? There is a Mrs. Thorndike and a Mrs. Cobb, two fashionable women, my neighbors in Beacon Street. If they fall in Mary's way, I wish she would be civil, as they are kind friends of mine. They have ample fortunes and are traveling for their health and amusement. And now I do insist upon it that you write your poor disconsolate old father and give me the earliest notice of the good Baron's movements, that I may be governed thereby. I must and will not live this gloomy, dreary life any longer.

God bless you all.
Your affectionate father
W. L.

To Mary, Baroness de Maltitz at London

Boston, April 20, 1837

I am still, my dear Children, without any letters from you. The great anxiety I experienced during the prevalence of the influenza in England was painful, such were the dreadful accounts we had here of its ravages. But that has subsided, and as the saying is, that no news is good news, I have reasoned myself into a belief you have escaped its harmful effects.

The papers again state that the Baron is coming here. I shall rejoice for one and be happy for a time at least, for God knows what is to become of us all here. Such distress was never known in this or any other country. It beggars all description, and reaches every grade of society. We have had failures from New Orleans to Boston for upwards of $80,000,000 and new ones daily occurring. Cotton, the staple of the country, has fallen to 8 and 9 cents, making a difference of $30,000,000 to the nation in its export. The planters will be ruined, as well as the merchant.

Real estate has fallen one third. Not a dollar is to be had; several of the smaller banks have failed, and others will no doubt follow suit. The dividends of stocks all fall short. I have already suffered by the fall in the sum of $1500. My income, which I fondly hoped would have gone nearly to $7000 this year, will I fear not amount to more than $3000! The panic is universal. My cook has gone to Lancaster, and as Mariette is much attached to her, she has gone with her to board at $1.25 cents a week. I have shut up my house, keeping only two rooms open for myself, and taking my meals at the Norfolk House very near to me, where I have found Alexander Everett,[14] our former Minister to Spain, and his charming wife, who have also shut up their house. All the world are flying to the country to live cheap. Boarding you know has always been the fashion here, though it is to my mind an execrable manner of living. The fare is wretched; but we must put up with it. I do not mean to spend for myself more than 40 or 50 dollars a month for this year.

William is seeking with some friends some cheap place in the country. Thomas is employed by the Government as engineer at $2000 per annum; so we shall get along. But what a change! If you were only within reach that I might fly to you to be cherished and assured! I should not care for all the rest. My constitution is firm, but an old man without a wife or children to comfort him is a wretched being.

God bless you all.
W. L.

To Mary, Baroness de Maltitz at London

Boston, August 1, 1837

I have received, my dear Mary, yours and Susan's letters announcing the Baron's appointment to The Hague, and of your speedy departure for Rotterdam. I congratulate the Baron on this distinguished mark of his sovereign's favor. The news to be sure has prostrated me, but I am an old man, and it is of but little consequence whether I am happy or not, during the short time I have to stay here in this troublesome world. The thought of once again embracing my children buoyed me up for many years, but that hope is fled and " hope deferred makes the heart sick." [15]

It seems as everything had combined this year to destroy my peace. By the best of management and strict economy, I had income in the net of from $5600 to $6200. Fifteen or $1800 is all I shall get this year. Bank stock is falling every day; several have failed, and none of the banks give any dividends. It is the same of insurance stock, life insurance stocks, house rents and everything else that this estate is composed of.

The people and Government are bankrupts. Such a state of things no country ever before exhibited. The loss of fortunes, the stagnation of business and distress of all classes beggars all description. What is to be the end of all this misery, God alone knows. Last year this country imported for eleven of millions of dollars from Lyons in silks. This year they will not import for one million. Privation will probably take place in Lyons for the want of work. In all these manufacturing towns in England distress will reign and the poor will be starving. We are their great consumers. They will curse us and who cares? I hate the nation. Old Jefferson said in his letter to Mme. de Staël they were a nest of pirates and a den of thieves.[16]

You will be pleased at The Hague if Susan can put up with peat and turf fires. In 1797 I spent a week or two there when Mr. Adams was our resident minister. If my income was free I would be with you as soon as this letter, but here I must remain to hold on, watch events, and die if it is so ordained by inches.

I spent yesterday afternoon with Mr. and Mrs. [John Quincy] Adams. They live six miles from me. They were delighted to see me. I sent them your two hire[d] maids. They are all sorely disappointed in your not coming out. Colden and his wife are both dead. He died poor. God bless you my dear Baron and my dear children. May you ever be strangers to the sufferings we endure here.

Your devoted &c
W. L.

On February 29, 1840, William Lee died, with only his elder son, William Barlow Lee, with him in Boston. The letter that follows is the one Mary wrote her brother from The Hague on April 20, 1840, after receiving the news of her father's death:

"My Dear Brother,

"Our grief and distress at the receipt of your letters of the 1st and 24th of March cannot be described. The news was so sudden, so unexpected! And yet, how uncertain is life! How ought we all to think of and prepare for death! to us the only event certain. Poor Papa! that we all could not be near him to soothe and comfort him the last years of his existence!

"Susan is quite overcome. She was to have sailed in the *Hollander* in May. We had no idea that Papa's constitution was so broken. Mrs. Bates painted him to us as being as well and cheerful as ever and enjoying life and company as usual. We thought his fits of illness transient and easily overcome by his good constitution. Still Susan had determined to devote herself to him and I had made up my mind to the separation; Poor Papa! How I wish now she had sailed with Miss Verveer! She came very near doing so. You at least, my dear brother, have had the painful satisfaction of being near him in his last moments.

"I will write you soon, my dear William. My heart now is too full to say more."

NOTES, CHRONOLOGY, AND INDEX

NOTE ON MANUSCRIPTS

The original of the diary of William Lee in two volumes, of the memorandum book, and of all the letters not specifically cited may be found in the Lee-Palfrey Collection at the Library of Congress. Sources of other letters are as follows.

The Madison Papers at the Library of Congress: William Lee to James Madison, December 10, 1807, November 1, 1808, January 1, 1812, May 24, 1812, September 6, 1815, February 16, 1816, November 8, 1816, November 17, 1816, November 9, 1830.

The Records of the Department of State at the National Archives: William Lee to James Madison, January 20, 1802, July 23, 1807; William Lee to James Monroe, January 20, 1813, March 4, 1814, March 20, 1814, March 12, 1815, two letters dated October 20, 1815; William Lee to the Prefect of Bordeaux, August 14, 1815; William Lee to Bergevin, Commissary of Marine, August 29, 1815; William Lee to Henry Jackson, Secretary of Legation, Paris, September 20, 1815.

The Jefferson Papers at the Library of Congress: William Lee to Thomas Jefferson, December 20, 1814, May 11, 1816, October 25, 1816, June 16, 1817, January 12, 1818; Thomas Jefferson to William Lee, August 24, 1816, January 16, 1817, June 6, 1817.

The Library of Columbia University in the Special Collections: Captain Charles Baudin to William Lee, July 16, 1815.

The Records of the Treasury Department at the National Archives: William Lee to Richard Rush, February 28, 1828.

I

YOUNG ENTREPRENEUR AND TRAVELER
1796–1798

1. From Alexander Pope, *Essay on Man*. Epistle I, lines 267–274. Lee made a few errors and omissions.

2. Benjamin Homans has given a good account of the wreck of the *Mary* on the coast of Soulac, Department of the Gironde. The ship's crew consisted of the captain, first mate, ten seamen, and two boys. These, added to three passengers mentioned by Lee (but not by Homans), make a total of seventeen souls on board the wrecked vessel. The cargo consisted of 221 tons of whale oil, salt beef, salt pork, 160 cases of candles, 100 small firkins of butter, biscuit, crackers, apples, potatoes, tobacco, and other things. Seven hundred seventy-five casks of whale oil were found, shipped to Bordeaux, and sold at public auction, evidently by Theodore Peters, whose signature appears on the account (Causten-Pickett Papers, Manuscripts Division, Library of Congress). The life of Benjamin Homans, Jr. (1765–1823), written by Benjamin Homans IV, states that in 1812 he was appointed chief clerk of the Navy Department by President Monroe. Homans spent the rest of his life in Washington, D.C., and in 1814 rendered a valuable service to his country by saving some of the public records from destruction by the British (Benjamin Homans Papers, Manuscripts Division, Library of Congress).

3. Probably Trémoille, the name of a well-known French family.

4. The Château Trompette was actually built during the reign of Charles VII and was merely enlarged by Louis XIV. Sébastien Le Prestre de Vauban (1633–1707), military engineer, was famous for building fortifications of French towns.

5. Probably the son of Harrison Gray, Loyalist, and brother of Elizabeth Gray, who married Samuel Allyne Otis (Lorenzo Sabine, *Biographical Sketches of Loyalists*, Boston, 1864, I, 489).

6. The only singer of the period whose name approaches "Sereuser" was Mme. Schreuzer (*Les Spectacles de Paris et de toute la France pour l'Année 1794. Suite de la quarante-troisième Partie*, Paris, p. 5).

7. Saint-André, which in fact antedates the Black Prince (1330–1376), its construction having been begun in the thirteenth century. Records of the architects commence only with Guillaume Albert, d. 1366 (Henri Stein, *Les Architectes des Cathédrales Gothiques*, Paris, 1909, pp. 101, 105).

8. Thomas Jefferson described this canal in notes taken on a journey into the southern parts of France in 1787. Jefferson said that the canal ended at Toulouse, where it had four communications with the Mediterranean. At the western end the canal communicates with the Atlantic Ocean by the river Garonne (*The Papers of Thomas Jefferson*, ed. Julian P. Boyd, Princeton, N.J., 1955, XI, 446–454).

9. Lee undoubtedly meant " chartrons." The Faubourg des Chartrons was a part of Bordeaux situated close to the Garonne River, presumably containing streets that ran along the water's edge (Map of Bordeaux, 1787).

10. *Décade*, ten days of the calendar of the first French republic; *décadi*, tenth and last day of the *décade*, observed as a holiday. Lee is undoubtedly referring to *décadi*, and the correction is made hereafter.

11. Paper money of the French republic.

12. Jesse Putnam (1754–1837), respected Boston merchant (Eben Putnam, *The Putnam Lineage*, Salem, 1907, p. 178). When Putnam was imprisoned for debt in France the following fall, Lee wrote to Talleyrand offering to take his place in prison (Letter of November 6, 1797, *Affaires Étrangères Correspondence Politique, Etats-Unis*, Vol. 48, Part VI; photostats, France, Library of Congress).

13. Mme. de St. Hilaire's home, 555 rue du Bac, was described in a report of the Préfecture de Police for March 19, 1803, seven years after William Lee had stayed there: " Her house is now marked as the meeting place of Chouans [Royalists] and émigrés, who are enemies of the government. Frightful plots are hatched here " (A. Aulard, *Paris sous le Consulat*, Paris, 1906, III, 758).

14. Of the people mentioned in this paragraph, Mr. S. Broome, Sr., was probably Samuel Broome. With his brother John (1738–1810) of Connecticut, he conducted an importing business, and during the Revolution fitted out privateers for the destruction of British commerce (*Appleton's Cyclopaedia*, I, 390; Louis F. Middlebrook, *Maritime Connecticut during the American Revolution, 1775–1783*, II). Joel Barlow (1754–1812) of Connecticut was to become important in Lee's life. Poet, statesman, known as one of the " Connecticut wits," he married Ruth Baldwin in 1781 and went to Europe in 1788, living in London and Paris. Having invested in French government securities, he was by 1794 a rich man. He was made

consul at Algiers and was instrumental in arranging treaties with that country and with Tunis and Tripoli. Returning to the United States in 1805, he bought his estate, Kalorama, in the District of Columbia, where Lee was a visitor. After Madison appointed him minister to France in 1811, Barlow sought to discuss with Napoleon a treaty between France and the United States, but he failed to reach the Emperor and died of inflammation of the lungs in December, 1812, near Cracow, Poland (*Dictionary of American Biography;* Charles Burr Todd, *Life and Letters of Joel Barlow,* New York, 1886). Dr. Brockenbrough was undoubtedly John Brockenbrough, surgeon in the Virginia Navy during the Revolution, and later a justice of Essex County, Virginia. He was the father of William Brockenbrough (1778–1838), jurist. Mr. Gelston was probably David Gelston (1744–1828), Collector of the Port of New York and member of the State Legislature (*New York Genealogical and Biographical Record,* I and II, 1870–1871, 134). François-Clément-Privat Garilhe (1759–1829), lawyer and legislator, was a member of the Convention and was imprisoned as a moderate during the Revolution. He was later elected a deputy to the Council of Five Hundred (Jean-François-Eugène Robinet, *Dictionnaire Historique et Biographique de la Révolution et de l'Empire, 1789–1815,* Paris [1899], II, 12).

15. The Bostonians whom Lee mentions include Richard Codman (1762–1806), member of the Boston firm of John and Richard Codman, who spent many years in Europe (Cora Codman Wolcott, *The Codmans of Charlestown and Boston,* Brookline, Mass., 1930, pp. 15–22). Samual Williams, eldest son of George Williams, went to Hamburg as a merchant in 1793 and soon became United States consul there; several years later he held the same post in London. He died in Boston in 1841 (*New England Historical and Genealogical Register,* 1851, V, 53–54). John Higginson, son of Stephen Higginson, was a Boston merchant (b. 1765). He lived in Paris for some years after 1792, marrying a Frenchwoman (Thomas Wentworth Higginson, *Descendants of the Reverend Francis Higginson* [Cambridge? Mass.], privately printed, 1910, pp. 24–26). Joseph Waldo (1722–1816) was a Boston merchant and Loyalist who died in England (Sabine, *Loyalists,* II, 392).

16. James Monroe (1758–1831), later Secretary of State and President of the United States. In 1794, Monroe was minister to France, but having pursued a course not in keeping with the desires of the State Department, he was recalled in 1796. William Lee made an affidavit regarding Monroe's residence in Paris, the text of which follows (original in the Monroe Papers):

To all whom it may concern.

The undersigned, having resided in France during the years 1796 and 1797, and having had the honor of being acquainted in the family of Mr. Monroe, the then minister from the United States of America near the French Republic. – CERTIFIES. – That during that period Mr. Monroe lived in a house which the undersigned knows he purchased with the intention and view of persuading the Government of the United States to take it at what it cost, it being a suitable house for their minister to occupy. That he frequently heard Mr. Monroe say he should offer it to the United States for that purpose. That Mr. Monroe purchased said house and grounds about it of an individual, and not of the nation, it being *patrimonial, unconfiscated property*, and not a *national domain;* and the said minister, when recalled, was under the necessity, before he could leave Paris, of selling the said estate, which he did, and for a sum not exceeding much (if any) the amount of the original purchase, with interest and repairs added thereto.

WILLIAM LEE

Boston, July 10th, 1799.

17. Fulwar Skipwith of Virginia (1765–1834) was appointed consul general to France in 1795 by George Washington, retiring from this post in 1799. He was later named commercial agent at Paris by Jefferson in 1802 and was appointed consul at Paris by Madison in 1815, but never held this position (Records of the Department of State, National Archives). Skipwith went to West Florida in 1809 and was a leader in the successful revolt against the Spanish in that region, called the West Florida Revolution, in 1810. On October 26 of that year Fulwar Skipwith was elected governor of the short-lived Commonwealth of West Florida. The following December a detachment of militia, sent by President Madison, took possession of West Florida in the name of the United States (*Louisiana Historical Quarterly*, 1934, XVII, 80–90).

18. Charles Le Brun (1619–1690), director of the Gobelin works, made the drawings for this series of tapestries illustrating campaigns of Alexander the Great (Adolphe Hullebroeck, *Charles Le Brun*, Paris, 1941, p. 29).

19. *Télémaque dans l'Ile de Calypso,* "ballet héroïque . . . ," music by Miller. Performed from February 23, 1790, to November 24, 1816 (*Bibliothèque Musicale du Théâtre de l'Opéra,* compiled by Théodore de Lajarte, Paris, 1878, vol. I, period from 1774 to 1807, p. 367).

20. Gaetan Vestris (real name Vestri), a famous dancer from 1748 to 1800 (Nérée Desarbres, *Deux Siècles à l' Opéra, 1669–1868,* Paris, 1868, p. 148).

21. Baritone at the opera from 1779 to 1823 (*Deux Siècles à l'Opéra*, pp. 85–86).

22. M. d'Hauteval (according to *The Autobiography of Colonel John Trumbull*, New Haven, 1953, p. 220) had been consul in Boston, where Trumbull knew him. M. Hauteval is perhaps better known as one of the personages in the " XYZ Affair " of 1797. Along with two bankers — Hottinguer and Bellamy — and a woman, Mme. de Villette, he unsuccessfully attempted to persuade the American commissioners to Paris (Charles Cotesworth Pinckney, John Marshall, and Elbridge Gerry) that the United States should lend money to the French government and pay a sum to the Directors and to Talleyrand. The three Frenchmen were referred to as Messrs. X, Y, and Z (Edward Channing, *A History of the United States*, New York, 1927, IV, 187).

23. Lee was in error here. In his *Essay of Superstition*, Bacon notes exactly the opposite point, stating that superstition *is* more dangerous than atheism.

24. Now the Place de l'Hôtel de Ville. From 1572 to 1789 the Place de la Grève had been the scene of execution of political prisoners and criminals, and upon its lamp posts the first victims of the Revolution were hanged by the mob (Karl Baedeker, *Paris*, Leipsic, 1891, p. 64).

25. *Giulietta e Romeo* (Milan, La Scala, January 30, 1796), considered the masterpiece of Nicola Antonio Zingarelli (1752–1837).

26. Now called the Place de la Concorde.

27. Now the Panthéon.

28. *Panurge dans l'Ile des Lanternes*, " comédie lyrique . . ."; music by Grétry; performed for the first time January 25, 1785. *Psyché*, " ballet-pantomine "; music by Miller: performed for the first time in 1790 (*Bibliothèque Musicale du Théâtre de l'Opéra*, I, 347, 369).

29. John Moore, M.D. (1729–1802), who traveled extensively on the continent of Europe and was the author of *A View of Society and Manners in France, Switzerland and Germany* (*The Dictionary of National Biography*).

30. On September 13, 1798, about two years and a half after Lee had made this entry in his diary, the Council of Ancients established a tax every bit as vexatious as that which had been abolished by the Constituent Assembly (Alfred Delvau, *Barrières de Paris*, Paris, 1865, pp. 9–12).

31. Jean-Lambert Tallien (1767–1820), French revolutionist. His wife, Theresia Cabarrus (1775–1835), was born at Saragossa, Spain. She was married first to the marquis de Fontenay, whom she di-

vorced. Imprisoned in Bordeaux and condemned to death, she was set free by Tallien, whom she married in 1794. By a third marriage, after divorcing Tallien in 1802, she became princesse de Chimay (*Autographes de Personnages ayant marqué dans l'Histoire de Bordeaux*, Société des Archives Historiques de la Gironde, vol. XXX, Bordeaux, 1895, pp. 343–344, 338–339).

32. Jazaniah Bussey, who was for some time in business with his older brother, Benjamin Bussey, according to Benjamin's manuscript autobiography deposited at Harvard University. Jazaniah died in Leeds, England, at the age of twenty-eight. (*Dedham Historical Register*, 1899, X, 71–72).

33. Velt: an old French measure, equivalent to 197 U.S. gallons.

34. Race of Alderney. That part of the English channel which lies between the island of Alderney and the Cap de la Hague, France, is a dangerous tidal race, or very rapid current.

35. Wear ship: a nautical term for changing the course of a vessel so as to bring the wind across the stern.

36. At this time " corn " was in common use as a name for various grains.

37. British naval and merchant vessels were formerly given a rating for insurance purposes (Joanna Carver Colcord, *Sea Language Comes Ashore*, New York, 1945, p. 19). Lee also spoke of seeing, on June 12, 1796, some " second rates " at Rochefort.

38. Hounslow Heath in Middlesex, near London, was the resort of highwaymen and the scene of many robberies.

39. Daniel Parker is described in 1787 by John Adams as an intelligent American (*Works of John Adams*, ed. Charles Francis Adams, Boston, 1856, VIII, 457). Parker resided for forty years in France, where he owned a beautiful country seat near Versailles. Here he entertained many noted persons until his death in April 1829. See also Note 6, Chapter II. For Codman see Note 15 above. For Judge William Tudor see Chapter II, Note 7. John Brown Cutting, apothecary general at Yellow Springs during the Revolution (*Virginia Magazine of History and Biography*, XV, 421; XVI, 59, 184, 188). John Quincy Adams spoke of John Brown Cutting several times in his *Memoirs*, especially as a former medical officer of the Revolution and a clerk in the War Department in 1828 (*Memoirs of John Quincy Adams from 1795 to 1848*, ed. Charles Francis Adams, Philadelphia, 1874–1877, VIII, 15).

40. Château d'Anet, built for Diane de Poitiers, was respected during the Revolution, but destroyed in the nineteenth century (Alphonse Roux, *Le Château d'Anet*, Paris, 1911).

41. The famous actress, Sarah Kemble Siddons (1755–1831), played Millwood in *The London Merchant, or the History of George Barnwell,* by George Lillo. Elizabeth Farren (1759?–1829) retired from the stage in April 1797 to marry Edward, twelfth Earl of Derby (*D.N.B.*).

42. Thomas Morton (1764?–1838). His five-act comedy, *A Cure for the Heart-Ache,* which was first performed at Covent Garden on January 10, 1797, soon became a stock play (*D.N.B.*).

43. The first notice of a Royal Menagerie in England places this establishment at Woodstock, where King Henry I kept a collection of animals. The menagerie was transferred from Woodstock to the Tower of London during the reign of Henry III (Edward Turner Bennett, *The Tower Menagerie,* London, 1829, Introduction).

44. Colonel Hore Browse Trist and his brother, Lieutenant Nicholas Trist, were officers in the British army at Boston in 1775. The colonel returned to England to attend to the Trist succession on the death of his father, who had been a member of Parliament (*Tyler's Quarterly Historical and Genealogical Magazine,* VI, 215). Having returned to the United States some years later, Trist was described as "the first American collector of the port of New Orleans, the second incumbent of that then important and distinguished office." He died in 1804. Thomas Jefferson, who had known Hore Browse Trist from childhood and thought very highly of him, sent for and brought up his two sons in Virginia (*Louisiana Historical Quarterly,* XXIV: 774, 782, July 1941; letter from John M. Gelston, October 15, 1804, Jefferson Papers, Library of Congress).

45. Amos Whittemore (1759–1828), inventor and manufacturer of cotton and wool cards. In 1797 he patented a machine for puncturing the leather and setting the wires in these cards, thereby revolutionizing their manufacture (*Appleton's,* VI, 492).

46. The battle of Gemappe (Jemappes) decided the fate of the Low Countries, since it witnessed the defeat of the Austrians under the Duke of Teschen by the French under the noted general Charles-François-Duperier Dumouriez, 1739–1823 (Charles-Francis Dumouriez, *The Life of General Dumouriez,* London, 1796, III, Book VI, pp. 322, 330–346).

47. Pierre Riel de Beurnonville (1752–1821), marshal of France (Lucien Graux, *Le Maréchal de Beurnonville,* Paris, 1929).

48. "It is related that another rich Antwerp merchant, Gasparo Dozzo, on being privileged to entertain the Emperor Charles V in his house, cast into the fire a promissory note for a large loan he had

formerly made to his sovereign " (Edward Neville Vose, *The Spell of Flanders*, Boston, 1915, p. 411). This is the same story told by Lee, although he gave a different name to the merchant. Gaspero, an Italian proper name, is used jestingly for a thief.

49. Quinten Matsys (Metsys or Massys, 1466–1530) was born at Louvain and settled in Antwerp. He was a blacksmith and later became a painter, although the story that he changed his calling for love is apocryphal (Harald Brising, *Quinten Matsys*, Upsala, 1909, pp. 8–9). He is commonly recognized as the painter of *The Misers*, at Windsor Castle (Jean de Bosschère, *Quinten Metsys*, Bruxelles, 1907, pp. 117–118).

50. Abraham Ortelius (Örtel, Ortels, Hortel, Bartolus, Bartholus Arameis, 1527–1598), Belgian geographer and cartographer (Leo Bagrow, *A. Ortelii Catalogus Cartographorum*, Gotha, 1928, Ergänzungsheft Nr. 199 zu " Petermanns Mitteilungen," pp. 11–25). Jean-Baptiste Gramaye (b. second half of sixteenth century at Antwerp, d. 1635 at Lubeck), Belgian *savant*, traveler, and historian (Jules de Saint-Génois, *Les Voyageurs Belges*, Bruxelles, 1846, II, 93–105). Rubens, Vandyke, and David Teniers the elder and David Teniers the younger were Flemish painters.

51. From Richard Savage's *Sir Thomas Overbury*, a Tragedy, Act I, Scene I, spoken by the Earl of Northampton. Lee's recollection of these lines differs interestingly from the text of the 1777 edition, which speaks of " false patriot's zeal," rather than " French patriot's zeal." The text runs:

> " You'll find the friendship of the world is show,
> Mere outward show! 'Tis like the harlot's tears,
> The statesman's promise, or false patriot's zeal,
> Full of fair-seeming, but delusion all."

52. Early name for Holland: the Batavian Republic, 1795–1806.

53. The Royal Palace, originally a town hall.

54. Two French versions of the famous Fielding novel had been made by that date: *Tom Jones*, a *comédie lyrique* by Poinsinet, 1765; and *Tom Jones à Londres* by a M. Desfarges, which played at the Théâtre Français in 1785.

55. An island of the Netherlands in the North Sea.

56. Martin Sherlock (b. *ca.* 1750, d. 1797), traveler, and author of *Lettres d'un Voyageur Anglois* (*D.N.B.*).

57. Inscriptions: inscribed securities, such as stocks and bonds. Lee may have meant "nationals' estates," or the estates of (American) nationals. The apostrophe was omitted.

58. John Quincy Adams writes in his *Memoirs* of such a trip on June 11, 1797: "We made a party this morning, Mr. and Mrs. Murray [note 62 below], Mr. and Mrs. Marshall [John, 1755–1835], Louis Marshall [1773–1866, brother of John], Mr. Vancouver [Note 60 below], Mr. Daindridge [Mr. Murray's secretary], Mr. Lee, and myself, to visit the little towns of Saardam and Broek, in North Holland. We crossed the river Y in a sail boat, and on the other side took carriages, which carried us in two hours to Broek. This village is distinguished for its extreme cleanliness." There follow descriptions of Broek and Saardam (Zaandam). (J. Q. Adams, *Memoirs*, I, 190–191.)

59. The principal curiosity of Zaandam is the hut said to have been occupied by Peter the Great in 1697, while he worked as a ship carpenter in order to gain a practical knowledge of this craft to take back to his countrymen.

60. American agriculturist. Between 1786 and 1793, Vancouver was engaged by the English government to report on agriculture in various English counties (*D.N.B.*).

61. An interesting aside to the Gutenberg-Coster Controversy is given by Hadrianus Junius in his work *Batavia*, 1568. He states that after Laurens Janszoon Coster of Haarlem invented printing from wooden blocks, one of Coster's workmen named Johannes (possibly Faust, although the last name is not mentioned) stole some of his master's tools and fled to Mainz with them. By 1442, says Junius, this printing office in Mainz had published some books with the type of Coster (Dr. A. Van Der Linde, *The Haarlem Legend of the Invention of Printing by Laurens Janszoon Coster*, London, 1871, pp. 61, 167).

62. The three American ministers mentioned by Lee were Adams, Pinckney, and Murray. John Quincy Adams (1767–1848), later Secretary of State and President, was appointed minister to the Netherlands in 1794, although he did not actually serve, as the French were in possession of the country when he arrived. Charles Cotesworth Pinckney (1746–1825) was sent on a mission to France in 1796 but, when the Directory would not recognize him, moved to Amsterdam. This was the "XYZ Affair." William Vans Murray (1760–1803), diplomat, succeeded Adams as minister to the Netherlands, arriving there on June 7, 1797 (*D.A.B.*).

63. Of Noël, John Quincy Adams notes in his *Memoirs* that he visited "the French Minister Plenipotentiary Noël" at The Hague, on October 20, 1795. A footnote says: "François Joseph Michel Noël, originally a littérateur, who, like many others of his class,

rose out of the vortex of the Revolution and filled a place in public life with credit and distinction. He survived until 1831 " (J. Q. Adams, *Memoirs*, I, 125).

64. A description of the contents of the *Musée Archéologique* in Ghent mentions a picture of historic interest signed by P. Heelant. It is said to recall the Ghent legend of the *fils bourreau de son père*. The statue stood on the " bridge of the beheading " (de la decollation). The legend says that a father and son were to be executed; the magistrate offered to pardon the one who became the executioner. At the insistence of his father, the son consented to do this sacrilegious act, but when he raised the sword it fell apart in his hand (Henri Hymans, *Gant et Tournai*, Paris, 1902, p. 54).

65. Nicholas, Count Luckner (1723–1794), marshal of France.

66. Samuel Miles Hopkins (1772–1837), lawyer in Connecticut and New York (*Appleton's Cyclopaedia of American Biography*, New York, 1888, III, 258). The Mr. Kidder to whom Lee refers was probably the mate of the ship, mentioned just below.

67. Snow: a small sailing vessel similar to a brig, but not identical with it (*A New English Dictionary on Historical Principles*, hereafter cited as *O.E.D.*).

68. The Georges Islands, a group of small islands at the mouth of Muscongus Bay, Maine.

69. Sable Island, thirty miles long, two miles wide, in the Atlantic off SE Nova Scotia, is the visible part of an extensive sand shoal and a major hazard to navigation. Cape Sable is the southern point of Nova Scotia, on an islet just south of Cape Sable Island, seven miles long, three miles wide.

70. James Spear Loring, Boston bookseller and author, wrote in *The Hundred Boston Orators* (Boston, 1852, pp. 200–201) an account of Harrison Gray Otis. In this he tells an amusing anecdote of a visit Otis made, accompanied by William Lee, to President John Adams at Quincy. According to Loring's report, Otis and Lee left hurriedly when they saw that a group of the Essex Junto had also come to visit Adams and to criticize him for sending Elbridge Gerry to France. But Lee had time to observe " the independent course which the president pursued towards the Essex junto committee," and " from that day forth became a convert to the Adams dynasty."

71. Thomas Boylston Adams (1772–1832), chief justice of the Norfolk County (Massachusetts) Court of Common Pleas from 1811 (information from L. H. Butterfield, Editor of the Adams Papers).

II

"CONSUL" AT BORDEAUX
1801–1808

1. The term "commercial agent" needs explanation. For all practical purposes the powers, rights, and duties of commercial agents were substantially those of consuls, and, in fact, William Lee was generally addressed as "consul at Bordeaux." However, the Treaty of 1800 between France and the United States stated that each country was free to appoint "commercial agents" (a sustitution for the term "consuls" used in the Treaty of 1788) for the protection of trade, to reside in France and the United States. The title may have been changed because Bonaparte, as First Consul of France, wished to distinguish between these appointees and himself. In any case, soon after the Treaty of 1800 expired in 1808, America's "commercial agents" in France and France's "commissaries of commercial relations" in the United States were officially known once more as consuls.

The Treaty of 1788 between France and the United States took up at length the subject of consuls, and hence was commonly called the "consular convention." Lee mentions the Consular Convention in his letter to James Madison, January 20, 1802.

2. Joshua Loring of Boston (1768–1862), merchant and master of a sailing vessel (Charles Henry Pope and Katharine Peabody Loring, *Loring Genealogy*, Cambridge, Mass., 1917, p. 98). He was the owner of the ship *Susan* and traveling agent for Perrot and Lee. William Stackpole of Boston was a frequent visitor at the house of William Lee in Bordeaux. In spite of accepting the hospitality of the Lee family, he tried to get Lee's consulship away from him. Thomas Lovell of Bordeaux was one of those having business connections with the house of Perrot and Lee (Records of the Department of State for Bordeaux. National Archives).

3. Mariette Ferrand, a Frenchwoman who took care of the Lee children at Paris and Bordeaux, and returned to America with the Lees, remaining with them until William Lee's death in 1840, when she went to Europe to live with Mary, Baroness de Maltitz. The entire family was extremely devoted to Mariette, and Lee's daughter, Susan, painted a miniature of her (see page 219).

4. The Reverend John Sycombe, or Secombe, of St. Matthew's Church, Halifax (since burned down). An Englishman by birth, he went from New Jersey to Halifax, where he baptized William Lee and most of his brothers and sisters (William Lee, *John Leigh of Agawam (Ipswich) Massachusetts, 1634–1671*, Albany, 1888, p. 187).

5. Also gallipot, a small earthen glazed pot, especially one used by apothecaries for ointments and medicines (*O.E.D.*). Seven lines later, the words " Sons of Cake " mean Scotsmen. In Scotland, as well as in parts of Wales and northern England, the thin hard-baked oaten bread which is common fare is referred to as " cake." Hence the name " Land of Cakes " was applied originally in banter — to Scotland and the Scottish lowlands (*O.E.D.*). The word " Guater," which occurs in the last line of the poem, probably means guitar.

6. Mrs. Henry Preble (who was Frances Wright) and her daughters lived with Daniel Parker, a rich American, at his country seat near Versailles. The younger daughter, Frances Anica, was married there to Thomas Barlow, Joel Barlow's nephew. In 1830, soon after the death of Daniel Parker, Mrs. Preble and her older daughter Harriet returned to the United States. Mr. Henry Preble, who had joined his younger daughter, Mrs. Barlow, in Connecticut, had died there five years before (G. H. Preble, *First Three Generations of Prebles in America*, Boston, 1868, family circulation, pp. 287–293).

7. Delia Tudor (1787–1861), daughter of Col. William and Delia Jarvis Tudor. She married Commodore Charles Stewart, U.S. Navy, in 1813, and her own daughter became the mother of the Irish patriot, Charles Stewart Parnell (William Tudor, ed. *Deacon Tudor's Diary*, Boston, 1896, pp. xvii xxii xxxvii). The Tudor family was very close to the Lee family. Lee frequently mentions Delia's father, William Tudor (1750–1819), judge advocate general of the army, who had been attached to the staff of General Washington during the Revolution. A Bostonian, Judge Tudor was one of the founders of the Massachusetts Historical Society (*Appleton's*, VI, 178).

8. " Mme. La Croix " was undoubtedly the widow of Charles Delacroix de Constant (1741–1805), lawyer. He was an important revolutionary figure, and voted in the Convention for the death of the King. He was elected deputy to the Conseil des Anciens and named its secretary; and he was minister of external relations under the Directory, replaced by Talleyrand. As prefect of the Gironde in 1803, he and William Lee had pleasant relations. Mme. Vernenac was their daughter (Robinet, *Dictionnaire Historique*, I, 376–377; Records of the Department of State for Bordeaux. National Archives). Lee's spelling has not been corrected.

9. Nathaniel Weld Johnston was the son of an Irishman, William Johnston, who established himself as a merchant in Bordeaux in 1743. In 1772 Nathaniel took over the direction of the commercial house founded by his father, later known as " Nathaniel Johnston and Son " (*Autographes de Personnages ayant marqué dans l'His-*

toire de Bordeaux, XXX, 256–258). William and George Johnston were two sons of Nathaniel by his first wife (Pierre Meller, *Les Familles Protestantes de Bordeaux d'après les Registres de l'état civil avant 1793*, Bordeaux, 1902, pp. 43, 46).

10. Christopher Meyer, then chancellor of the American consulate at Bordeaux (Records of the Department of State for Bordeaux, National Archives).

11. Thomas Newel Lee (1789–1811). "Died single at sea near Bermuda." There is in existence a very nice miniature of this Thomas (*John Leigh of Agawam*, p. 188). Appleton was probably Samuel Appleton (1766–1853), merchant, philanthropist; the Boston shop which he ran with his brother, Nathan, was so successful that from 1799 to 1819 he made frequent business trips abroad (*D.A.B.*). Nancy Lowell was Anna Cabot Lowell of Newburyport, Mass. (1768–1810). Daughter of Judge John and Sarah Higginson Lowell, she was reputed to be "a woman of fine talents and both a poetical and prose writer" (Delmar R. Lowell, *The Historic Genealogy of the Lowells of America*, Rutland, Vt., 1899, p. 58).

12. John Armstrong (1758–1843), soldier and diplomat, was minister to France from 1804 to 1810. Toward the end of this mission he accepted a note from the French foreign minister, Cadore, without making any attempt to ascertain its true purpose, which was to deceive the United States government into thinking that the Berlin decree (1806) and the Milan decree (1807) were no longer in force, and hence there would not be any more interference with our commerce. Almost immediately afterwards every American vessel in a French port was illegally confiscated. Martin Van Buren is said to have described Armstrong as "eminently pugnacious" *D.A.B.*; and James Truslow Adams, *New England in the Republic*, Boston, 1926, p. 265).

13. James Monroe and William Pinckney.

14. Joseph Fenwick of Maryland was consul at Bordeaux from 1792 until William Lee was appointed. Fenwick's testimony that the cargo of the ship *Molly* was American, whereas it was actually entirely French, led John Quincy Adams to speculate in his memoirs about what sort of officers the American government had placed in their consular service (J. Q. Adams, *Memoirs*, I, 135–136). William Lee himself described Fenwick in a letter dated October 8, 1815, to Count Tournon, prefect of the Gironde. Lee wrote that Fenwick had made a considerable fortune while consul, but that, as he was an American, he should not be taxed to support the Emperor's military campaigns (Records of the Department of State for Bordeaux, National Archives).

15. Christophe Gernon belonged to one of the most ancient families of Dublin, Ireland. In 1754 he assumed the management of his father's commercial house, founded at Bordeaux in 1742, and occupied himself principally with armaments (*Autographes de Personnages. . .* , p. 257). The neighbor Martin, mentioned two paragraphs above, was probably Henri Martin, merchant (*Les Familles Protestantes. . .* , p., 53).

16. George-Louis Leclerc, comte de Buffon (1707–1788), naturalist, for nearly fifty years was *intendent* or steward of the Jardin du Roi, and wrote the monumental forty-four volume *Histoire naturelle, générale, et particulière.*

17. Mrs. Lee's brother, John Palfrey. Son of William and Susan Cazneau Palfrey, he was the father (by his first wife, d. 1803) of the distinguished historian John Gorham Palfrey. From 1804 until his death in 1843, he lived in the Louisiana territory. His second wife, Miss Hannah Phillips, actually came from "Middleton" (Middletown), Connecticut (Hannah Palfrey Ayer, *A Legacy of New England*, Portland, Maine, privately printed, 1950, I, 11).

18. The greater number of the persons concerned in these rumors were connections of Napoleon I. Joseph, Louis, and Jerome were his brothers; the grand duke of Berg (Murat) was a brother-in-law, having married Caroline Bonaparte; Eugène Beauharnais was the son of the Empress Josephine; Jean-Baptiste-Jules Bernadotte (later King of Sweden), married Désirée Clary, the sister of Joseph Bonaparte's wife. Francis I was the Emperor of Austria; the grand duke Constantine Pavlovitch was the brother of Alexander I, Czar of Russia; Charles-Louis, archduke of Austria, was the brother of Francis I. Old families of Naples were Anjou, Aragon, and Bourbon. Naples was under Napoleonic domination from 1806 until 1815, and then it was returned to the Bourbons.

19. The kingdom of Tuscany, now to be called Etruria, was established in 1801, and on the throne were placed Louis I, son of the Duke of Parma, and Maria-Luisa, daughter of Carlos IV of Spain. After reigning only fifteen months, the King died and the widowed Queen acted as regent for her young son until December, 1807, when Etruria was taken over by Napoleon (Paul Marmottan, *Le Royaume d'Etrurie*, Paris, 1896, pp. 3, 122, 254).

20. Andoche Junot, duc d'Abrantès (1771–1813), French general. He commanded the French invasion of Portugal in 1807, but was driven out by Wellington in 1808.

21. George William Erving (1769–1850), diplomat, was born in Boston and educated at Oxford, Erving was appointed by Jefferson to a succession of posts, including agent for seamen in London,

secretary of legation and chargé d'affaires in Madrid. He was made special minister to Denmark in 1811 and later served as minister to Spain (*D.A.B.*).

22. Jean-Joseph-Régis Cambacérès, duc de Parme (1753–1824), legislator, second consul, and minister, was grand chancellor of the Empire (Robinet, *Dictionnaire Historique*, I, 320–321).

23. João (John 1769–1826), son of Queen Maria I of Portugal, took control of the state in 1792 when his mother went insane, becoming Prince Regent in 1799. When the Peninsular War broke out the royal family took refuge in Brazil, then a Portuguese colony. Queen Maria died in 1816 and John succeeded to the united thrones as João VI (Charles E. Nowell, *A History of Portugal*, New York, 1952, pp. 172–183). The arrangements for the departure for Brazil of the Prince Regent and his family were made by Sir William Sidney Smith (1764–1840), Admiral, R. N. Smith sent several of the ships under his orders to convoy the Portuguese squadron (*D.N.B*).

24. Jean-Baptiste Nompère de Champagny, duc de Cadore (1756–1834), replaced Talleyrand as minister of foreign affairs in April, 1807, and was in turn succeeded four years later by Maret, duc de Bassano (Adolphe Thiers, *Histoire du Consulat et de l'Empire*, Paris, 1845, VIII, 67; XIII, 48–51).

25. André-Charles la Bonninière, comte de Beaumont (1768–1836). Under the empire he became the first gentleman-usher of the Empress Josephine. Created baron of the empire in 1811, he entered the legislative corps in 1813 and remained until the end of the empire (Robinet, *Dictionnaire Historique*, I, 134).

III
GOSSIP FROM PARIS
1809–1810

1. Joel Barlow, for example, had written of calling for Kosciusko and dining with the " Hotingers " in 1804; and John Trumbull spoke kindly of " M. D'Hauteval," who called on him in Paris in 1797. Neither Barlow nor Trumbull mentions the third agent, Bellamy, but Madame de Villette, the woman who had served as liaison between the American ministers and Messrs. X, Y, and Z, was apparently well received by some Americans. Thus, a letter from Mrs. Barlow to Mrs. Lee on October 17, 1811, tells of the Barlows' intention to spend a few days with Mme. de Villette at her château near Paris.

2. The Minister of the Interior was Jean-Pierre Bachasson, comte de Montalivet, 1766–1823 (Martha-Camille Bachasson, comte de

Montalivet, *Fragments et Souvenirs,* Paris, 1899, Son père, pp. vi–xv). Laurent de la Faurie de Monbadon (1757–1841), chevalier de l'empire, 1808, comte de l'empire, 1809. He was mayor of Bordeaux in 1805, senator in 1809, peer of France in 1814 (Le V'te. A. Révérend, *Armorial du Premier Empire,* Paris, 1896, III, 20–21).

3. David Bailie Warden (1772–1845), diplomat, author, and bibliophile. Born in Ireland, he became a United States citizen and went to Paris as private secretary to General John Armstrong, by whom he was designated in 1808 to act as consul *pro tempore.* Later Warden was appointed consul at Paris; but he was removed from this office in 1814 ostensibly on the ground that, during the period which elapsed between the death of Joel Barlow and the arrival of William H. Crawford as the next minister, he had assumed the role of consul general, with which he had not been invested (*D.A.B.*).

4. From *The Spectator,* No. 195, Saturday, October 13, 1711. The passage from Addison reads: "For my part, when I behold a fashionable table set out in all its magnificence, I fancy that I see gouts and dropsies, fevers and lethargies, with other innumerable distempers lying in ambuscade among the dishes."

5. Sawney, a derisive nickname for a Scotsman (*O.E.D.*), was used in fun by Lee for his friend James Ronaldson, who was born in Scotland about 1780 and settled in Philadelphia. Engaged in the cotton textile industry and one of the country's leading type founders, he was first president of the Franklin Institute of Pennsylvania, 1824–1842 ("Historic Philadelphia," ed. Luther P. Eisenhart, *The Transactions of the American Philosophical Society,* vol. 43, part 1, 1953, p. 276).

6. Louis-François-Armand de Vignerod du Plessis, duc de Richelieu et Fronsac (1696–1788), marshal of France. He was a person of extremely loose morals even for the times (*Memoirs of Duke de Richelieu,* New York, 1904, vol. I, Biographical Sketch by Léon Vallée).

7. A process for preventing chimneys from smoking, so called after its inventor, Benjamin Thompson, Count von Rumford (1753–1814), who was born in North Woburn, Mass. While in London, where the problem of smoky chimneys was virtually ubiquitous, Rumford discovered the principles upon which fireplaces and chimneys have since been constructed (G. Curtis Gillespie, *Rumford Fireplaces and How They Are Made,* New York, 1906).

8. From *The Lousiad,* Canto II, by John Wolcot (1738–1819), English satirist and poet, who used the pen name Peter Pindar (*D.N.B.*).

9. (Mrs.) Ann Ward Radcliffe (1764–1823), English novelist, noted for her " Gothic " novels, particularly *The Mysteries of Udolpho (D.N.B.)*.

10. From *The Deserted Village* by Oliver Goldsmith, line 158.

11. Anne Lenclos, called Ninon de Lenclos (1620–1705), a beautiful, charming, and unconventional Parisienne, whose salon was frequented by many French notables (*Life, Letters and Epicurean Philosophy of Ninon de L'Enclos*, translated and edited by Robinson-Overton, Chicago, 1903). Having heard of the child prodigy François-Marie Arouet (who later changed his name to Voltaire), Ninon arranged a meeting with the eleven-year-old boy (George R. Havens, *Selections from Voltaire, with Explanatory Comment upon his Life and Works*, New York, 1925).

12. Mathieu-Louis Molé (1781–1855), director of French roads and bridges from 1809 to 1813 (Mathieu-Louis, comte de Molé, *The Life and Memoirs of Count Molé*, edited by the Marquis de Noailles, London, 1923, vol. I).

13. William Lee was undoubtedly familiar with the common nautical terms: to ship — to put on board; to unship — to detach from a vessel. Although in his letter Lee said " on ship," he undoubtedly meant that the sleeves could be put on the dress or removed from it.

14. Francis James Jackson (1770–1814), English diplomat, gained his nickname from the special mission to Denmark, to which he had been sent before the bombardment of Copenhagen by the English in 1807. Shortly before Lee's mention of him, Jackson was named minister plenipotentiary to Washington following the recall of Lord Erskine, whose arrangements in the dispute concerning H. M. S. *Leopard* and the U. S. frigate *Chesapeake* in 1807 the British government had refused to ratify. Jackson was also recalled to England at the request of the U. S. government in November 1809 (*D.N.B.; Register of the Department of State corrected to March 1, 1874*, p. 113).

15. Charles-Maurice, duc de Talleyrand-Périgord, prince de Bénévent (1754–1838), was minister of foreign affairs from 1797 to 1807 and grand chamberlain from 1808 to 1810.

16. From 1791 to 1816 this depository for church art was the Abbey of the Petits-Augustins and was administered by Alexandre Lenoir. In 1816 Louis XVIII placed in the restored church of Saint-Denis the tombs of the kings and returned to other churches the monuments that had formerly belonged to them (*Inventaire Général des Richesses d'Art de la France. Archives du Musée des Monuments Français*, Paris, 1883, I, 21–23, 25, 436–439). The modern *Musée des*

Monuments Français, established in 1879, is housed in the Palace of Chaillot.

17. Valentine Visconti, who married Louis, duc d'Orléans, second son of Charles V of France in 1389. When the duke was assassinated in 1407, the duchess tried unsuccessfully to have Jean-Sans-Peur, the assassin, punished for the deed. She herself died in 1408 and her body was eventually placed at the side of her husband in the chapel of the Celestins in Paris (Frances Marjorie Graves, *Quelques Pièces Relatives à la Vie de Louis I, duc d'Orléans et de Valentine Visconti, sa Femme,* Paris, 1913, Introduction, pp. i–x).

18. Honorable John Douglas (1756–?), son of James Douglas, Earl of Morton, was the man undoubtedly meant by William Lee. In 1809 he was appointed one of the commissioners for the care of sick and wounded seamen and for the care and custody of prisoners of war (John Philip Wood, *The Peerage of Scotland,* Edinburgh, 1813, pp. 276–278).

19. Louis-Alexandre Berthier, prince de Wagram et de Neufchâtel (1753–1815), marshal of France and legislator. He was appointed vice high constable in 1807 and master of the hounds in 1808 (Ernest Lavisse, *Histoire de France Contemporaine,* Paris, 1921, III, 228).

20. The Palais de l'Élysée, erected in 1718 by comte Evreux, acquired the name "Elysée Bourbon" from its prolonged occupation under Louis XVI by the duchesse de Bourbon (Baedeker, *Paris,* 1878, p. 157). Since 1873 this palace has been the residence of the Presidents of the Republic.

21. The women Lee mentions are the duchesse de Raguse — formerly Mlle. Perregaux — wife of Auguste-Frédéric-Louis Viesse de Marmont, duc de Raguse (1774–1852), marshal of France (Marmont, *Mémoires du duc de Raguse de 1792 à 1832.* Paris, 1857, I, 348–349); Madame Portalis, wife of Jean-Étienne-Marie Portalis (1745–1807), a distinguished lawyer (Robinet, *Dictionnaire Historique,* II, 664); and Madame Hottinguer, wife of Jean-Conrad Hottinguer, 1764–1841), merchant and legislator of Zurich. Establishing himself in Paris, M. Hottinguer became a rich merchant and was made Regent of the Bank of France (Robinet, *Dictionnaire Historique,* II, 180). Hottinguer was the Monsieur X in the XYZ Affair, and made part of his fortune by financing the French armies. He had traveled widely in the United States and later became a financial intimate of John Jacob Astor (Stewart Mitchell, ed., *New Letters of Abigail Adams,* Boston, 1947, p. xxxvii).

22. Lieutenant-Colonel Antoine de Cazenove d'Arlens, who lived at Lausanne on Lake Geneva. Mme. de Staël, the celebrated writer,

was a close friend of Mme. d'Arlens (*Journal de Mme. de Cazenove d'Arlens*, Paris, 1903, Introduction).

23. From *A Father's Legacy to his Daughters*, 1774. This was written for his children, who had been left motherless, by John Gregory (1724–1773), professor of medicine at Edinburgh University (*D.N.B.*).

24. Lee may have been speaking of Montmartre when he said "Mont Calvaire." Montmartre was the scene in 1806 of a celebration of the discovery of the cross (the Calvaire) at that site (Charles Simond [Paul Adolphe van Cleemputte], *La Vie Parisienne à travers le XIXe Siècle: Paris de 1800 à 1900*, Paris, 1900, I, 138).

25. Elizabeth Patterson of Baltimore, who married Jerome Bonaparte (1784–1860) in 1803 without the consent of Jerome's family, although he was a minor (Lavisse, *Histoire*, III, 196). Refusing to recognize this marriage, Napoleon made Jerome king of Westphalia and married him to Charlotte of Württemberg.

26. Conyers Middleton (1683–1750), English divine. Traveling in France in his youth, he wrote these verses, which Voltaire translated:

> A nation here I pity and admire,
> Whom noblest sentiments of glory fire;
> Yet taught by custom's force, and bigot fear,
> To serve with pride, and boast the yoke they bear:
> Whose nobles born to cringe and to command,
> In courts a mean, in camps a gen'rous band;
> From priests and stock-jobbers content receive
> Those laws their dreaded arms to Europe give:
> Whose people vain in want, in bondage blest;
> Tho' plunder'd, gay; industrious, tho opprest;
> With happy follies rise above their fate;
> The jest and envy of a wiser state.

(*Oeuvres Complètes de Voltaire. Les Honnêtetés Littéraires*. Vingt-sixième Honnêteté, Paris, 1879, vol. XXVI. Mélanges V, pp. 159–160.)

27. Jean-Siffrein Maury (1746–1817), the foremost preacher and orator of his time. In 1789 he entered the États Généraux, where he eloquently defended the clergy against abuse (Mgr. [Antonie] Ricard, *L'Abbé Maury (1746–1791)*, Paris, 1887, pp. 206–208).

28. *Picard:* native of Picardy. According to Larousse *picard* may possibly be traced to an old French word signifying a quarrelsome person.

29. James Fordyce, D.D. (1720–1796), Presbyterian divine and

poet. His *Sermons to Young Women*, 1765, were reprinted many times (*D.N.B.*).

30. From " Corin's Profession or the Song of Constancy," by John Wolcot. See Note 8 above (*The Works of Peter Pindar*, Esq. London, 1796, IV, 334).

31. Elisabeth-Pierre, comte de Montesquiou-Fézensac (1764–1834), French statesman. He replaced Talleyrand as grand chamberlain in 1810 (Thiers, *Histoire du Consulat et de l'Empire*, X, 19).

32. Charles Rollin (1661–1741), noted French historian.

33. This was the work of François-Joseph-Michel Noël, who turned from literature to diplomacy and was minister to the Netherlands (see Note 63, Chapter I).

34. Colonel Seth Hunt (1780–1846) of Massachusetts, who traveled abroad extensively (Thomas Bellows Peck, *The Bellows Genealogy*, Keene, N. H., 1898, pp. 164–166). Hunt and Elbridge Gerry furnished the necessary bond for Lee when he was appointed to Bordeaux.

35. Isaac Cox Barnett of New Jersey. After serving as unofficial agent at Bordeaux from 1799–1800, he was agent for seamen there for the following year, until William Lee took over the agency. Barnett later went to Antwerp and from 1814 to 1833 was consul at Paris (Records of the Department of State for Bordeaux and Paris, National Archives).

36. *La Vestale*, lyric tragedy in three acts, words by Jouy, music by Spontini, presented for the first time on December 11, 1807 (Clément et Larousse, *Dictionnaire des Opéras*, p. 1137).

37. The first two of these three lines are from William Congreve's *The Mourning Bride*, Act I, Scene I, lines 1–2.

38. Gideon Granger of Connecticut (1767–1822), lawyer and public official. A supporter of Jefferson, he was appointed postmaster general in 1801, resigning at the request of Madison in 1814 (*D.A.B.*). By the " Louisiana purchase " Lee must have meant some private business deal in Louisiana. He certainly was not speaking of the well-known Louisiana Purchase of 1803.

39. Joseph Fouché (1759–1820), a revolutionist, was minister of police in 1799 and again from 1804 to 1810, when he was appointed governor of Rome. Already in Italy, he heard that his refusal to return his correspondence with the Emperor was about to cause his arrest. He relented and obtained permission to return to Paris (Fouché, *Memoirs Relating to [Joseph] Fouché*. Translated from the French by E. Jules Méras, New York, 1912, Introduction, pp. vi–ix). The " Minister of State " was probably Cambacérès, President of the Council of State.

40. " After bleeding the Spanish monarch as long as there was any blood or money left, Napoleon decided to take possession of Spain and Portugal. . . . The Spanish royal family was removed to France and a Napoleonic brother [Joseph] substituted. In May 1808 the Spaniards rebelled " (Channing, *History of the U. S.*, IV, 394).

41. Joachim Murat (1767–1815), general and marshal of France, who married Caroline Bonaparte, sister of Napoleon I. He was King of Naples.

42. Henri-Jacques-Guillaume Clarke, duc de Feltre et comte d'Hunebourg (1765–1818), French soldier and statesman of Irish descent. He was minister of war from 1807 to 1814 (Robinet, *Dictionnaire Historique*, I, 417–418).

43. Ferdinand VII (1784–1833) became King of Spain in 1808 but was replaced by Napoleon's brother, Joseph. He returned to the throne after the French had been driven out, in 1814 (Louis Bertrand and Sir Charles Petrie, *The History of Spain*, New York, 1934, Part II, 440–449). While in banishment in Valençay in 1810, Ferdinand wrote to Napoleon and asked him to adopt him as a son and give him as consort a princess of his dynasty. This request was treated with ridicule. Hence he did not marry the daughter of Lucien Bonaparte (*Memoirs of Ferdinand VII*, translated by Michael J. Quin, London, 1824, pp. 11, 103).

44. The second of these puns about court life revolves around *beau harnois* (handsome harness — clothes, ornaments) and Beauharnais, the first husband of Josephine. The third involves the play on the words *cire* (wax; *bougies* are wax candles) and *Sire* (the title given to kings and emperors in direct address).

45. Henry Brockholst Livingston (1757–1823), jurist, was judge of the New York Supreme Court and for seventeen years after 1806 he served on the United States Supreme Court (*D.A.B.*).

46. William Patterson. According to a letter from Joel Barlow to James Monroe, December 10, 1811, Patterson thought the President was wrong in revoking his consulship at Nantes, and Barlow found him well regarded (Records of the Department of State for Paris). William Patterson was recalled by Robert Smith, Secretary of State, on May 10, 1810 (Consular Dispatches, Nantes, Vol I., National Archives).

47. Marie-Louise, who became Napoleon's second wife in April 1810. She was a great-niece of Marie-Antoinette.

IV

A YANKEE AT NAPOLEON'S COURT
1810–1812

1. Louis XIV married Marie-Thérèse, eldest daughter of Philip IV of Spain on June 9, 1660, at St. Jean de Luz (François Combes, *Histoire Générale de la Diplomatie Européenne*, Paris, 1854, pp. 302–303).

2. George Colman, the younger (1762–1836), wrote *The Heir at Law*, a comedy famous for its presentation of Dr. Pangloss as a greedy, pompous pedant (*The Oxford Companion to English Literature*, p. 176).

3. André Masséna, duc de Rivoli, prince d'Essling (1758–1817), French marshal, commanded in the Peninsula, 1810–1811 (Pierre Sabor, *Masséna et sa Famille* . . . *(1758–1794)*, Aix-en-Provence, 1926, pp. 213–263).

4. A *trincadoure* is a kind of launch used on the coast of Spain. These strong, well-constructed, though narrow boats had well-cut sails and were very seaworthy (Pierre-Marie-Joseph, baron de Bonne – foux et Edmond Paris, *Dictionnaire de Marine à Voiles et à Vapeur*, Paris [1848].

5. This fire in the hotel of the Austrian Ambassador, Prince Charles of Schwarzenberg (1771–1820), in the midst of the fetes marking the marriage of Napoleon and Marie-Louise has been described in several reports. Among them are an account by Prince Metternich in his *Memoirs* (ed. Prince Richard Metternich, tr. Mrs. Alexander Napier, New York, 1880, I, 298–305) and a full description in Simond's *La Vie Parisienne* (I, 208–211). There is also mention made by Paul Bondois in *Napoléon et la Société de son Temps* (Paris, 1895, pp. 272–273). The victims included the wife of the consul of Russia (Labensky), who was killed by a falling luster; Princess Pauline, wife of Prince Joseph Schwarzenberg; her second daughter was badly burned; and Prince Kourakin, the Russian ambassador, was gravely injured, but finally recovered.

6. Lucien Bonaparte (1775–1840), prince of Canino and brother of Napoleon I, fled from Italy (when the Pope, his protector, was taken prisoner) and went to Sardinia. There the English captured him and took him to Malta. Three months later he was taken to England, where he lived the life of a country gentleman on an estate that he purchased (A. Hilliard Atteridge, *Napoleon's Brothers*, London, 1909, pp. 230–231, 260–264).

7. Louis Bonaparte (1777–1846), brother of Napoleon I. When

Holland's commerce was ruined by the blockade, he abdicated on July 1, 1810 (Lavisse, *Histoire*, III, 419).

8. In 1801 the ship *Margaret* of Salem had made a successful voyage to Japan and back, only to founder in an Atlantic storm in 1810. On board were thirty-one passengers, many of them seamen of American vessels which had been confiscated by order of Napoleon in the harbors of the Mediterranean. The long boat with a few survivors was sighted and the men were picked up by the brig *Poacher* and landed in America. Three men on the yawl were also taken from the sea and arrived at home a month later. The survivors published a pamphlet describing the wreck (Ralph D. Paine, *The Ships and Sailors of Old Salem*, Boston, 1923, pp. 233–237).

9. Robert Fulton (1765–1815), artist, civil engineer, and inventor. He became a friend of Joel Barlow and of William Lee while working on his steamboat in Paris (*D.A.B.*).

10. Albert Gallatin (1761–1849), statesman and diplomat. He was Secretary of the Treasury from 1802 to 1814 (*D.A.B.*).

11. Robert Smith (1757–1842), Secretary of the Navy and Secretary of State (*D.A.B.*).

12. William Eustis (1753–1825), born in Cambridge, Mass., was Secretary of War under Jefferson and Madison. In 1810 he was married to Caroline Langdon of Portsmouth, N.H. (*D.A.B.*).

13. Barlow's house, called "Kalorama," was built about 1750 and purchased by Barlow in 1807 for $14,000 from its third owner, William Augustine Washington. Although it remained largely in the family of Joel Barlow and his wife, Kalorama was occupied in 1811 by Louis Sérurier, French envoy extraordinary and minister plenipotentiary from 1811 to 1816; in 1819 Friedrich Greuhm, the minister from Prussia, lived there. The name Kalorama (Greek: *calorama* — fine view) reflects the prevailing vogue for classic names (Corra Bacon-Foster, "The Story of Kalorama," *Columbia Historical Society, Records*, Washington, 1910, XIII, 98–118). Although the house itself has been torn down it has given its name to two neighboring streets in the national capital.

14. John Barney (b. 1785) was a captain and assistant district quartermaster general in the U. S. Army, 1814 to 1815. Elected to Congress as a Federalist in 1825, he died in Washington in 1857 (*Biog. Dir. Am. Congress*). He and his older brother Louis Barney (1783–1850) were the sons of Commodore Joshua Barney (William Frederick Adams, *Commodore Joshua Barney*, Springfield, Mass., 1912, privately printed, p. 77).

15. Robert R. Livingston (1746–1813), chancellor of New York,

statesman, diplomat, and farmer. He sailed in 1801 as minister to France (*D.A.B.*).

16. John C. Payne, younger brother of Dolley Payne Madison. In a letter to the Secretary of State dated September 11, 1809, George Davis, consul at the Regency of Tripoli, speaks of Payne as secretary of the consulate. On March 15, 1810, the consul wrote to Payne that, since he was leaving for home, he would put the affairs of the consulate in Payne's hands until the pleasure of the President should be known (Records of the Department of State for Tripoli, National Archives). The Mrs. Washington mentioned by Lee was Dolley Madison's younger sister, Lucy Payne, who had eloped with George Steptoe Washington in 1793, when she was fifteen years old and he was but nineteen (Irving Brant, *James Madison, Father of the Constitution*, Indianapolis, 1950, p. 405).

17. All three of these men served in the United States Senate: Timothy Pickering (1745–1829), administrator and public official, was a senator from Massachusetts, 1803 to 1811 (*D.A.B.*). James Lloyd (1769–1831) represented Massachusetts in the Senate from 1808 to 1813 and again from 1822 to 1826 (*Biog. Dir. Am. Congress*). Nicholas Gilman (1755–1814) was elected in 1805 as a Democratic senator from New Hampshire, and was re-elected in 1811 (*Biog. Dir. Am. Congress*).

18. Lizard Head or Lizard Point: the southernmost point of England. Land's End: the southwesternmost tip of England.

19. Count Rumford, who had discovered the principles for improved chimney and fireplace construction (see Note 7, Chap. III), also advocated earthenware glazed with common salt as being more durable and wholesome than enamel-covered iron for use in cooking utensils (*The Complete Works of Count Rumford*, Boston, 1870–1875, III, 340–345).

20. Charles Jared Ingersoll, *Inchiquin, the Jesuit's Letters, during a late residence in the United States of America, being a fragment of a private correspondence accidentally discovered in Europe by some unknown foreigner*, New York, 1810, Bailey tracts, Vol. 57, No. 3.

21. William Lyman of Massachusetts (1755–1811), representative in Congress 1793–1797, was brigadier general of State militia, 1796–1800, and U. S. Consul at London from 1805 until his death (*Biog. Dir. Am. Congress*).

22. William Bass, son of Henry Bass of Boston, was secretary of the agency at Bordeaux. He desired to be consul at Antwerp in 1808, a position for which William Lee recommended him, but to

which he was not appointed (Records of the Department of State for Bordeaux, National Archives).

23. Louis-Philippe, comte de Ségur (1753–1830), senator and grand master of ceremonies under the Empire (*The Memoirs and Anecdotes of the Count de Ségur,* translated by Gerard Shelley, London [1928]). Bernard-Hugues Maret, duc de Bassano (1763–1839), lawyer, ambassador, minister, and legislator, made Minister of Foreign Relations in 1811 succeeding Champagny (Robinet, *Dictionnaire Historique,* II, 512–513).

24. Pauline Bonaparte (1780–1825), sister of Napoleon I and wife of Prince Camille Borghese.

25. Hortense de Beauharnais (1783–1837), daughter of Josephine and wife of Louis Bonaparte, King of Holland.

26. The mother of Napoleon I, Laetitia Romolino Bonaparte (1750–1836).

27. Stephen Higginson (1743–1828), one of the leading Boston merchants, at one time was reputed to be worth a half million dollars. He later lost about two thirds of his fortune (*D.A.B.*). One of his sons was Henry Higginson, 1781–1838 (Higginson, *Descendants of Reverend F. Higginson,* p. 21).

28. Daniel Gustier (1755–1847) headed a house for the manufacture of armaments at Bordeaux. Later he was president of the Chamber of Commerce and one of the founders of the Bank of Bordeaux (*Autographes de Personnages,* XXX, 260).

29. The Navy uniform was prescribed by Thomas Jefferson in a " Circular of the Consuls and Vice-Consuls of the United States," New York, August 26, 1790, as follows:

The consuls and vice-consuls of the United States are free to wear the uniform of their navy, if they choose to do so. This is a deep blue coat with red facings, lining and cuffs, the cuffs slashed and a standing collar; a red waistcoat (Laced or not at the election of the wearer), and blue breeches; yellow buttons with a foul anchor, and black cockades and small swords.

Judging from his portrait, Lee's uniform was not like that of a Navy officer. Family tradition has it that William Lee designed his own uniform to suit himself.

30. Mlle. Tascher, niece of the Empress Josephine, had married the duc d'Arenberg (Metternich, *Memoirs I,* 293–294).

31. The *Promenade du Boeuf Gras,* a celebration before Lent, had been suspended in 1790 and was resumed in 1805 (Simond, *La Vie Parisienne* I, 111–112).

32. From "The Deserted Village," by Oliver Goldsmith, lines 261–264.

33. From 1766 for a number of years many political pamphlets were written in England under the pseudonym of *Junius*. The exact identity of this writer, who attacked the King's party, has never been discovered (*The Cambridge History of English Literature*, X, 454–463).

34. Jean-Louis Brown, merchant of Bordeaux, was born at Copenhagen. His eldest son, David Brown, was president of the Tribunal of Commerce, and father of John-Lewis Brown (1829–1890), well-known French painter (*Les Familles Protestantes de Bordeaux*, p. 72).

35. David Sears (1787–1871) of Boston, Massachusetts, was married in that city, June 13, 1809, to Miriam Clarke Mason. " He read law for a time, and soon after his marriage in 1809, sailed for Europe with his wife, and passed several years in foreign travel, at a most interesting period in Continental history." The Mrs. Sears mentioned by William Lee was Mrs. David Sears, and the diamond cross, which he so much admired, is still in the possession of a member of the Sears family (Samuel P. May, *The Descendants of Richard Sares (Sears) of Yarmouth, Mass.*, Albany, 1890, p. 261).

36. From " The Rape of the Lock," by Alexander Pope, Canto II, lines 7–8. The correct version reads:

> On her white breast a sparkling cross she wore,
> Which Jews might kiss, and infidels adore."

V

WAR AND INTRIGUE
1812–1816

1. Bertrand Clauzel (or Clausel, 1772–1842), soldier, marshal of France, legislator, made a baron of the Empire in 1810, eventually escaped to the United States.

2. The Prince of Wales (later George IV of England) had become Regent on February 5, 1811, after recognition of the insanity of his father, George III (*D.N.B.*). The Prince Regent's Manifesto of April 21, 1812 (printed in the London *Times* April 23, 1812), says that, although the French have pretended to revoke the Berlin and Milan decrees, these, on the contrary, are still in force. But if these decrees are unconditionally repealed, the British Orders in Council of January 7, 1807, and April 26, 1809, shall be wholly and absolutely revoked (*The Annual Register . . . for the Year 1812*, London,

1813, pp. 338–342). Joel Barlow in a letter (May 1, 1812) to the duc de Bassano, a copy of which was sent to the Secretary of State, emphasizes that the Manifesto declares that the British Orders in Council will not be revoked: that this fact is " beyond all question." On May 12, 1812, Barlow wrote to James Monroe, Secretary of State, that the duc de Bassano had shown him the decree of April 28, 1811, which had long been concealed from him, was not found in the archives of the American legation, and had never been published. This decree stated that the Berlin and Milan decrees were (as related to the United States) unconditionally repealed (Records of the Department of State, 1812, for Paris. National Archives).

3. The severest of these Orders in Council issued in 1807 declared Napoleon's coasts in a state of blockade and practically required all neutrals to trade through British ports (Walter Phelps Hall and Robert Greenhalgh Albion, *A History of England and the British Empire*, Boston, 1937, p. 570). The Order in Council, April 26, 1809, declared certain ports and places of the countries " lately styled the kingdom of Holland " to be strictly blockaded (*The Annual Register . . . for the Year 1809*, London, 1811, State Papers, p. 763). On June 23, 1812, the objectionable Orders in Council were substantially modified, as related to the United States of America. But war had already been declared, on June 18th, by the Congress (*The Annual Register . . . for the Year 1812*, London, 1813, pp. 379–381).

4. The seizure of American ships at San Sebastian by the French, who had occupied the Spanish frontier town. See Lee's letter of January 16, 1810.

5. For George William Erving see Chapter II, Note 21.

6. William Carr Beresford, Viscount Beresford (1768–1854), English general. After the battle of Orthez, " he was detached with two infantry divisions and two brigades of cavalry to Bordeaux, where, Wellington was informed, a strong party existed for the restoration of the Bourbons, and was in command there when the duc d'Angoulême hoisted the white flag again " (*D.N.B.*).

7. Louis-Antoine de Bourbon (1775–1844). He was the son of comte d'Artois and a nephew of Louis XVIII.

8. Nicolas-Jean-de-Dieu Soult (1769–1851), one of Napoleon's generals and commander in chief of the army of Andalusia, designated head of the army of Spain after the peace of Tilsit ([Jean] Sarrazin, *Histoire de la Guerre d'Espagne et de Portugal de 1807 à 1814*, Paris, 1814, pp. 379–399).

9. The war of the Vendée was an uprising of peasants in this department in Western France against the republic from 1793 to 1795

(Pierre-Victor-Jean Berthe de Bournisseaux, *An Historical Sketch of the Civil War in the Vendée*, Paris, 1802).

10. William Harris Crawford (1772–1834), Senator, Cabinet member, and from 1813 to 1815 minister to France (*D.A.B.*).

11. Prince Eugène de Beauharnais (1781–1824), son of the Empress Josephine by her first husband.

12. Marie-Thérèse-Charlotte (1778–1851), daughter of Louis XVI and Marie-Antoinette, and niece of Louis XVIII. The duc d'Angoulême was her first cousin as well as her husband.

13. Charles-Philippe, comte d'Artois (1757–1836), brother of Louis XVI and Louis XVIII, became Charles X of France in 1824 and reigned until 1830.

14. The final action of the War of 1812 came in the battle of New Orleans on January 8, 1815, when Andrew Jackson won a decisive victory over the English forces. The Treaty of Ghent, which ended the war, had been signed on December 24, 1814, but the combatants were not aware of this.

15. Christopher Hughes (1786–1849), secretary to the American Peace Commission at Ghent. He was, in fact, given a copy of the treaty to convey to Washington, but, delayed by a stormy crossing, he did not reach the United States until after the arrival of Henry Carroll, who had a duplicate (*D.A.B.*).

16. This quotation is from Cicero: " Opinionis enim commenta delet dies, naturae iudicia confirmat." It is translated thus by H. Rackham: " The years obliterate the inventions of the imagination, but confirm the judgements of nature " (Cicero, *De Natura Deorum Academica*, Loeb Classical Library, New York, 1933, Book II, pp. 126–127).

17. Trophime-Gérard, marquis de Lally-Tollendal (1751–1830), applauded the coming of Louis XVIII, who made him minister of state (Pierre La Mazière, *Lally-Tollendal, 1702–1766*, Paris, 1931, pp. 233–249).

18. Joseph-Henri-Joachim Lainé (1767–1837), a lawyer and member of the council of the duc d'Angoulême, who appointed him prefect of the Gironde. As president of the Chamber of Deputies, he protested against the usurpation of power by Napoleon during the Hundred Days (Adrien Bonnet, *Éloge de M. Lainé*, Bordeaux, 1844).

19. George Ramsay (1770–1838), ninth earl of Dalhousie in the peerage of Scotland, and commander of the British seventh division in the Peninsula and France, 1812–1814 (*D.N.B.*).

20. Art treasures that had been seized by Napoleon's orders in countries overrun by his armies were now returned by order of the

allies. Such major works as the four bronze horses from St. Mark's in Venice, the Apollo Belvedere, and paintings of Raphael and Rubens went back to Italy and the Low Countries. The French were bitter about this enforced restitution and some interpreted it as a manifestation of the English resolve to insure the preeminence in art of the British Museum as against the Louvre (Dorothy MacKay Quynn, "The Art Confiscations of the Napoleonic Wars," *The American Historical Review*, April 1945, L: 437–460).

21. "Now therefore ye are cursed, and there shall none of you be freed from being bondsmen, and hewers of wood and drawers of water for the house of my God." Joshua 9:23.

22. The seminary for the deaf and dumb in Paris was instituted by the abbé l'Epée, who was succeeded upon his death in 1789 by the abbé Sicard. Sign language and the manual alphabet were taught (Edwin John Mann, *The Deaf and Dumb*, Boston, 1836, pp. 44, 233).

23. This letter from Jefferson to Lee is dated August 24, 1816. The Dr. Mitchell mentioned by Jefferson in the letter was Samuel Latham Mitchill (1764–1831), physician, Senator and Representative from New York. He was professor at the College of Physicians and Surgeons, and for two decades physician to the New York Hospital. He was a supporter of Thomas Jefferson (*D.A.B.*). Jefferson's spelling and capitalization have been preserved in all his letters.

Monticello, Aug. 24. 16

Dear Sir

Your letters of Dec. 20. 14. and May 11. 16. are yet to be acknowledged: and my thanks to be returned for the book which accompanied the former on the subject of Great Britain and America. that able exposition prepared the European mind for receiving truths more favorable to us, and subsequent events have furnished facts corroborating those views. I believe that America, & by this time England also are more justly appreciated. some greatly enlightened minds in Europe are in science far beyond anything we possess; but leaving them out of the account (& they are but few) the mass of their people, within which term I include from the king to the beggar, is returning to Gothic darkness while the mass of ours is advancing in the regions of light. during the paroxysm of Anglomany lately raging in Bordeaux you must have had a mortifying time. that rage cannot last. the English character is not of that cast which makes itself be loved. I was just about publishing Mr. Garde's letter when I saw in the newspapers that addressed to Dr. Mitchell. his position in a populous city, and convenient to others, being so much more favorable than mine for the view of M. Garde, I rejoiced to see his letter in so good hands and surceased medling in it myself, my inland & rural situation affording me no facilities for promoting it's object. should you have occasion to write to Mr. Garde, I will thank you to throw in a line of explanation and to tender him my respects & best wishes for his success.

Not doubting that after so long a residence in France your wishes are still there, I heartily sympathise with them and hope the circumstances are not very distant, which may render your return agreeable and useful. Accept my salutations and assurances of perfect esteem and respect.

Th. Jefferson

24. Emmanuel Grouchy, marshal of Napoleon. He fought at Waterloo and spent the years 1816 to 1820 in the United States (Emmanuel Grouchy, *Mémoires du Maréchal de Grouchy*, Paris, 1873, I, Introduction). A letter from General Grouchy to William Lee, written from Bordentown, N. J., is in the Special Collections at the Columbia University Library.

25. Jean-Augustin Pénières (1767–1821), a republican member of the French National Assembly who voted for the death of Louis XVI. Proscribed in 1816, he took refuge in America, and eventually engaged in agriculture in Alabama (Albert James Pickett, *History of Alabama*, Sheffield, Ala., 1896, pp. 625, 627). That plans for the settlement continued is evidenced by this letter from Jefferson to Lee dated January 16, 1817:

Monticello Jan. 16. 1817

Dear Sir

I received three days ago a letter from M. Martin 2d Vice-president and M. Parmantier Secretary of 'the French agricultural & manufacturing society' dated at Philadelphia the 5th. instant. it covered Resolutions proposing to apply to Congress for a grant of 250m [250,000] acres of land on the Tombigbee, and stating some of the general principles on which the society was to be founded; and their letter requested me to trace for them the basis of a social pact for the local regulations of their society, and to address the answer to yourself, their 1st Vice President at Washington. No one can be more sensible than I am of the honor of their confidence in me, so flatteringly manifested in this resolution; and certainly no one can feel stronger dispositions than myself to be useful to them, as well in return for this great mark of their respect, as from feelings for the situation of strangers, forced by the misfortunes of their native country to seek another by adoption, so distant, and so different from that in all its circumstances. I commiserate the hardships they have to encounter, and equally applaud the resolution with which they meet them, as well as the principles proposed for their government. that their emigration may be for the happiness of their descendants, I can believe; but from the knolege I have of the country they have left, & it's state of social intercourse and comfort, their own personal happiness will undergo severe trial here. the laws however which are to effect this must flow from their own habits, their own feelings, and the resources of their own minds, no stranger to these could possibly propose regulations adapted to them. every people have their own particular habits ways of thinking, manners etc. which have grown up with them from their infancy, are become a part of their nature, and to which the regulations which are to make them happy must be accomodated. no member of a foreign country can have a sufficient sympathy with these. the institutions of Lycurgus, for example would not have suited Athens nor those of Solon Lacedaemon. the organisations of Locke were impracticable for Carolina, and those of Rousseau and Mably for Poland. turning inwardly on myself from these eminent illustrations of the truth of my observation, I feel all the presumption it would manifest, should I undertake to do what this respectable society is alone qualified to do suitably for itself. there are some preliminary questions too which are particularly for their own consideration. is it proposed that this shall be a separate state? or a county of a state? or a mere voluntary association, as those of the quakers, Dunkars, Menonists? a separate state it cannot be, because from the tract it asks, it would not be of more than 20. miles square, & in establishing new states, regard is had to a certain degree of equality in size. if it is to be a county of a state, it cannot be governed by it's own laws, but must be subject to those of the state of which it is a part. if merely a voluntary association, the submission of it's members will be merely voluntary also; as no act of coercion would be permitted by the general law. these considerations must control the society, and themselves alone can modify their own intentions and wishes to them. with this apology for declining a task to which I am so unequal, I pray them to be assured of my sincere wishes for their success and happiness, and yourself particularly of my high consideration & esteem.

Th. Jefferson

A few things in the letter need explanation. Solon: Athenian lawgiver; Lycurgus traditionally reformed the constitution of Sparta, whose inhabitants were the Lacedaemonians. John Locke (1632–1704), English philosopher, was one of the " lords " proprietors of Carolina. He wrote in 1669 a model constitution for the government of the colony. Jean-Jacques Rousseau wrote " Considérations sur le Gouvernement de Pologne." Gabriel Bonnot de Mably (1790–1785), French publicist, counseled the Poles on constitutional reform. Quakers: Society of Friends, religious body originating in England. Dunkers: German Baptist brothers. Mennonites: sect of Protestant Christians originating in Switzerland.

26. A settlement of immigrants proscribed from residence in their native country. While there is no record of a community by that name, there are accounts of a later colony called Demopolis, settled in 1818 by " The Vine and Olive Colony " of French refugees on the southern bank of the Tombigbee River at its confluence with the Warrior River in Alabama (Thomas McAdory Owen, *History of Alabama and Dictionary of Alabama Biography*, Chicago, 1921, I, 480–483). The two earlier settlements of European refugees mentioned by Lee were Vevay in Indiana, founded in 1801 by a group of Swiss immigrants soon noted for their vineyards (*Indiana, a Guide*

to the Hoosier State, Program of the Work Projects Administration, New York, 1941, p. 376); and Harmony, north of Pittsburgh, Pennsylvania, founded in 1803 by George Rapp of Württemberg and several others. The Harmony Society, organized in 1805, consisted of some 600 working men who raised crops and ran a woolen mill (Charles Nordhoff, *The Communistic Societies of the United States,* New York, 1875, pp. 63–95).

VI

THE TREASURY DEPARTMENT, WASHINGTON
1817–1822

1. This was Jefferson's letter of June 6, 1817, the text of which follows. The Mr. Barnes to whom he refers was his good friend and confidential agent, John Barnes (1730–1826), born in England, and later a prominent citizen and collector of customs in Georgetown (Cordelia Jackson, " John Barnes, a Forgotten Philanthropist of Georgetown," *Columbia Historical Society. Records,* Washington, 1904, VII, 39–48).

Monticello June 6. 17.

Dear Sir

The National Intelligencer informs us there is a numerous party of Swiss stocking weavers arrived at Washington, and Mr. Barnes of Georgetown now here, tells me he thinks they are under your patronage. believing it for their interest to distribute themselves to good posts in the country, I take the liberty of stating that I think there is no better stand for one or two of them than the town of Charlottesville, 3 miles distant from me. it is a mountainous country, of course healthy, inhabited by an industrious, thriving & independent yeomanry, whose wives & daughters would furnish much of the spun material, and all would buy that ready-woven. I have enquired and found they can be accomodated with comfortable quarters, paying from 20. to 30.D. a year for a good room. European goods are dear, but the necessaries of life very cheap. I have the promise of the merchants of the village that they will do every thing in their power to prosper them. if a family or families should come with bulky baggage, they had better come round by water to Richmond in the vessels constantly passing from your district to that place, where they will always find open batteaux coming up the river to Charlottesville. single persons may come direct in the stage from Washington to Charlottesville. a silversmith, if any among them, would find great employment at the same place & would be particularly well received. we have there a fine watchmaker, a Swiss from Neufchatel, finding much more work than he can do, and taking in money as fast as he can earn it. he finds himself peculiarly happy and delighted with the country & his own situation. if you can encourage good subjects from among these emigrants you will ensure their success, accomodate this vicinege and do an acceptable favor to

your friend & serv't

William Lee esq.   Th. Jefferson

2. Stephen Decatur (1779–1820) was a brilliant naval officer and prominent member of Washington society. He was on the court of inquiry that heard testimony on James Barron (1769–1851), a naval officer who commanded the *Chesapeake* when it was fired on by the British vessel *Leopard* (Barron refused to allow the British to search his ship, but in the end he was forced to give up to the *Leopard* several alleged English sailors). Decatur opposed Barron's reinstatement in the navy after a five-year suspension, and some time later, Barron sent Decatur a challenge. In the ensuing duel Decatur was killed. He was buried in a tomb on Joel Barlow's estate, Kalorama, his remains later being transferred to Philadelphia (Myra L. Spaulding, " Dueling in the District of Columbia." *Columbia Historical Society. Records,* Washington, 1928, XXIX–XXX, 132–157; *D.A.B.*).

3. James Cutbush, chemist, was chief medical officer of the United States Military Academy from 1820 to 1821. He died at West Point in 1823 (*Appleton's Cyclopaedia,* II, 45).

4. Daniel Parker of Massachusetts (*d.* 1846), paymaster general of the army from 1821 to 1822 (Heitman's *Historical Register and Dictionary of the United States Army,* 1789–1903, Washington, 1903, I, 769).

5. Louis Malesherbes Goldsborough (1805–1877), later a rear admiral, had gone to Annapolis at the age of eleven (J. T. Headley, *Farragut and our Naval Commanders,* New York, 1867, pp. 196–198).

6. Eldest son of William Wirt, attorney general of the United States from 1817 to 1829. Robert went to West Point in 1820 and died at Le Havre, France, in 1824 at the age of nineteen (John P. Kennedy, *Memoirs of the Life of William Wirt,* Philadelphia, 1849, II, 117, 189).

7. Smith Thompson (1768–1843), secretary of the navy from 1819 to 1823, and his daughters, were undoubtedly the persons who are referred to here as having water in the cellar of their house at 14 Jackson Place (Wilhelmus Bogart Bryan, *A History of the National Capital,* New York, 1916, II 7). The Joseph Bradley Varnum (1750–1821), referred to in the next sentence, was a senator from Massachusetts (*D.A.B.*).

8. Colonel John Tayloe (*d.* 1828) built as a winter residence the famous Octagon House in Washington, D. C., at the suggestion of

his close friend, George Washington. He is described as "a very wealthy man for those days, having an income of $75,000 a year and owning the immense country estate at Mount Airy, Va. He owned five hundred slaves, built brigs and schooners, worked iron mines, and converted the iron into plowshares, all by the hands of his own subjects" (Frank J. Metcalf, "Octagon Houses of Washington and elsewhere" *Columbia Historical Society. Records*, Washington, 1924, XXVI, 100–101).

9. This letter from Mary Lee to her father tells of the progress of the family in their search for a healthful climate for Mrs. Lee. Dr. Physick was the well-known Philadelphia physician, Philip Syng Physick (1768–1837), called the "Father of American Surgery." He was professor at Pennsylvania University and President of the Philadelphia Medical Society (Howard A. Kelly, *A Cyclopedia of American Medical Biography from 1610–1910*, Philadelphia, 1912, II, 270–272).

To William Lee at Washington

Philadelphia, June 4, 1822

My dear Papa:

Dr. Physick has decided in favor of Schooley's Mountain, and disapproves of our going to Bedford, Saratoga, or any other spring. He says we only want change of air, moderate exercise, and quiet. Schooley's Mountain is proverbially healthy. Every person whom we have consulted speaks in the highest terms of it. Mr. Ronaldson has made inquiries for us as to the best mode of going. He says we can go from here in the steam boat to Trenton, and from Trenton ride fifty miles through a beautiful hilly country to Schooley's Mountain, where the air is so cool that one can sleep all summer under a blanket. In short every one here speaks so highly of the place that Mamma has decided to go there immediately without waiting to hear from you.

Dr. Physick says that she has nothing more to do than take the rhubarb pills once or twice a week, and that change of air is better for her than all the physic in the world. As to our remaining here much longer, it is impossible. The air is too confined, and the house not to be borne. Another and better reason, if possible, is that Miss Dallas has admitted, without being aware of it, an *Actress* into the house. The poor girl is very much distressed that it should have happened; especially as she can devise no means to get rid of her. She came yesterday and told Mamma of it immediately. Mamma told her that, as we were to remain only two days longer, it made very little difference. I do not dine downstairs in consequence; and we are very badly served in our rooms.

All these reasons you see are very good ones for not staying. We shall try and get off to-morrow. You may direct your letters to some one in Trenton, who will send them to us. Mr. Carey says a stage goes from there every day to Schooley's Mountain. I shall write you from Trenton. Mr. Collins was here last evening. I saw him. He also speaks highly of Schooley's Mountain. Susan is rather better today.

Yours affectionately
Mary.

10. One of the four children of Thomas Munroe (1771–1852), postmaster of the city of Washington from 1799 to 1829, and a neighbor of Lee's in the " Seven Buildings " during 1822. The other children were Columbus, Emily, and Frances (Madison Davis, " A History of the City Post-Office." *Columbia Historical Society. Records*, Washington, 1903, VI, 157–170). The Miss Onis to whom Lee refers was undoubtedly the daughter of the former Spanish minister, Luis de Onis.

11. Red Jacket was a Seneca Indian chief and noted orator who customarily wore a scarlet jacket given him by a British officer (J. Niles Hubbard, *An Account of Sa-Go-Ye-Wat-Ha or Red Jacket and His People*, Albany, 1886, pp. 9, 19, 35).

12. Lee refers in this paragraph to the following friends and neighbors. The captain — Captain James Harvey Hook of Indiana, formerly captain of the 38th infantry, then clerk commissary general of subsistence in Washington, living in the " Seven Buildings " (Heitman's *Historical Register* I, 540; *Washington Directory* for 1822). Mrs. Lear — undoubtedly the third wife of Tobias Lear and now his widow, who was a niece of Martha Washington (*D.A.B.*). Mrs. Ramsay — probably the wife of Andrew Ramsay, clerk in the paymaster general's office (*Washington Directory* for 1822). Mrs. John Ewing Calhoun — the mother-in-law (he had married his cousin, Floride Calhoun) of John Caldwell Calhoun (1782–1850), vice president of the United States from 1825 to 1832 (*D.A.B.*). Mrs. Hawley — wife of the Reverend William Hawley, from 1817 until his death in 1845 rector of St. John's Episcopal Church, Lafayette Square, Washington, D. C., and living in the " Seven Buildings " (Alexander B. Hagner, " History and Reminiscences of St. John's Church, Washington, D. C.," *Columbia Historical Society, Records*, Washington, 1909, XII, 89–114).

13. The " First Unitarian Church " of Washington had been organized in 1821 and was dedicated June 9, 1822. The 1822 convention, held at St. John's Church, voted to establish an Episcopal seminary in the national capital. But because of a difference of opinion, the Virginia Theological Seminary was opened instead in Alexandria in the following year (Bryan, *History of the National Capital*, II, 184, 203). William Lee was apprehensive, undoubtedly because of the sermon which had been preached by the rector of St. John's

about the Unitarian, Jared Sparks, when he was chaplain of the House of Representatives. This incident is mentioned by John Quincy Adams in his *Memoirs*, December 23, 1821, V, 458–459.

14. Stratford Canning, first Viscount Stratford de Redcliffe (1786–1880), envoy extraordinary and minister plenipotentiary from Great Britain to the United States, 1820–1823 (*D.N.B.*). The James Baker of whom Lee writes was private secretary to the British consul general, Anthony St. John Baker (*Washington Directory* for 1882).

15. The Vice President was Daniel D. Tompkins (1774–1835), formerly the governor of New York. During the War of 1812 Governor Tompkins backed up the credit of the United States government when New York banks refused to lend money on U. S. Treasury notes without his endorsement. His popularity decreased while he was Vice-President, 1816–1824; there were accusations about the heavy expenditures during the war and he was even charged with dishonesty. These charges, it is now clear, resulted solely from the inaccuracy and confusion in his accounts. He was so distressed by these allegations that his mind became unhinged and he took to drinking heavily. The Congress, at the recommendation of President Monroe, authorized payments to Tompkins of over $95,000 for losses incurred in the public service (*D.A.B.*). Other people cited by Lee in this paragraph are the following: Henry Baldwin (1780–1844) of Connecticut, half-brother of Mrs. Joel Barlow; elected to Congress in 1816 and twice thereafter, he resigned because of illness in 1822 and was made an associate justice of the Supreme Court in 1830 (*D.A.B.*). George Bomford (1782–1848), soldier, was made a colonel in 1832; his wife was Clara Baldwin, sister of Mrs. Barlow (*D.A.B.*). Colonel Nathan Towson (1784–1854), paymaster general of the army (*Appleton's Cyclopaedia*, VI, 151). James Lloyd (1769–1831), Senator from Massachusetts 1822–1826, was elected to fill the vacancy caused by the resignation of H. G. Otis and then reelected (*Biog. Dir. Am. Congress*). The commander of the *Franklin* at that time was Commodore Charles Stewart who took with him on this South American cruise his wife Delia Tudor Stewart (see Chapter II, note 7). G. Hyde de Neuville was envoy extraordinary and minister plenipotentiary from France, 1816–1822 (*Register of the Department of State, corrected to March 1, 1874*, p. 111).

16. Margaret Freeman, also called " The Dowager." She was the wife of Lee's cousin, Constant Freeman (1757–1824), who was made fourth auditor of the U. S. Treasury after having served in the army (Frederick Freeman, *Freeman Genealogy*, Boston, 1875, private edition, pp. 389, 404–405).

17. By the "Duke of Vinegar" Lee must have meant the first auditor of the Treasury, the person directly over him in rank. This was Richard Harrison (1750–1841). Appointed by George Washington in 1791, he was continued as first auditor through successive administrations until Nov. 1, 1836 (*Appleton's Cyclopaedia*, III, 100–101).

18. After the battle of Waterloo, Joseph Bonaparte (1768–1844), eldest brother of Napoleon I, came to Bordentown, N. J., where he purchased a large estate, and was known as Count Survilliers. His wife remained in Europe with her daughters. One of the daughters, Zenaïde, was married in 1822 to her cousin Charles Lucien Bonaparte, eldest son of Lucien and heir to the principality of Canino. The daughter and her new husband went to visit Joseph in Bordentown, and was the "Countess" mentioned by Lee (Atteridge, *Napoleon's Brothers*, pp. 470–476). Joseph seems to have left Schooley's Mountain rather hurriedly without having come in contact with the Lees.

19. Mahlon Dickerson (1770–1853), adjutant general 1805–1808; governor of New Jersey 1815–1817; Senator from New Jersey 1817–1829, lived in Morris County (*Biog. Dir. Am. Congress*).

20. A clerk in the Treasurer's office, according to the *Washington Directory* for 1822, Benjamin B. Beall was married in Baltimore on May 21, 1822, to Miss Caroline Matilda Warner of Baltimore (*Daily National Intelligencer*, Washington, Monday, May 27, 1822). Mrs. Hill was the wife of George Hill, clerk in the general land office, who lived on Pennsylvania Avenue opposite the "Seven Buildings" (*Washington Directory*, 1822).

21. In this sixth mayorality contest for Washington, D.C., Roger Chew Weightman (1787–1876) was narrowly defeated by Thomas Carbery. Charging that many of Carbery's votes were illegal, Weightman, who represented the moneyed aristocracy, carried the case to the court, and the contest continued until Carbery's term expired. The next elected mayor died and Weightman was put by the Council in the vacant place. In 1826 he won the election against Carbery (Allen C. Clark, "General Roger Chew Weightman, a Mayor of the City of Washington," *Columbia Historical Society, Records*, Washington, 1919, XXII, 62–104; Clark, "The Mayors of the Corporation of Washington; Thomas Carbery," *Columbia Historical Society, Records*, Washington, 1916, XIX, 61–98). John Law was a wealthy Washington lawyer (George Alfred Townsend, "Thomas Law, Washington's First Rich Man." *Columbia Historical Society, Records*, Washington, 1901, IV, 222–228, 237). William Winston Seaton (1785–1866), president of the board of Aldermen,

himself became mayor from 1840 to 1848 (Allen C. Clark, " Colonel William Winston Seaton and his Mayorality," *Colombia Historical Society, Records,* Washington, 1928, XXIX–XXX, 1–15).

22. Although these two lines, according to Bartlett, have been attributed to Swift and Pope, they appear as an Epigram on the Feuds between Handel and Bononcini in John Byrom, *Miscellaneous Poems* (Manchester, 1773), I, 343–344.

23. The *Washington Directory* for 1822 mentions Charles Hay, clerk in the office of the Secretary of the Navy, and G. A. Bibby, clerk in the engineer's office. The Randalls were Captain Thomas, who married Laura Wirt, daughter of Judge William Wirt; and Henry, who married Emily Munroe, daughter of the postmaster (Kate Kearney Henry, " Richard Forest and his Times, 1795–1830," *Columbia Historical Society, Records,* Washington, 1902, V, 92–93).

24. Lewis Salomon, clerk in the Registrar's office, lived on Pennsylvania Avenue near the " Seven Buildings " (*Wash. Dir.,* 1822).

25. Daughter of the solicitor-general of Massachusetts, Daniel Davis, and of Louisa Freeman Davis, b. 1798, d. during or after 1887 (Freeman, *Freeman Genealogy,* pp. 407–408).

26. Charles Lefebvre Desnouettes (1773–1822) was a distinguished cavalry officer in Napoleon's army, where he rose to the rank of lieutenant-general. When his life was in danger after Waterloo, he fled to the settlement of French refugees known as Demopolis in Alabama. Having obtained permission from Louis XVIII for his return to Europe, Desnouettes set sail on the *Albion,* but was drowned when that vessel was wrecked near the coast of Ireland (Thomas McAdory Owen, *A History of Alabama,* Chicago, 1921, III, 483).

27. John Peter Van Ness (1770–1846), representative from New York, major general, 1813, mayor of Washington, 1830–1834, and president of several banks (*Biog. Dir. Am. Congress*).

28. Henry Huntt (1782–1838), hospital surgeon in the U. S. Army in 1814–1815, first health officer of Washington, president of the Board of Health, 1822–1833, and an incorporator of the Medical Society of the District of Columbia (*History of the Medical Society of the District of Columbia, 1817–1909,* Washington, 1909, Part I, 149–150, 214).

29. David Montagu Erskine (1776–1855), eldest son of Thomas, lord chancellor and the first Lord Erskine. In 1799 he married the daughter of General John Cadwallader of Philadelphia, one of the leaders of the American Revolution. Erskine was minister to the United States from 1806 to 1809; his marriage to an American may have been the reason for his lack of diplomatic employment upon his return to England (*D.N.B.*).

30. See Note 6 above.

31. Henry Middleton (1770–1846) of Middleton Place, near Charleston, S.C., a former governor of South Carolina and Congressman; minister to Russia from 1820 to 1830 (*Biog. Dir. Am. Congress*).

32. From Alexander Pope, "Essay on Man," Epistle IV, line 331. Hogarth's "Enraged Musician" depicts the musician at an open window, bow in hand and a finger in each ear, as, with a distressed expression, he tries to keep out the noises from the street below (Rev. John Trusler, *The Works of William Hogarth*, London, [18..], I, 63. Reproduced as a steel engraving).

33. Jonathan Russell (1771–1832), statesman from Rhode Island and one of the five Ghent commissioners. John Quincy Adams believed that in 1882 Russell was trying to destroy his (Adams') political fortunes in the West by representing him as having been one of the commissioners ready to trade free navigation on the Mississippi for the restoration of the northeastern fisheries. Adams had the better of this controversy, and in New England slang, " to Jonathan Russell " an opponent meant to overwhelm him in a dispute (*D.A.B.*).

34. Mrs. Samuel Lawrence Gouverneur was the former Maria Hester Monroe (1803–1850), a daughter of James Monroe. With her marriage in 1820 she became the first daughter of a president to be married in the White House (Reginald Buchanan Henry, *Genealogies of the Families of the Presidents* Rutland, Vt., 1935, pp. 149–150).

35. L'abbé François-Metel de Bois-Robert (born *c.* 1592, *d.* 1662) was a canon at Rouen, and entered the service of Cardinal Richelieu, who banished him for an indiscretion. When the cardinal became ill his doctor said to him, " Je ne sais plus que vous donner, si ce n'est trois dragmes de Bois-Robert après le repas." The abbé was recalled ([Gédéon] Tallemant des Réaux, *Le Cardinal de Richelieu, Sa Famille, Son Favori Bois-Robert*, Paris, 1920, pp. 179–217).

36. Samuel Harrison Smith (1772–1845), at Jefferson's invitation in 1800, followed the government to Washington, where he started the *National Intelligencer and Washington Advertiser*. In 1804 he bought " Turkey Thicket," a country estate that later became part of the grounds of the Catholic University (*D.A.B.*). The letters of his wife have been published in a volume called *The First Forty Years of Washington Society*. Dr. Thornton, who was present at the party mentioned by Lee, was William Thornton (1761–1828), architect of the first Capitol building, which was later burned by the British (Marian Graham Bell, " Sketch of the Life of Dr. William

Thornton," *Columbia Historical Society. Records,* Washington, 1917, XX, 225–227).

37. From James Beattie, *The Minstrel,* Book II, line 413.

38. In June 1821, the old theatre, which had been burned, was rebuilt, and in 1822 it reopened as the "Washington City Assembly Rooms" (A. I. Mudd, "Early Theatres in Washington City," *Columbia Historical Society, Records,* Washington, 1902, V. 64–86).

39. George McDuffie, statesman of South Carolina, fought a duel on June 8, 1822, with Colonel Cummings of Georgia. Each thought that the other was the author of certain articles in a Georgia paper. Both were mistaken, and no explanation was offered on either side. McDuffie was wounded in the back and did not recover from the wound for the rest of his life (Lorenzo Sabine, *Notes on Duels and Duelling,* Boston, 1855, p. 242).

40. This letter of July 18th, which said that Mrs. Lee was no better and slept most of the time, was followed by an even more poignant letter of July 20, which follows:

To William Lee at Washington

> Schooley's Mountain,
> Saturday, July 20, 1822,
> 2 o'clock

Dearest father:

Ever since daylight Mamma has been in a very dangerous state, and this moment, for the first time, do we begin to feel a ray of hope. Every remedy that could tend to relieve her has been administered by a physician, who stays here, and has been indefatigable in his attentions. And Mrs. Mason and her daughter are the kindest of beings. . . .

How I grieve to make you so unhappy, dearest father. You have no one to soothe you. Do pray come. Summon all your resolution, and come to us. We have great reason to hope that all may yet be well, but it is necessary to prepare for the worst. Susan is better than she has been for months, and I feel a degree of fortitude which astonishes me. Dearest father! How I wish I was with you. My heart is wrung with anguish, when I think of your feelings on receiving this. Pray come as soon as you can.

> Your affectionate
> Mary.

VII

WASHINGTON SOCIETY
1823–1829

1. A position he held until he was eighty-eight years old. In William Barlow Lee's obituary (October 24, 1895), the New York *Tribune* said that he served through the various grades in the Department and "in the war was Chief of the Record of Division." The

article went on to say that he " had a wonderful memory, and was retained by various Secretaries long after his usefulness in other capacities . . . was at an end."

2. Louisa Kalisky's diary, written in German, was translated by a member of her family; extracts from it can be found in the Division of Manuscripts, Library of Congress.

3. Ann Phoenix was a slave but was employed by William Lee. In later years she often went to see the family of William Barlow Lee in Washington.

4. This letter of June 20 is evidently a draft, with many revisions, of a letter sent to Baron de Maltitz, probably in reply to a note of uncertain date in 1824 from the Baron to Lee. The text of the Baron's note follows:

Mon cher Monsieur Lee. Je vous supplie de ne point écrire à Mlle. Mary et de ne pas lui envoyer ma lettre qu'avant de m'avoir permis de vous entretenir encore une fois sur l'affaire la plus importante de ma vie. J'attands avec confiance de votre bonté l'accomplissement de cette prière.

Tout à vous
M.

5. The Roxbury residence of John Lowell (1769–1840) and Rebecca Amory Lowell (Arthur Theodore and Ella Lyman, *Letters and Journals prepared by their daughter, Ella Lyman Cabot,* Menasha, Wis., 1932, privately printed, I, 86–87). The other members of the Lowell and Amory families referred to in this letter are John's father, Judge John Lowell (1743–1802), the " patriarch," a delegate to the state Constitutional Convention, 1779–1780 (*D.A.B.*) Sarah (" Sally ") Champney Lowell (1771–1851), daughter of Judge John Lowell and Sarah Higginson Lowell and sister of John and Anna Cabot Lowell (Delmar R. Lowell, *The Historic Genealogy of the Lowells of America, 1639–1899*, Rutland, Vt., 1899, p. 59). Mary Amory Bethune (1773–1844), daughter of John and Catherine Greene Amory and wife of George Bethune, 1769–1859 (George Ticknor Dexter, *The Amory Family of Boston*, broadside, 1897).

6. Andrew Law (1748–1821), clergyman, musician, compiler and teacher of sacred music (*D.A.B.*). Born in Connecticut, he was associated musically with New England, particularly Salem and Boston, where he had a singing school in 1802 (H. Earle Johnson, *Musical Interludes in Boston, 1795–1830*, New York, 1943, p. 292).

7. " L'absence diminue les médiocres passions et augmente les grandes, comme le vent éteint les bougies et allume le feu." La Rochefoucauld, *Maxims*, No. 276.

8. George Ellisen, counselor of the Russian legation, had actually

ceased being chargé d'affaires in April 1823. He was succeeded by Baron de Tuyll, envoy extraordinary and minister plenipotentiary from 1823 to 1826, at which time Maltitz became chargé d'affaires (*Register of the Department of State, corrected to March 1, 1874*, p. 120).

9. David Porter (1780–1843), naval officer. He had been commissioner of the Navy Board from 1815 to 1823 and had used the money gained from captured prizes to build a large residence directly north of the White House called " Meridian Hill," which became a social center of official Washington. In 1823 he became commander-in-chief of the West India Squadron (*D.A.B.*).

10. Aaron Vail (1796–1878), diplomat, was at that time a clerk in the office of the secretary of state. He lived with his brother, Eugene, a clerk in the general land office, and with his widowed mother (probably Elizabeth Dubois Vail) in one of the " Seven Buildings " (*Wash. Dir.*, 1827).

11. Captain Joseph L. Kuhn, paymaster in the Marine Corps (*Wash. Dir.*, 1822). Mrs. Pleasanton: probably the wife of Stephen Pleasanton, fifth auditor (*Wash. Dir.*, 1822).

12. Ezekiel Freeman, eminent lawyer and landowner in Maryland, brother-in-law of Mrs. Constant Freeman (Freeman, *Freeman Genealogy*, pp. 389, 406).

13. This was the Franklin House, a hotel at the northeast corner of I Street facing Pennsylvania Avenue and 21st Street, purchased in 1824 by John Gadsby (Bryan, *History of the National Capital*, II, 60–61).

14. Sir George Jackson (1785–1861), commissioner to Washington from 1823 to 1827, under Article I of the Treaty of Ghent for the settlement of American claims (*D.N.B.*). Count de Medem carried dispatches from Russia to Baron Tuyll, the minister from that country; he took back with him the ratified Northwest Coast Convention. (In this treaty of 1824, " Russia agreed not to allow any establishment by its subjects south of 54°40′ and the United States agreed not to permit its citizens to make establishments north of that latitude.") In 1825 Great Britain made a similar treaty with Russia (Samuel Flagg Bemis, *A Diplomatic History of the United States* New York, 1936, p. 274; J. Q. Adams, *Memoirs*, VI, 409, 482).

15. Thomas Randall of Maryland was brevetted captain in 1814 and held that rank until he resigned in 1817 (Heitman, I, 814–815). See also Chapter VI, Note 23.

16. Daniel Brent of Virginia was chief clerk in the State Department, 1817 to 1833, when he resigned to become consul at Paris (*Register of the Department of State, corrected to March 1, 1874*,

p. 56). From a study of the *Washington Directory* for 1822 and 1827 it does not appear that his marriage with the widow Graham took place.

17. The Corporation consisted of the Mayor, the Board of Aldermen, and the Board of Common Council (*Wash. Dir.*, 1822).

18. "L'hypocrisie est un hommage que le vice rend à la vertu." La Rochefoucauld, *Maxims*, No. 218.

19. The Honorable Daniel Davis (1762–1835), solicitor general of Massachusetts. He was married to Lois Freeman, daughter of Captain Constant Freeman by his first wife Lois Cobb, William Lee's aunt (Freeman, *Freeman Genealogy*, pp. 407–408). By the "Essex Scouts" Lee probably meant the disgruntled Federalists of New England, formerly called the "Essex Junto."

20. Benjamin Bussey (1757–1842) was the son of a seaman. After enlisting in the Revolutionary army, he went into business at Dedham, first as a goldsmith, then as a fur merchant. He amassed a large fortune, some of which he left as a bequest to Harvard College. The Bussey Institution (a college of agriculture and horticulture connected with Harvard University) was opened in the period 1869–1870 in accordance with his wishes (Memorandum on Mr. Bussey's life as detailed by him, *The Dedham Historical Register*, 10, 1899, 71–76; *Boston Daily Advertiser*, Feb. 10, 1842).

21. John Pickering, *A Vocabulary or Collection of Words and Phrases* . . . peculiar to the United States of America . . . (Boston, 1816).

22. Charles Stewart (1778–1869), naval officer, was a cabin boy in the merchant service at thirteen, and rose to become master of a merchantman. He entered the Navy, distinguished himself in the war with Tripoli, and made a brilliant record as commander of the *Constitution*. In 1813 he married Delia Tudor; in 1816 he was given command of the ship of the line *Franklin*. In 1862 he was made a rear admiral on the retired list (*D.A.B.*). This case, which was decided in August 1825, involved the secreting aboard the *Franklin*, while Stewart was commander, of a foreigner called "Madrid, or by some other name." This man came on board from a Genoese merchant ship carrying with him letters from two ladies who had interested themselves in his behalf. These he presented to Mrs. Stewart, who directed the steward to feed him in the pantry. With the consent of First Lieutenant William M. Hunter, this man was transported on the *Franklin* from Callao to Quilca in southern Peru, remaining on board ship for three weeks. Hunter did not report the incident to Commodore Stewart, believing, as he later testified, that Stewart already knew of it. It developed that "Madrid" had withheld the

information that he had been in the military service of one of the contending parties in South America. Stewart was court-martialed, but cleared of the four charges against him. Hunter was also court-martialed, but was probably acquitted, since he remained in the Navy and rose to the rank of Captain (Records of Proceedings of General Court Martial and Court of Inquiry (" Court-martial record "), case No. 433, from Record Group 125. Navy Records, U. S. National Archives).

23. A first cousin of William Lee, the Reverend James Freeman, D.D. (1759–1835), was minister at King's Chapel, Boston (Freeman, *Freeman Genealogy*, pp. 405–406).

24. William Lee's guests were: Mrs. John Quincy Adams, wife of the then Secretary of State; Mrs. John Ewing Calhoun; Mrs. William Wirt; Mrs. Nathan Towson; Mrs. Joseph L. Kuhn; Mrs. Andrew Ramsay.

25. The visit of Lafayette to Washington in 1824 was one of the season's leading events. He arrived in an elegant landau, drawn by four greys, accompanied by General Jacob Brown (commander in chief of the army from 1815 until his death in 1828) and Commodore Thomas Tinguey, U.S.N., and a military escort. An address of welcome was delivered by the Mayor, General Weightman; and John Brown Cutting, the local laureate, addressed the general in prose and poetry. Lafayette was then received at the Executive Mansion by President Monroe (Clark, " General Weightman . . . ," *Columbia Historical Society Records*, XXII, 67–74). The other men mentioned in connection with Lafayete's visit are Major General Alexander Macomb, who was commander in chief of the army from 1828 to 1841, succeeding Brown (*D.A.B.*) and Charles W[ashington] Goldsborough, who represented the aldermen on the committee for the reception of the French general (Clark, XXII, 68).

26. Mrs. Greuhm had been in mourning for her husband since December 1823. A former governess in the Middleton family when they lived in Kalorama, she returned to that estate as its mistress on her marriage to Friedrich Greuhm, minister from Prussia (Bryan, *Hist. of Nat. Capital*, II, 52–53).

27. Cadwallader David Colden (1769–1834), lawyer and statesman, was mayor of the city of New York from 1818 to 1820, a member of Congress in 1821, and state senator from 1825 to 1827 (*D.A.B.*).

28. Baron de Krudener, Russian Minister from December, 1827, to August, 1836.

VIII
LAST YEARS
1829–1840

1. " City Arabs are . . . bound by no obligation and utterly ignorant or utterly regardless of social duties " (*O.E.D.*).

2. A term applied to naval captains retired as rear admirals in H. M. fleet without being attached to a particular squadron (red, white, or blue). To make a " yellow admiral " of, to retire a person (*O.E.D.*).

3. Lee is probably referring to Calvin's action with respect to the Spaniard Michael Servetus, who opposed some of Calvin's religious doctrines. When Servetus arrived in Geneva, Calvin had him arrested, thrown into prison, and tried for blasphemy. Servetus was condemned by the Council of Geneva and burned at the stake. Calvin apparently agreed with the sentence, but would have preferred the sword rather than fire as the instrument of Servetus' death ([Albert Rilliet] *Calvin and Servetus*. From the French: with notes and additions by the Rev. W. K. Tweedie, Edinburgh and London, 1846).

4. Mungo: typical name for a black slave, hence a Negro (*O.E.D.*).

5. John McLean (1761–1823), merchant, founder of the McLean Asylum. He bequeathed $100,000 to the hospital (Massachusetts General) and $50,000 more to be divided between that institution and Harvard (Samuel Adams Drake, *Old Landmarks and Historic Personages of Boston*, Boston, 1873, pp. 307, 377).

6. Brother of Ann Amory McLean Lee. John Lowell was, of course, Mrs. Lee's brother-in-law.

7. Lemuel Shaw (1781–1861), jurist. He studied law and practiced in Boston, then served for thirty years at a considerable financial sacrifice in the Massachusetts Supreme Court, replacing Chief Justice Isaac Parker (*D.A.B.*).

8. Catherine Amory Codman (1796–1850). The daughter of John Amory, who was a brother of Ann Amory McLean Lee, she married Henry Codman, 1787–1853 (George Ticknor Dexter, *The Amory Family of Boston*, broadside, 1897). This letter is undoubtedly one of the 77 circular letters that Lee sent to his second wife's legatees (mentioned in his letter to his daughter Mary on September 20, 1834).

9. Winfield Scott had in 1817 criticized an order of his superior officer, General Jackson, as mutinous. Jackson never forgave this. Impatient at what he regarded as Scott's delay in prosecuting the

war (1835–1842) against the Creeks and Seminoles in Florida, Jackson relieved him and placed him before a court of inquiry. The court not only exonerated Scott but praised his " energy, steadiness, and ability " (*D.A.B.*).

10. Both James Farley Izard of Pennsylvania and John F. Lane of Kentucky were cadets at the Military Academy as of July 1, 1824. Both died in 1836 — Izard of wounds received in action with the Seminole Indians in Florida, Lane while a colonel with the Creek volunteers (Heitman, I, pp. 566, 614).

11. The Augustus Thorndikes lived at 52 Beacon Street during 1835 and 1836. Richard Cobb also lived on Beacon Street, and these must have been neighbors of Lee in 1833 and 1834 when he lived at 44 Beacon Street (*Boston Directories*).

12. Son of Thomas and Diana Cobb Newell and a first cousin of William Lee, whose mother was Mary Cobb. *The Improved Cheltenham Guide,* Bath (1822?), p. 71, lists a Mr. Newall of 5 St. George's Place as "surgeon Extra to the Prince of Wales" and member of the Royal College of Surgeons.

13. Boeotia was a district of ancient Greece proverbial for the stupidity of its inhabitants.

14. Alexander Hill Everett of Massachusetts (1790–1847), editor, diplomat (minister plenipotentiary to Spain, 1825–1829), brother of Edward Everett. In 1816 he was married to Lucretia Orne Peabody (*D.A.B.*).

15. Proverbs 13:12.

16. Jefferson wrote of England to Mme. de Staël on May 28, 1813: " Bonaparte will die and his tyrannies with him. but a Nation never dies. The English Government and it's pyratical principles and practices have no fixed term of duration. . . . England is in principle the enemy of all maritime nations, as Bonaparte is of the continental. . . . No, my dear Madam; the object of England is *the permanent dominion of the ocean,* and the *monopoly of the trade of the world* . . ." (Jefferson Papers, Library of Congress).

1772	December 31	Born in Halifax, Nova Scotia
1790	Fall	Became commission merchant in Boston, connected with Lyman and Williams
1794	June 26	Married Susan Palfrey
1795	April 8	Daughter, Susan Palfrey, born in Boston
1796	January 1	Embarked for Bordeaux on mercantile business
1798	March 31	Sailed for America
1799	May 12	Daughter, Mary Elizabeth, born at Roxbury
1800	June 24	Twin daughters, Charlotte Barlow and Nancy Lowell, born at Roxbury (both died within three months)
1801	July 26	Left Boston for Bordeaux with his wife and two daughters to take up duties as United States commercial agent
	September 8	Daughter, Julia Barlow, born at La Rochelle (died on September 24)
1802	January 26	Confirmed as commercial agent at Bordeaux
	October 26	Daughter, Julia Barlow, born at Bordeaux (died on February 9, 1803)
1805	January 28	Son, William Barlow, born at Bordeaux.
1808	August 7	Son, Thomas Jefferson, born at Bordeaux
1810	July 8	Sailed for the United States
1811	February	Barlow appointed minister to France; asked Lee to be secretary of legation
	August 5	Lee and Barlow sailed on the *Constitution* for France
1812	June 18	U.S. Congress declared war on England
	December 26	Death of Barlow in Poland
1814	March 12	British captured Bordeaux
	April 12	Napoleon abdicated, succeeded by Louis XVIII
	December	*Les Etats-Unis et L'Angleterre* published at Bordeaux

1816	February 16	Asked President Madison for leave to return to U.S.
	June 16	Sailed with family for America
	November 17	Accepted position as accountant in War Department, Washington
1817	March 6	Made second auditor of the Treasury
1822	July 22	Death of Mrs. Lee at Schooley's Mountain, N.J.
1825	June 6	Marriage of daughter, Mary Elizabeth, to Baron de Maltitz, secretary of the Russian legation
1826	July	Graduation of son, Thomas Jefferson, from West Point
1827	December 20	Departure of Mary and her husband for European posts
1829	March 21	Removal of Lee from auditor's position by President Jackson
	September	Susan joined her sister Mary in Berlin
		Lee moved to Boston
1830	November 4	Married Ann (Amory) McLean
1834	September 11	Death of Ann McLean Lee
1840	February 29	Death of Lee at Roxbury

INDEX